The Female Dominant: Games She Plays

From the review by Zak Jane Keir of *Desire* magazine:

"Varrin has put together a comprehensive collection of stories drawn from her own life, detailing scenes, tips, tricks, and fun had with casual clients to long-term lovers. Shot through with the respect and compassion essential for good kinky action, this book packs quite a punch. Very readable and entertaining. Highly recommended."

From the review by Beverly Glick of *Skin Two* magazine:

"In this companion volume to her other highly rated works, Varrin sets forth a series of short stories to inspire play and reflect the many different levels of a mistress's relationships: Casual Toys, Friends, Lovers, and Multiples. Male creatures are invited to become aroused by her words and fellow doms encouraged to add Varrin's inventive experiences to their repertoire."

Female Dominance: Rituals and Practices

From the review by David Jackson of *DDI* magazine:

"Varrin's latest and best work is her new book, *Female Dominance: Rituals and Practices,* is an insider's perception of romantic consensual BDSM. Preceded by *The Art of Sensual Female Dominance*, this newest effort deals with new techniques in cross-dressing, humiliation, bondage, fabulous fetishes, and even vampirism."

From the review by Helen Lane of *Skin Two* magazine:

"Varrin imparts knowledge, wisdom, and deep insight in a sensitive and often touching way. This book is so well written, it invokes the mysterious symbiosis between dominant and submissive, and the charismatic relationship between dom and sub, without the psychoanalytical jargon and clinical opinion many an explanation of this exotic sexuality resorts to. Instead it communicates the potential beauty and fulfillment of a BDSM relationship. Thoroughly recommended for dom and sub alike."

Erotic Surrender: The Sensual Joys of Female Submission

From the review by Lisa Sherman of *Skin Two* magazine:

"Like her previous book, *The Art of Sensual Female Dominance, Erotic Surrender* is a useful discussion aid, and Miss Varrin vividly communicates the delight that can be found in the delicious depravity of sensual submission."

The Art of Sensual Female Dominance: A Guide for Women

From the review by Lisa Sherman of *Skin Two* magazine:

"Full of solid practical advice that no one ever tells you and plenty of ideas to keep you inspired and interested, Varrin proves that the skills of dominance are easily within reach of any adventurous woman."

FEMALE SUBMISSION:

The Journals of Madelaine

Claudia Varrin

CITADEL PRESS
Kensington Publishing Corp.
www.kensingtonbooks.com

CITADEL PRESS BOOKS are published by

Kensington Publishing Corp.
850 Third Avenue
New York, NY 10022

Copyright © 2006 Claudia Varrin

All Kensington titles, imprints, and distributed lines are available at special quantity discounts for bulk purchases for sales promotions, premiums, fund-raising, educational, or institutional use. Special book excerpts or customized printings can also be created to fit specific needs. For details, write or phone the office of the Kensington special sales manager: Kensington Publishing Corp., 850 Third Avenue, New York, NY 10022, attn: Special Sales Department; phone 1-800-221-2647.

CITADEL PRESS and the Citadel logo are Reg. U.S. Pat. & TM Off.

First printing: November 2006
First trade paperback printing: October 2007

10 9 8 7 6 5 4 3 2 1

Printed in the United States of America

Library of Congress Control Number: 2006929664

ISBN-13: 978-0-8065-2838-0
ISBN-10: 0-8065-2838-9

To Meris

Anna and Frank, Josephine, and Nancy

and

Phillip D'Drennan

February 14, 2005

and

Eva Norvind

May 13, 2006

Rest in Peace

CONTENTS

Disclaimer   viii

Acknowledgments   ix

About the Book   x

Prologue   1

The Journals of Madelaine   5

Epilogue   219

Glossary: A Bit o' British Slang   220

About the Author   221

Disclaimer
Read this . . .

This book relates controversial, risky, and sometimes dangerous sexual activities written from the author's journals. The following pages are for *entertainment purposes only* and not meant for instructional purposes. This publication does not imply that these practices are anything other than the highly personal experiences of one woman. Neither the author nor her publisher assume *any responsibility whatsoever* for the exercise or misuse of the practices described in this book.

Practitioners of BDSM are keenly aware of the danger, both physical and emotional, in what they do. All care should be taken and all precautions followed to reduce risk, anticipate problems, and understand them when they happen—but most important—to avoid them completely. Related reading is suggested before and after perusing this book.

Additionally, practitioners of BDSM make a real and explicit distinction between consensual acts between adults for mutual pleasure, and any and all acts of violence against non-consenting and/or underage partners. Imposing any sexual activity on an unwilling partner is immoral, morally reprehensible, offensive, and in some places, constitutes rape. Furthermore, these laws vary from state to state as well as from country to country. In some jurisdictions, these activities are illegal even between consenting adults.

What does this all mean? It means that *if you screw up, you are on your own, baby.*

ACKNOWLEDGMENTS

For Anna, my dearest grandmother who has passed on. To the gorgeous Mistress Antoinette for her sweet nature, and Betsey Rochette for a being of a like mind. To D'Drennan: Long Live the Regent, the Regent is Undead! To Mistress Elizabeth for a fantastic realization of an alter ego and to ESS, for wet latex dreams. To Eva and our friendship and to Franco for giving me something I always wanted and never had. To the Fanciful Sovereign. For Frank, my dearest grandfather who is now with Anna; and for my beloved Aunt Josephine, who has passed on. To Juls, my Gentle Giant.

To Johnnie, Joey and "The Dish" for excursions in the night and Margo, the Russian Terror, for her love and protection. To dear Miss Toni for our mutual understanding. For Nancy, my dear grandmother who has passed on. To Pat B. for never forgetting my birthday. To Rosemary for her friendship in life, whether near or far. To Mistress Shane for generously letting me use her boy. To Ted and Di, my wild things, for their cat class and cat style, To Tim the Slim for just being him. To Tim Woodward, Tony Mitchell, and the staff at *Skin Two Magazine* for their support over the years.

ABOUT THE BOOK

Dear Reader, please allow me to introduce myself. Although my name is Claudia Varrin, my submissive name was Madelaine. I sometimes laughingly referred to myself as "Mad Elaine." This was not intentional when I took that name; I took it because I liked the way it sounded when said with a French, or any European, accent. I thought it sounded pretty and I wanted to be called a pretty name when I explored my lifelong submissive desires. But as you read, will you be able to discern when I was "Madelaine" or "Mad Elaine"?

If you have read *Erotic Surrender: The Sensual Joys of Female Submission*, then you already know something about yourself, and about me. Admitting in print that I was professionally a dominant, but preferred the submissive role in my personal life brought me grief from all quarters. Fem doms claimed that I couldn't be "truly dominant" if I had submissive fantasies or acted the role of submissive. Fem doms came on to me to submit to them. Fem subs looked smug and said to themselves, "I knew it all along." Countless male doms, many I never met, claimed to have "mastered" me. Truth is, I don't consider myself to be dom or sub, I consider myself to be an author, a "creative type," and a bit of the bohemian, whose sexual experiences can help enrich the lives of others.

But it didn't stop there. When *Erotic Surrender* was first published, it was, in general, a very misunderstood book. Dominant men scorned it as a "vanilla woman's fantasies," and experienced submissive women waved it away with a "nothing new here." But *Erotic Surrender* was not written for either of them. It *was* written for "vanilla women." *I* was a vanilla woman as far as sexual submission was concerned when I had those experiences; I had never played with a master and explored my desires as a slave before. *Everyone* is vanilla until they have had their first experience, and the experiences in these journals are what inspired me to write *Erotic Surrender*. Experienced female submissives didn't really need it because, well, they had experience, didn't they? And the men? If their criticisms weren't so stupid, I would have laughed.

Erotic Surrender was written for the woman whose deepest, most secret fantasies revolved around being a sex slave or slave girl, or being the pampered pet of a dominant male. It was written to make her proud of her state of sexual submission in a society where female submission is ridiculed and stereotyped. My heart filled with joy when a reader wrote that after she had read *Erotic Surrender* she was no longer deeply ashamed of her sexually submissive desires, and had stopped mutilating herself.

Female Submission: The Journals of Madelaine is a very special book which peeled back the years and transported me to faraway places; to places of gut-wrenching eroticism and consensual sadism that I hadn't visited in too long of a time; distant and exotic places that made my spirit soar and sing for what I had and weep for what I had lost. I share with you the very journals that I kept during that wild, wonderful, and sometime roller-coaster journey, to the Midnight World. As I transcribed these journals and fleshed out the players, I found myself feeling emotions and actual physical sensations I had not felt in many years. Desires I thought I was inured to rose to the surface and reconnected me with the hesitant yet eager woman/child in the journals.

This book is not a sequel to *Erotic Surrender,* but it certainly could be called a pre-quel to it. In this book, I will be sharing with you, my dear reader, the thoughts and experiences that led up to the writing

of *Erotic Surrender*. Painfully transcribed from the handwritten journals I kept at the time, each entry was lovingly written the very day
after the experience described so that nothing would be forgotten. I
think that as I wrote these journals, it was in the back of my mind
that this would be an experience I would like to write about someday
and share with other women. But the experience was so emotionally
intense, and the bottom of the spiral so far down, that it took me
eight years to summon up the courage to open these journals again;
eight years to reconcile the person I was then with the person I am
today, and only with some degree of success. I will freely admit to feeling confused and unsettled by the emotions writing this book has
brought to the fore. I freely admit that I almost allowed myself to
become deluded by the fantasy once again but caught myself just in
time.

Having decided to publish my journals, I had to go back into the
past and find "Madelaine." In order to find Madelaine, I had to reconnect with Niles to make him the romantic leading male I needed him
to be. Then, dear reader, having found Madelaine, I had to once again
become her; to become her, I had to be with the master. Being with
the master was a dangerous game. In spite of the glowing phrases
and words I use in here, in spite of the freeing of my spirit and the
downward masochistic spiral that left me knowing so much about
myself yet so very confused, this ("this" being my entire experience
as a sexual submissive) was a *research project* first and foremost. And
since I fell in love with the master, I consider it to be the only
research project I have failed at. The researcher is not supposed to
fall in love with the subject. And what strange things can happen
when things veer so far off course. So read on, dear reader, because
I have gone on this journey to share it with you. What a long, strange
trip it's been. . . .

FEMALE SUBMISSION

PROLOGUE

How does one describe the search for a master? Is it the same as looking for a vanilla boyfriend? Having done both, I would have to write, "No, I don't think so." It has some of the same elements, of course, and in most cases the search is just as unrewarding and frustrating until the right one comes along and the world glows. But what one looks for in a master versus what one looks for in a boyfriend differs when one is exploring the Midnight World of male dominance and female submission. Let me elaborate just a bit.

When looking for a boyfriend, one might consider whether he is "marriage material," a "good provider," a "suitable father," and the new "M" word: monogamous. However, when looking for a master, none of these criteria may apply. It may be more important that the master is a skilled dominant, that he is creative, strong yet sensitive, and that he exudes raw erotic power. Sometimes part of the master's allure may be his desirability to other women so monogamy becomes unimportant. Whether he may be "marriage material" becomes irrelevant because one's sexual needs are being met rather than one's need to have a roof over their head. Many male dominant/submissive female (male dom/fem sub) relationships are not based on the house at the end of the road with the white-picket fence, a two-car garage, a big fluffy dog and 2.3 children, but rather on exploring the dark side of their sexual psyche.

These requirements may make the master something of a "bad boy," a "dangerous type," or the "one your mother warned you about."

You know the kind I mean. We all have one of our very own and he differs from person to person as widely as we differ from each other. If we compared them all, yes, we could categorize them into Jungian archetypes, but why spoil the fun? We know our bad boys for who and what they are as soon as they walk into the room. Some of us flee from them like deer bounding out of a burning forest. Are these the smart ones? Who knows? I am not one of them. Others toy with their bad boy, telling themselves over and over that they have their desires under control and can stop any time they wish. Sometimes it even works out that way. Sometimes.

And then there are the rest of us. We are the ones, who upon seeing danger enter the room, fly at it like moths to the flame. I am a moth, albeit a rather attractive moth. And no matter how many times I singe my wings, I promise myself that next time "it" will be different. Once in a great while, it is. I call people like me "hopeful romantics." I prefer to think of it, and myself, that way because it's better to be a hopeful romantic than a "hopeless romantic"; hopeless has such a negative implication. Sometimes the hopeless ones lapse into the bitter promiscuity of the failed romantic. I am not one of those unhappy souls. I am a moth *and* a hopeful, if cautious, romantic.

Even though he is physically available, my flame, my dangerous type, is emotionally unavailable; his very unattainability is exactly what attracts me to him. I will be the one who will break down his walls, I will be the one who he falls for—and falls hard.

This man comes in many packages but no matter what others' perceptions of his looks are, to me he must be handsome, exude raw erotic power, have great confidence in himself and his abilities, and be able to enact with me those fantasies I most desire without being given a detailed script as to what those fantasies are. Specifically, a master who can portray the part of Romantic Sadist, a taller, handsomer version of the Marquis de Sade; one who could play really hard and would take me where I wanted to go by reading my body; a master who never thought to stop and ask if I was "okay." A master who could enslave me with his charm, who could quell me with one look, and who could give me the rough sex that I craved. A master who could look into my soul, see the romantic submissive masochist that lurked beneath the surface and bring that sexual persona forth in full force. A master that could humble me and yet still make me proud to be his submissive.

The standards above might seem quite high, but these are the general characteristics and qualities I was looking for in my master. I found most of them in one man. As time went on, I came to learn that he liked meat at every meal and that when he drank whiskey, he got mean. Exploring every inch of his body, I found him to be beautiful: from the ridge of his hairline scar to his well-rounded, firm buttocks; from his flat-stomached, hairless torso to his lovely, slender feet with their second toes longer than the big toes. The master's feet are the only feet I have ever worshipped, ever had in my mouth. I learned that the master could, at will, produce those pheremones that drove me wild and that when he smiled, two deep dimples disarmingly appeared in his cheeks.

Despite all this, his charm, his skill, and his creativity as a dominant, and the rugged handsomeness, there was still his emotional unavailability and this was a great challenge to me. But how can one hope for true romance with the emotionally unavailable? One cannot. Realizing that, I now look upon my time with him as a joyous, magical time in which he gave me all he could give me and made the dream come true. I woke up from the dream, but the sweet memories of it have almost become fantasies again.

When I met my master, the one I call the Fanciful Sovereign (because of his uncanny ability to look into my soul; to give me exactly what I want and plan the scenario to the smallest detail) I made the fatal mistake of merging fantasy with reality. I imbued the master with every human personality trait and characteristic that I found desirable and bestowed these upon him as if they were part of his real psychological makeup. I took a mere man and made him into the supreme and extreme Master I wanted him to be and fell head over heels in love with the fantasy. Not that the master wasn't every bit as wonderful, creative, and handsome as these pages (and *Erotic Surrender*) relate. Not that he doesn't charm me into breathlessness to this day, but no man could have possibly lived up to the paragon of vice and virtue manifest in my made-to-measure master, my very own Marquis de Sade.

Armed with this fantasy master, I plunged into the darkest side of the Midnight World, not stopping to consider the consequences of living in its intensity. But before that you need to know how it all began, how I came to be in London, and how I met my master, the Fanciful Sovereign. My journey into the Midnight World started in New York City almost eight months prior to the night the master and I met at a BDSM club in London.

Greetings and felicitations, I am Mad Elaine and I will be your guide on this journey.

The Journals of Madelaine

ONE

As with most personal searches, my search for a master began near to home, in New York City, where I lived at that time. How could I know when I began my search to explore my submissive desires that none of the local masters would prove to be suitable? Time after time, upon meeting them, there was no spark, nothing that made me want to submit to them. Their desires and mine were ill matched.

Then one weekend I met Oliver, from Germany, currently living in the UK. Oliver was attending a big BDSM weekend in New York, an event I was also attending with my friend, Walt. Oliver was young and handsome in a blond-haired, blue-eyed Germanic way and he certainly exuded raw erotic power. Being German, one knew he would be precise, an excellent master and trainer. His power shocked me into a shy silence. Physically he was not one of my "types," but I was fascinated by him all the same. There wasn't anyone like him in my neck of the woods.

Since Oliver was German and had traveled from the UK just to attend this event, everyone was doing their very best to speak with him. Naturally, they were very flattered that he had come so far to attend their anniversary celebration. Being a German master added to his allure, and in no time at all, Oliver had acquired an entourage. Walt was somewhat jealous at all the attention Oliver was getting. As another dominant male, Walt felt Oliver to be competition and he couldn't have been more correct. Walt didn't understand what "the attraction was about that guy" and made his opinion clear to all who cared to listen. I felt the pull of Oliver's attraction, but because I was there with Walt, I didn't want to offend him by running off and joining Oliver's ever-growing following. So I stood there, struck with awe, as Oliver walked by me, his court trailing behind him. The moment had passed but I knew there would be another opportunity. There were parties all weekend and I was sure to meet Oliver at one of them.

The next night there was a private party held in one of New York's most elaborate and exclusive houses of domination. Walt asked me to attend it with him and confirmed that Oliver would be there, reiterating that he didn't know what that attraction was about "that guy." Walt sounded a little peevish to me, so I chose to go alone and try to meet Oliver without the encumbrance of Walt. It would be a chance to strike up a conversation with Oliver and perhaps give him my phone number. I can't, for the life of me, remember what I wore that night, which is very odd indeed. Reflecting on how important this was to me then, and being the vain clothes horse that I unabashedly am, I think I should have remembered my outfit. I do recall that I had put tiny braids in my hair when it was wet, let it dry, then brushed the braids out. This was as close to curled as my impossibly straight hair would allow, and everyone liked it. The braids gave me a headache but it felt sooo good to take them out and brush my hair. Did I mention that I was something of a masochist?

I did get to speak with Oliver privately that night and he did accept my phone number, something a gentleman/master was under no obligation to do. We met at my apartment one afternoon in late June. We sunbathed on the roof, what all New Yorkers called "tar beach," then had lunch at a local Mexican restaurant. After lunch, we returned to my apartment and Oliver tested my responsiveness to him by pinching my nipples between his fingers, very slowly at first then building up more and more pressure. My response pleased him and he decided that we would conduct a master/slave phone and postal relationship before I visited him in England. He was a guest of Wetherole, the local lord in Susingham, and I would be staying in Wetherole's Manor with the two of them. Oliver gave me an assignment that I was to perform each day for seven minutes: I was to get on my knees, spread them wide, and place my head and shoulders on the floor, with my hips held high. Then I was to reach back and spread my cheeks and expose my anus so that my hole was open. As I held this position, I was to think of him and of being his slave. I faithfully did this every day and it had the intended effect on me. I thought more and more about being submissive to him.

This also inspired me to buy a little silver box. One night, I trimmed my pubic hairs onto a sheet of waxed paper and carefully placed them in the box. I would present this gift to Oliver at the appropriate time.

I spent many months of long-distance phone calls at odd hours of the day and night talking with Oliver, and many hours at the word processor writing stories of a master and his slave. I had a friend over to take Polaroids of me in every outfit I owned, and some in no outfit at all, and sent them to Oliver along with stories and other things I thought he might enjoy. All of this helped pass the time, as did performing my ritual, working at my day job, and doing domina sessions at night and on the weekends. Oh, yes, and having fantasies, lots and lots of fantasies.

TWO

Finally the departure date arrived. I was so nervous I almost canceled the trip, but everything was packed and Oliver was awaiting my arrival, so I gathered up my courage and left for the airport. I took the last overnight flight from New York to Heathrow so Oliver wouldn't have to get up too early to meet me. I thought that was the considerate thing to do and I wanted to impress Oliver with my thoughtfulness. Though the flight was unfortunately and unexpectedly crowded, at least there were no babies screaming their way across the Atlantic and I was able to get some sleep. I awoke in plenty of time to monopolize a bathroom and change into the fresh clothes I had in my carry-on bag, put on makeup, and freshen up in general. I didn't want to greet Oliver looking bedraggled and travel weary. I wasn't looking for a mate; I was looking for a master—The One—and my preparations were made with that one thought in mind. Could it be Oliver, awaiting me at the gate?

After the chaos of deplaning, I anxiously scanned the waiting faces for Oliver and found him accompanied by the lord of the manor, Wetherole. Wetherole's nickname was Toby, and he loved having guests in his home. Toby and I had spoken many times in the long months between my agreement with Oliver and my arrival in London. First I greeted Oliver with the traditional European kiss on each cheek, then I turned to Toby, did the same, and graciously thanked him for making the trip and having me as his guest. Oliver took charge of my baggage and pushed the cart up the ramp while Toby and I walked behind him. Oliver's butt looked great in his jet-black jeans and I smiled to myself. Toby was intent on watching Oliver's butt, too, and when Toby and I caught each other's eye, we smiled conspiratorially. Then Toby whispered to me that he was Oliver's collared slave and served no other. Surprised but not shocked, I told Toby that he was a lucky man. Up until that moment, I had no idea that Toby or Oliver were bisexual. I was more than a bit thrilled that Oliver liked men as well as women. Truthfully, it really turned me on.

During the ride to the Manor, I felt like I was in the Twilight Zone. I love waking up under foreign skies but the immediate countryside around Heathrow looked very much like New Jersey! As we drove farther south the scenery began to look more like the "England" I expected. By the time we reached the little hamlet of Susingham, it was as picturesque as I could have hoped for. The hedged one lane road that led to the Manor was also a barrier for the livestock of which Toby, as the local lord, owned a large share.

A charming sprawl of old buildings, the Manor was set well back from the road. To the left were stables and the carriage house, which had two apartments upstairs for the caretaker and the gardener. The lower carriage house sheltered Toby's collection of exotic cars. Straight ahead was the Manor with its two entrances: one for the family of privilege and the other, leading into the kitchen side of the house, was for the now-gone servants. We used the servants' entrance although we all slept in the "family" side of the second floor. Behind the Manor was a pond, a lovely garden, and a small maze. I had never been in a "lord's" house before and I was fascinated.

This was all very nice, but what interested me most was the air raid shelter that Oliver had spent considerable time outfitting as a dungeon. The thought of a party in this private dungeon with such skilled, experienced players thrilled me. It was one of the reasons I had suppressed my initial nervousness, gathered up my courage, and undertaken this journey. I had never played as a slave before, although as a female dominant, I certainly knew how to turn that around and play the role of slave-girl. As I entered the Manor, I turned back for another look at the air raid shelter–turned dungeon and wondered what mysteries about myself I would unravel within its timeless black walls. It was like being at Roissy, the famed slave-training chateau from *The Story of O*. Seeing my wide-eyed attention, both Oliver and Toby laughed. Oliver said I wouldn't have to wait long for my first experience because he had planned a private dungeon party there after a trip to a BDSM club the following night. A frisson ran up my spine as I stepped over the threshold and into the house.

Each carrying a piece of luggage, we clambered up the stairs to the second floor and the family bedroom wing. Oliver and Toby led me to a small but charming room with a working fireplace, armoire, desk, and a twin bed piled high with soft blankets and pillows. My room overlooked the front of the house and the tree-lined path to the air raid shelter with its roof covered in grass from years ago to keep it undetectable from the air during bombings. The other bedrooms were much larger, more elegantly appointed than mine, and overlooked the garden, pond, or maze. But I felt that my room was the best in the house because it adjoined Oliver's room. I thought it was fitting that the slave slept in the smaller room connected to the master's spacious one, ready and waiting for his call, and the connecting door could only be locked from the master's side. To sleep in a genuine British manor from long ago and serve a handsome skilled master was all that a hopeful romantic like myself could ask for.

THREE

Once I had settled into my room, Oliver invited me to take a nap with him in his room. How wonderful to take a nap with the master in his queen-size bed all a-tumble with lots of pillows and piles of downy-white comforters! I was so tired from traveling and from adjusting to the new environment that I thought I would drop off right away. But my nervous excitement got the better of me, and Oliver's presence, his warm and strong body against mine, was more of a distraction than a comfort. Finally I settled down and slept. Our nap lasted right up until Toby called us for dinner. I woke up first then gently awoke Oliver. Together we scrambled to the staircase on wobbly legs like puppies hearing their bowls being filled.

Downstairs, the huge kitchen table in the servants' side of the house was beautifully set for three. Toby had made one of his specialties and Oliver's favorite dish, Chicken Lebanese, which was excellent. Toby had unknowingly prepared one of my favorites, too, Potatoes Lyonnaise, so I complimented him lavishly on his cooking. I started to chatter about the house and ask about its history, especially if there were any ghosts in residence. Toby smilingly obliged me, but I was a little disappointed when he said there were no ghosts that he knew of. After dinner, Oliver and I had a relaxing cigarette while the water boiled for tea. This gave me the opportunity to look around the kitchen.

The floor was set with foot-square gray slate, cold and slightly uneven, and quite old, but in keeping with the rustic decor one would expect in a servant's kitchen. The nicked and distressed wooden dining table was very large and wide and could seat twelve comfortably. The walls were hung with many wooden cabinets, some with glass doors, containing all of the usual kitchenware. One long countertop held an impressive collection of silver tea services, including serving trays, tea pots of various sizes, lidded bowls filled with white and brown lumps of sugar, creamers, tiny sugar spoons, and cups and saucers. A large wooden hutch displayed Toby's collection of china. Although there were modern double sinks under a large window and a microwave oven, the stove was unlike anything I had ever seen. It was enormous and used wood and coal to heat the top burners but used gas for the oven and the "grill," which is what we would call the broiler.

There seemed to be only one house rule and Toby carefully explained to me what they called the "door policy." If the door to the person's room was open, you could just walk in. If the door was ajar, you would knock, announce yourself, and then enter. But if the door was completely closed, you would knock, wait to be invited in, or have the door opened for you. I thought that this was so sensible as well as polite and such a wonderful way of preserving privacy that I adopted Toby's door policy as my own. How else does one get along when living with several people?

After tea, Oliver and Toby drifted away from the kitchen, each up to his own room to relax. I stayed in the kitchen with the remains of dinner. I cleared the table and washed the dishes, happy to be there yet happy to have a little privacy to absorb this new adventure. When I finished in the kitchen, I went up to my own little slave's room with the intention of taking a nice shower and getting into clean clothes. It was quite chilly in my room and I wished I had asked Toby to show me how to make a coal fire. And little did I know that a "shower" was not very British and nothing like a shower in the states, though I was soon to find that out.

The bathroom was next to my room and it was all the bathroom any female could want. It was a dream room, a real room, not the usual undersized five-by-seven box common in so many big-city apartments. The room was spacious enough to accommodate not only the expected sink, toilet bowl, and bathtub, but also an antique vanity with chair, a chest of drawers containing bubble bath, shampoo, bars of soap and the like, and a cedar chest used for storing towels. There was a large window framed in lace curtains, and on the opposite wall was a lovely working fireplace. Best yet, there was still plenty of room to stretch out full length like a cat on the Aubusson rug in front of the fire! I felt like I had stepped back in time and landed in the nineteenth century. I couldn't have been more delighted.

I decided to take a "bird bath," which was to sit in a tub filled with a few inches of water and bubble bath and use the handheld shower head to slough the soap off my body and rinse the shampoo and conditioner out of my hair. Afterward I discovered that a full bath would have warmed me up considerably, and from then on I did just that. Stepping out of the shower curtain–enclosed bathtub into the freezing cold room was quite a shock to my system, and I hurriedly dried my hair, dressed in a sheer floor-length black jacquard robe, and put on light makeup. Exiting the bathroom, I was happy to see Oliver's door wide open. I went into his room, and as I crossed the floor, I could feel his eyes on me, looking me up and down, taking me in. Although my eyes were downcast, I used the old trick all submissives know: how to peek at the dominant through your eyelashes. Oliver was wearing only a pair of dark purple briefs. I knelt next to his bed, head down, hands behind my back, and waited to be acknowledged.

Oliver got up and bade me to stand. Smiling pleasantly, he used his hands to bend me into a wonderfully uncomfortable position that thrust out my derriere and made my breasts dangle like ripe peaches. Oliver stepped up behind me, raised my robe, and spread my cheeks. He began to rub his hardening member between them and I felt myself getting wet. Suddenly he reached his arm up between my legs, picked me up, and flipped me upside down! He twirled me like a baton, round and round, until he held me right-side-up in his arms before setting me on my feet. I felt a delightful lightness and was giddy and needed to sit down to preserve the feeling. I wish I could describe to you exactly how he did this but I haven't been able to reconstruct it, although I was to meet one other person later who knew how to do it.

When I became steady on my feet, Oliver asked me to give him a back massage, not too hard. I was glad to offer this service to him. I had massage oils with me and knew I had a natural talent as a masseuse. I returned with the oils and he selected the scent and texture he liked best: almond essence oil. I rubbed the oil between my hands to warm it up before starting the massage. His skin was warm and pale and nearly hairless, and smooth like a youth's. He allowed me to straddle him because it was easier for me to give him an equal-sided massage while astride him. From his sighs and soft moans, I knew he was pleased with my ministrations, so I was happy. It came time to massage his buttocks, legs, and feet. I climbed off him, and when he rolled over, I noticed a creamy white spot on his purple briefs. When I laughingly told him this, he said he would think about a good punishment for me overnight and then punish me tomorrow. I wondered if he would forget.

The final step of the massage was to cover him with a comforter and let him relax under its warmth. I knelt next to the bed and awaited his next command. Shortly, he returned to Earth and turned to me, smiling. He asked me to stand up and take off my robe, acknowledging that it was a little cold in the room but that I would humor him. He said he wanted to see his new pleasure toy. I was overjoyed at finally being able to display myself for him. I knew I had a lovely figure: a slender body and legs with the muscle tone of the dancer I used to be, a nice round derriere, and medium-size round breasts. I wanted him to see my body; I wanted him to be pleased with it and become filled with desire to have me as his toy. I felt his blue eyes on my flesh, not cold blue eyes but hot ones. I realized that I was no longer cold.

In his look, I could read his thoughts about my body, and my heart leapt. He ran his hands over me, touched me intimately, but did not penetrate me. Instead, he put me into different positions meant to expose me and strip me of any lingering shame I might be feeling under his gaze. When he put me into a position that pleased him, he would command me to hold the position while he rubbed his member on me. Then he put me on my belly, spread my legs wide, and left me there for several minutes. As I felt his gaze upon me, I began to cream and my thick opaque juice formed a little puddle under me. Soon I heard him cover himself with a sheath.

I felt another warm rush when Oliver first knelt between my parted thighs. My breathing became faster and more ragged as I waited for him to enter me. He thrust into me hard, wanting to hurt me and observe how I would react to it. Although his member was only of average size and this was a disappointment, it *was* pierced, a Prince Albert with a large thick ring to be exact. The ring added a much-needed extra inch to his length. He took me hard, ramming into me deeply. My hips rose up to meet him as he pounded into me. I am small and tight and even though it didn't hurt very much because he was just average, I thought it was the most lovely little pain I had ever experienced. I had many small orgasms as he stroked me with his ring, which he needed to reach my hot spot. My mind kicked into high gear and off I went. I arched my back and thrust my hips up further, moaning like an animal, my hands clutching the comforter beneath me; Oliver went into what I recognized as a come stroke. With a very deep thrust, he allowed me to have a smashing orgasm by touching my hot spot just once before he himself came.

Oliver pulled out of me slowly and stripped off the sheath while kneeling between my spread thighs. He tied off the sheath, and with perfect aim tossed it into the dust bin. Then he stretched out beside me. I curled up next to him, my head on his shoulder, still making little moaning sounds. He laughed delightedly and reached for the cigarettes. He lit one for each of us and we smoked in silence, the ashtray balanced on his hairless chest. Several minutes later, Oliver asked me if I would like to spend the night in his bed. My very first night there! I was happy to have pleased him so much in spite of my initial nervousness. It was heavenly to sleep with him, just to be near him after such a long wait. I was sure I had made the right choice by coming here.

FOUR

I awoke the next morning after a lovely night's sleep in Oliver's bed. Shortly after, Toby came in to clean the room. I arose and helped him while Oliver looked on with amusement as we scurried around toiling on his behalf. Then Oliver remembered that he "owed" me a punishment; I guess our cleaning inspired him. Doing his laundry was to be my punishment, he announced. Then he laughingly collected a small mountain of dirty clothes, seven loads in all. I started on it right away, but seven loads of a wash with no tumble drier took quite a bit of time since after each load I had to run up and down stairs to the boiler room to hang the wet clothes on clothes line. As each load washed, I helped Toby with the usual household chores of dusting, vacuuming, brushing the rugs, washing dishes, et cetera. When the chores were finished and all seven loads had been hung up to dry, Toby prepared a lamb chop dinner, which the three of us fell upon like starving creatures.

Oliver and I were going to the Whiplash party that night, which, in the usual style of major cities, lasted until four o'clock the next morning with the cool people arriving between eleven thirty and midnight. After that, Toby was holding the invitation-only party in his air-raid dungeon, which Oliver had mentioned. He and I took a nap so we would have the energy to party until whenever. Then it came time to dress. I asked Oliver what I should wear and he chose a black latex hobble dress with long sleeves, high neck, and a back line that plunged to my waist. Before I went to bathe, I presented him with the silver box containing my shorn pubic hairs. Never having been given a gift like this before, he was very happy with the novelty of it and the thought behind it. I dropped to my knees and kissed his feet. He knew my pussy wasn't clean shaven and commanded me to shave it bare when I bathed. A thrill ran through me. A request like this was not considered a casual one among "our people"; a shaven pussy was a sign of commitment.

The club was membership-only and Oliver introduced me to the club promoters, Adam and Roger, who humorously insisted that I open my coat for "dress-code inspection." Of course, the latex dress Oliver had picked out for me to wear was perfect and I passed muster. Once inside, I was amazed. There was nothing at all like this in the States! Seeing my wide-eyed curiosity, Oliver allowed me to go off on my own to explore. The club had two levels. Downstairs in the front was a bar that opened onto a well-lit dance floor. On the darker outskirts of the dance floor and in deep corners of the room was a selection of dungeon equipment such as St. Andrew's crosses, spanking benches, bondage chairs, and other pieces I knew the use of but not the names for. The second floor was a "chill zone" lit only by red lights, filled with large chairs and comfortable sofas. The smell of incense lingered in the air and the music was quieter there. The whole atmosphere struck me as a den of iniquity where secret desires were discussed, trysts and assignations were made, and, if so desired, physical compatibility could be explored in full view of the other denizens or in a semiprivate corner.

It was easy enough to find Oliver in the crowd; his paleness shimmered in the dim light and called to me. Rejoining him, he introduced me to Niles, Charmaine, Rowan, and Esme. Niles and Charmaine were an on-again-off-again couple, and I was immediately attracted to the strong-featured, handsome, and sexually powerful Niles. His strong pheremones had a hypnotic effect on me. I asked myself if my attraction to Niles was a betrayal of Oliver. Immediately, I decided not; after all, my relationship with Oliver was just a day old, and I didn't feel that the eight months between our first meeting and this one really counted as a "relationship."

Although I was a bit shy at having met four such distinguished members of the London scene all at the same time, Charmaine was bubbly and friendly and put me at ease. Rowan was the club's house mistress and Esme was her personal slave. Rowan had great presence and exuded natural power and strength. About five-foot-eight, she had large full breasts, a small waist, and a beautiful heart-shaped derriere. Her eyes were hazel, her complexion creamy, her lips generous and sensual, and her long tightly curled hair was a rich brown. Magnificently dressed in latex, her tightly laced corset accentuated her small waist and plumped out her breasts and derriere. In her swing-back black latex coat and stiletto-heeled over-the-knee boots, she indeed commanded attention. Esme was very slender and had the body of a dancer or swimmer. Her small breasts, small bone structure, flat stomach, long legs without an ounce of fat, and short blondish hair was a perfect contrast to Rowan's imperious stance and luscious figure. Esme was Rowan's lover as well as her personal slave.

In addition to Esme, Rowan had several other slaves who were contracted to her, six in all. As soon as Rowan made her entrance, her slaves approached her respectfully and offered her the gifts she required of them: colorful containers filled with dried fruits and nuts, baskets of cheese, crackers and creamy spreads, and long-stemmed red roses. Imperially yet graciously, Rowan collared each slave presenting the gift and accepted him into her service. After all six were collared, Rowan produced a chain leash with a leather handle and a large ring at the end. Connected to the ring were six double-sided clip hooks: one side clipped to the ring and the other to a chain about three feet long. At the end of that chain, there was another double-sided clip hook with one end clipped to the chain and the other to the ring in each of the slaves' collars. In this manner, she had full control of them, the only exception being Esme who was collared but not chained and assisted Rowan with the slaves.

As Rowan's well-trained personal slave, Esme, although not in the capacity of a co-top, demonstrated to the other slaves how to follow Rowan's creative and demanding commands. As a working domina always looking for new ways to control my own slaves, I watched this ceremony carefully, impressed with Rowan's creativity and ability to control so many slaves at once. It was obvious that the English played much harder than their American counterparts and took their roles more seriously. This was going to be a learning experience for me, not only as a submissive but as a dominant as well.

While absorbing the dark pleasures of the night, I found myself sitting next to the dangerously attractive Niles. Nervous and shy, I attempted opening up a conversation in what I hoped to be a playful way. Wearing only the latex dress, I was very cold; Niles had on a brown leather bomber jacket. Leaning in close, I whispered a proposition to him. Telling him I was cold, and that his jacket looked warm and cuddly, I offered to trade him drinks all night for the use of his jacket. He turned to me, and for the first time, I was able to look into his eyes. He was a flame and I was captivated, surreptitiously taking in his features while I awaited his answer. This flame had rugged good looks, was tall, and had long, straight golden brown hair, neatly restrained by a black barrette. A high forehead with a small and very sexy scar just below the hairline and two generous eyebrows stood guard over his beautiful green eyes. A sensually cruel mouth was set above a cleft chin and well-defined jaw and below a strong, once-broken nose. His leather pants fit him as if they were part of his personality. His Lord Byron shirt was worn tucked into his pants, and ruffles cascaded out of the collar and cuffs of his brocade coat. Black leather boots hugged his feet and calves. His pheromones were so strong: I could smell them from where I was sitting. His deep voice, precise way of speaking, and crisp London accent made him all the more desirable—British accents have that effect on me.

Then he smiled. I giggled in delight. I never would have expected his strong face would dimple when he smiled. The overall effect was utterly charming and I felt myself falling under his spell.

Standing, he took off his jacket, flung it over my shoulders, and tucked it around me. The scent of his pheromones assaulted me again and I became a bit giddy. Laughingly, I reached for my purse, handed him a ten-pound note, and asked if that would be enough for starters. Bowing slightly, he took the proffered tenner and said that it would be plenty. Then he thanked me and headed toward the bar. Although I didn't know if he would return and sit with me, I knew he would be back. After all, I did have his jacket. But after hitting the bar, he did return to my side and asked if I would like to go upstairs with him. I accepted immediately and followed him up the stairs to the red-lit den of trysts and assignations. He chose a plump cushioned love seat and we sat down, shoulder to shoulder. There was only one other person in the den, and I noticed that Niles kept a close eye on this man as we spoke. After just a few short minutes, Niles whispered to me that this man was a "bobby," a cop, and that we should go back downstairs. I was very disappointed but understood the caution.

After we returned downstairs, he drifted off and I took a seat with a good view of the dance floor where Rowan was putting her slaves through their paces. I arrived midscene, just in time to see the preparations to corporally punish one of the slaves. Rowan had unchained them all and had the other five slaves on all fours, alternating head to buttocks to make a human spanking bench. The one to be punished bent at the waist and laid his upper body across the human bench, holding his hips high to make an appealing target for Mistress Rowan's flogger. Esme stood at the head of the bench, grasped his wrists, and stretched his arms out, making his body taut and thereby enhancing the pain of the flogging. Once he was in the proper position, Rowan went to work on his buttocks and upper back, using an overhand stroke that was very similar to my own. After each stroke, the slave called out, "Thank you, Mistress." I was familiar with this practice but did not employ it myself because I found it too distracting. My own method was to administer the punishment in silence until I was satisfied or until the slave said his safe word. No one had ever "worded up" on me; I had a gift for knowing when the last stroke *was* the last stroke.

The punishment over, the slaves were ordered to stand and Rowan re-collared and re-chained all of them with the help of Esme. Stepping back from the collared group and leaving some play in the leash, Rowan then commanded them to dance. The song was not the usual fast-beat multilayered trance music played in the clubs, but a rather well-known tune by the Rolling Stones. Anyone should have been able to dance to it. Well, anyone except this particular collection of slaves! Obviously, they had yet to discover Elvis and were totally clueless, not even knowing enough about dancing to bend their knees. The sight of these six struggling to dance to a song that my ancient grand-mother could have managed a good wiggle to was absolutely hilari-ous. Knowing that outbursts of laughter so close to a scene could very well disrupt it, I literally had to clamp my hand over my mouth! I made my way to Charmaine, who was in a corner farther away from the dance floor watching the scene. Plopping down in the chair next to her, we read each other's minds and burst into side-splitting laughter.

When we had recovered from our mutual laughing fit, we began to chat. Charmaine was about my height and weight but we had entirely different builds. A few years younger than I, she had tiny little titties, flat stomach with an out-ty belly button, slightly wide hips, and very nice legs. Her hair was very short and bleached very blond and she had a fair complexion, but her two most beautiful attributes were her amazing blue eyes and her mouth, especially when she smiled. Char-maine was so well known in the scene that she didn't even have to meet the dress code for entry to a club or party. She told me that she had a son in lower school and that she was a single mom. She and her son lived about a ten-minute walk away from Niles in a "maisonette," a small house with many split levels and two bedrooms on the upper floor. She worked freelance selling advertising with BDSM overtones to large companies and booking outlandish entertainers for corporate functions.

Since this was a midweek party and the next day was a workday, the club started to clear out about two in the morning. But we stayed on, having no such mundane obligations, and as the others left, the club became more like a private party of our own. As I sat next to Charmaine, my eye caught a man at the edge of the dance floor. His back was to us and as he danced, he reached back and took the barrette out of his hair. Shaking it free to the music, he danced alone without inhibition. He danced very sensually and his movements hypnotized me. I couldn't take my eyes off of him. Then he turned and I saw his face. It was Niles. I felt my attraction to him building as he continued dancing as if no one was watching him. From the corner of my eye I saw that Charmaine was watching him, too, smiling. Still wearing his jacket, I hugged it closer to me and inhaled the delicious smell of his pheromones.

FIVE

The club was nearly empty at three o'clock, and Oliver signaled it was time for us to leave. Oliver, Niles, Charmaine, and I piled into one car and Rowan and Esme into their vehicle and off we went, back to Susingham for a private party in the air raid dungeon. Forty five minutes later, Toby was awaiting us at the door to welcome us in. Resplendent in a tightly laced silver corset and tight black pants, he was very happy to see us, his guests and party animals. Rowan and Esme were staying overnight and while Toby took them up to their room, the rest of us congregated in the kitchen and made tea. Except for me. I ran up the stairs to my room as fast as the hobble dress would allow and changed into warm stretch pants and a sweater, but, keeping in mind the dungeon party, underneath I had on thigh-high lace top stockings and a lacy thong. I completed this outfit with high-heeled shoes.

I rejoined the group in the kitchen and saw Niles looking at me and my trim figure. This pleased me greatly. Shortly after, Rowan and Esme joined us, also in street clothes. Before I sat down for my cup of tea, I noticed that Niles, Charmaine, and Oliver were smoking. I knew that I was soon to join them and that there wasn't an ashtray in sight. The only ashtrays were in Oliver's room and my room, so again I ran upstairs, taking them two at a time, and returned with the ashtrays and placed them near the smokers just in time. Rowan noticed this and invited me to sit next to her. As we chatted she said what at the time I thought was a very strange thing. She told me to watch my heart. I didn't know what she meant, but I remembered her comment.

Oliver was the first to finish his cigarette. He excused himself, gestured to Toby, and left the room. They returned with a little wooden box, holding it with all the respect one would give an ancient artifact. I was intensely curious about the little box and the heads-together conversation Oliver and Toby were having. I was soon to find out what they were discussing.

Almost ceremonially, Oliver opened the box and handed each of us a little beige pill. It was Ecstacy! The lovey-dovey kind, not the speedy kind, therefore perfect for a play party with friends. It was an unwritten rule that when in a professional session, the dominant was never drunk or high, but in a social setting that rule was generally abandoned. I had of course heard of ecstacy and knew people who did it but I had never tried it myself. In the UK , they called Ecstacy "E" and when one was using it they were "on E," but the stateside people called Ecstacy a "roll" and when one was on it they were "rolling." As each person accepted their roll from Oliver, Toby poured each a small glass of orange juice. He explained to me that orange juice was one of the best catalysts for Ecstacy. We waited until everyone had their pill and orange juice before we popped the pills into our mouths and toasted ourselves and the night with the glass of orange juice. I joined in, thinking of all the wonderful things my friends had told me about rolling. This was turning out to be an evening of many firsts.

At long last, it was time to make our way down the moon-lit, tree-lined path to the dungeon. Covered in grass with the exposed walls painted black, it was a little difficult to locate in the dark, even for Oliver. Upon entering, we were in an enclosed entranceway facing another door. The double door was to help keep it warm inside so that when anyone left the chamber, those remaining inside were not hit by a nasty blast of cold air. Inside the second door was a galley kitchen with a fridge, working sink, cabinets, and the usual assortment of dishes, glasses, cutlery, and a coffee- and tea-maker. The galley kitchen led to the main room with its black walls and floors. A small table and two chairs were set in one corner with a large bowl of condoms, gloves, lube, and binder clips atop it, and right behind this was a door leading to a tiny isolation chamber. The chamber was very small and also all black, and had a slot in the door so those outside could look in. There was a music system but I couldn't see it, only hear it.

A bondage table was suspended from one wall, which could be secured up against the wall, to make more play space when not in use. Two mattresses were set against one wall next to each other on the floor and were piled high with comforters and pillows for relaxation or sex. We used them for both. The "pillars of Hercules" were the main feature and dominated the middle of the chamber. The wooden columns were used for upright bondage and were lined with eye hooks, some of which had leather wrist and ankle restraints hanging from them. Around the corner from the galley kitchen, to the extreme right and off of the main chamber, was a tiled shower stall the size of a small bedroom. There was a shower nozzle and a drain was set in the middle of the floor, but there was no toilet.

Everyone else had started to feel the effects of the E and were getting all smiley and touchy-feely. Not knowing what to expect, I couldn't tell if I was high and just didn't know it. When I spoke of this, they all told me to wait, that I would know when I was rolling because the "world would glow" and everyone would look sexy and desirable to me. (As if they weren't sexy and desirable already.) During this time, Oliver stayed by me, going slowly with me and letting me absorb it all at my own pace. After I had oriented myself and taken it all in, Oliver sent me back up to the house for tea bags, sugar, instant coffee, and milk. I was also to bring back a large bowl, towels, and soap with which I was to wash his feet. Putting my coat over my shoulders, I bolted off to the house to gather up the required items and was happy that I was able to find the things quickly, and more important, find the dungeon door upon my return. I had an image of myself wandering the surrounding woods trying to locate the door while a search party was organized to find me!

Arms full, I clambered through the second door. I saw that everyone except Niles had shed most of their clothes, so when I took off my coat, I also took off my sweater and stretch pants, leaving me clad in only my thigh-high stockings, shoes, and my thong. Rowan complimented me on my figure and Niles's eyes were so hot when he looked at me that I could feel them burning into me. Hurriedly, I put the tea and such in its proper place in the kitchen. When I was finished with that, Oliver ordered me to fill the bowl with nice warm water and wash his feet. I was to perform my first public service for him! Small as this service was I was delighted to do it. He had positioned himself at the end of one of the mattresses to await me. First, I laid towels under his feet, then I wrapped his feet in them to keep them warm. I filled the bowl from the sink, put the bar of soap in it, and as I turned to serve him, I realized that the Ecstacy had taken effect. His pale blond body shimmered and glowed in the dark light of the dungeon, beckoning me to him.

When I saw him glowing, I realized the E was working its magic on me. Suddenly, I could feel the warmth emanating from his body and see the orange glow it cast around him. I felt myself glowing, wondering if the others could see it, too. The warm sexy glow engulfed the room and embraced everyone in it. My whole body tingled and was tuned in to every sensation, even the feeling of my own hair on my back. *This* was the feeling they were talking about. It was great! It was a totally new, mind-blowing, peace-love-and-sex experience, and I loved it.

I made my way to Oliver without spilling a drop from the bowl. Standing in front of him, I gave him a minute to appreciate his new toy before I gracefully dropped to my knees to begin his foot bath and massage. I bent his knee and placed one foot in the bowl and began to wash it. My technique was to use the soap as a lubricant for the massage, which I performed at the same time as the foot bath. Knowing how I liked my feet to be washed and massaged, I used my desires as a guide for what he would like. I recalled that I often closed my eyes as I massaged the foot and let my hands see for me. In my mind's eye, I could see his foot, the bones and muscles under the skin and where the massage would feel the best.

Starting at the top, I did each toe separately and gave the tip a little squeeze. This elicited a moan from him, so I assumed he liked it. Using my thumbs, I paid careful attention to the shy area right beneath his toes, then used a little more pressure on the ball of his foot. Making a fist, I used my knuckles on his insole and elicited more moans. After each area but before the next one, I held his foot in one hand and used the other to pour more water over it, ensuring that the foot would always be soapy and lubricated. I made my way down his foot, cupped his heel in my hand, and used my palm and my fingers to massage it in a circular motion. Finished with his heel, I began to massage his ankles and the muscles up the back of his calf. His whole foot now bathed and massaged, I rested it in the bowl and filled my cupped hands to rinse away any lingering soap bubbles.

Moving the bowl to the side, I first used a towel to dry his foot, then as a sign of submission, I ritualistically dried his foot with my long hair. I wrapped his freshly washed foot in a clean towel and then went to refill the bowl with fresh water for the other foot. I had never felt so in touch with anyone, especially just their foot, before this. And strangely, it didn't matter whose foot it was, as long as I could make this deep and spiritual connection. Before he dismissed me to empty the bowls and clear away the towels, he told me I had a talent for massage.

When I returned to Oliver's side, Niles was there, speaking with Oliver in low tones I couldn't hear. I knelt and kept my head down, waiting to be told what to do next. Oliver told me that Niles had asked for me and that he was giving me to Niles. Niles rose and signaled me to follow him, but before I could follow Niles, Oliver pulled me close and whispered in my ear, "it's all right to have limits." I looked askance at him but he said no more, so I went to Niles. He led me to the table and chairs in the corner, casually tossed a pillow on the floor, and gestured for me to kneel on it. He turned the chair away from the table, pulled the chair close to me, then sat down facing me, his legs open so that I was kneeling between them. I clasped my hands behind the small of my back so that my breasts jutted out and spread my knees wide.

I wish I had the words to describe to you how I felt at that moment. The excitement of the club, the trip to the dungeon, my first public experience as a submissive, the mind-expanding effect of the E, my earlier attraction to Niles . . . and now here I was, kneeling before him wearing only a pair of shoes and stockings, and a thong.

He leaned forward and began to speak softly into my ear. I don't even remember what he said. I was enthralled by his rugged handsomeness, his long hair, green eyes, the smell of his leather pants, the overpowering scent of his pheromones, the sound of his deep voice, and his sexy British accent. He ran his large warm hands over my body, touching me gently, fondling my breasts, and pinching my nipples. I took especial note of his hands: They were very large and strong yet slender, with long straight fingers and shiny nails. Beautifully and almost delicately shaped, they belied the great strength and masculinity he possessed. I loved having them on me and I melted under his touch. His face was very close to mine, and as he touched me, I rested my head on his shoulder, making little sounds of pleasure and moaning softly. My responsiveness to him pleased him, and I could feel his breath getting heavier as his hands roamed my body.

Wrapping his arms around me, he stood and lifted me up all in one motion; I was still in a kneeling position. He carried me over to the mattress and laid me down next to Charmaine. Charmaine started to kiss me and touch me, but not for one minute did I take my eyes off Niles, who was undressing. He removed his ruffled shirt first, and I beheld his almost hairless chest, flat stomach, and muscular arms with their dark fine hair. He shook his head and his hair flowed around his shoulders. With only his leather pants and boots on, he looked like a satyr from an ancient forest. He bent and took his boots off and tossed them aside. Standing up again, he unbuckled his belt and pushed his pants down; as they cleared his hips, his cock sprung free, thick and long and hard and gorgeous. His balls were high and tight with ridged skin; his thighs were muscular and he had well-developed calves, both covered in the same dark hair as his arms. Niles's ass was gorgeous, too, round yet manly and very firm. Even his feet were beautiful, echoing the form and masculine delicacy of his hands. Using one foot then the other to hold down the legs of his pants, he stood naked before me, letting me take in his physique.

As I looked up at him, the pagan god with his huge priapus, I ate up

every inch of him with my eyes, then felt the welcome lovely sticki-
ness between my legs, felt myself cream onto my thighs and almost
screamed with pleasure. Charmaine moved away from me and I
opened my mind, my legs, and my arms to Niles.

Niles lay on his side next to me and ran his hands all over my body,
stopping at my quim to tease it gently. When he felt how wet I was, his
intake of breath was audible and he growled like the wild thing he
looked to be. His growl sent me whirling, my mind filled with nothing
but thoughts of him, fantasies of him having his way with me and of
me surrendering to him. The dungeon drifted away. The god of the
wood had me in his world and I went willingly into the dark forest with
him—no one else existed, nothing mattered but his hands on me and
how he would take his pleasure on me. One strong arm went under my
back and lifted me slightly up off the mattress, arching my back. One
large warm hand covered my quim as he started to bite my neck and
growl and sniff me loudly. He bit my nipples until I cried out and I
began to grind my hips against his hand. But he still didn't penetrate
me. I clung to his neck, moaning mindlessly, savoring the pain and
wanting more. His pheromones exuded from his body, conquered me,
and rendered me a willing, compliant thing whose only thought was to
be possessed by him.

Suddenly he withdrew his arm from underneath me and removed
his hand from my quim. I cried out at the abrupt deprivation of him
and begged him for more. I ripped off my thong, fondled my breasts, and
drew my knees up to expose myself to him to encourage him to play
with me. He knelt between my legs and, catching my eye, let me know
he was looking at my wet quim and spasming asshole. Charmaine, forgotten all this time, leaned over me and spread my lips and felt around
for my clitoris. Finding it and showing it and my opening to Niles, she
remarked that my clit was right on top of my opening and that the
hole was very small.

Niles smiled. His gorgeous cock was much larger than my opening
and with my clit being so close to it, I could have clitoral as well as
vaginal orgasms. Charmaine held me open and used her upper body
to keep my knees up while Niles covered himself with a sheath.

Charmaine moved to the side, still holding my lips open. I was coming and coming, thrashing my head against the pillow, clenching the comforter in my hands, begging Niles to penetrate me. He inserted his tip while Charmaine held my lips apart. Once his head was in me, Charmaine let my lips go and moved away. Niles fell on top of me and plunged his cock deep into me, stretching me, filling me, making me cry out in relief and pain and pleasure and release. He took me hard, enjoying my tight hole and the pain his huge cock was causing me. With each almost violent stroke, I became more and more pliant, more and more focused on his cock inside of me, until I was screaming mindlessly, completely unaware that Rowan, Esme, Oliver, Toby, and Charmaine were watching us. Niles manipulated me into several positions, each one meant to stretch me farther and give him the maximum penetration possible. Loving rough sex, I was a willing rag doll, letting him move me and penetrate me however he pleased as long as he didn't stop.

And he didn't stop for a very long time.

After an eternity that ended too soon, Niles rolled off of me. I lay panting on the comforter, limp, spent, my thighs smeared with my own juices, a rather large wet spot beneath me. He lay on his back and I put my head in the crook of his shoulder. Charmaine spooned against my back and soon Niles turned on his side so that I was between him and Charmaine. They started kissing, and as they kissed, I felt one of Charmaine's hands and one of Niles's hands exploring my quim. Breaking their kiss, they started talking about my quim as if I weren't there, saying how wet I was, how big my hole had gotten after Niles's rough attention to it, that it was more fun to shag someone with a beautiful body, how limber and pliable I was, and so on. Clenching each other tightly, they crushed me between them, and as their lips met, they began to grind against me; Niles's still-hard cock pounded my belly and Charmaine's softly furred pudendum rubbed and thrust against my buttocks. Delightful frissons of electrified humiliation ran through me. A vision of the three of us, greatly enhanced by the E, exploded in my mind. I imagined I was being publicly used as a human blow-up doll for Niles's and Charmaine's pleasure. Yet another fantasy fulfilled!

During the time that Niles, Charmaine, and I were shagging and roughhousing, Rowan and Esme had been enacting a scene of their own. Rowan was very adept at rope bondage and she had ingeniously secured Esme to the pillars of Hercules. Starting at Esme's small perky breasts, Rowan had made a bra of rope, ran the two ends down Esme's back, and made a crupper which is basically a g-string made of rope. Attaching more rope to the bra, Rowan ran the ropes up Esme's arms to her wrists cuffed with leather restraints and secured the restraints to eye hooks in the ceiling. Using another length of rope, Rowan secured this rope to the crupper, ran the ropes down Esme's legs, cuffed Esme's ankles with leather restraints, and secured those ropes to eye hooks at the bottom of the pillars. The visual effect was amazing and Rowan's rope work was artistic as well as inescapable. One look at Esme's face told us she had been transported to another world.

Esme was nude, and Rowan was wearing only a man's white dress shirt, cuffs rolled up and unbuttoned from the collar to right below her voluptuous breasts, and over-the-knee leather boots. A CD that Rowan loved began to play and she started to dance with the bound Esme. Standing behind her, Rowan pulled Esme back as far as the ropes would allow. Putting her hips to Esme's buttocks, Rowan commenced to bump and grind Esme in time to the music, rubbing her large breasts on Esme's back and flinging her long wild hair around. Esme responded immediately, and from where we sat we could see the ropes of the crupper digging into Esme's quim, intensifying her excitement. As Rowan ground into her from behind, Esme reacted by thrusting her hips back to meet Rowan's pudendum, tossing her head, flinging her short blond hair, and moaning in ecstacy. Their positive energy, their intuitive responses to each other, and their overall raw sexuality was tangible. We were intoxicated and couldn't tear our eyes away from them.

Several songs later, the breathless and panting Rowan draped herself over the suspended Esme. Although supporting Rowan's weight should have been quite an exertion for the slim Esme, both had been transported to the Midnight World we all love so much and Esme bore Rowan's voluptuous frame easily. They hung there together, limbs entwined, Rowan's head over Esme's shoulder, her mass of long curly hair cascading down the front of Esme's slender form. Esme's head was thrown back, resting on Rowan's opposite shoulder, her neck exposed as if awaiting the kiss of a vampire. Floating motionlessly, bound together in utter stillness, framed by the pillars of Hercules, they were completely unaware of us.

Returning to Earth, Rowan disengaged herself from Esme and began untying her. All this time, Toby and Oliver had been sitting together at the table, watching but not participating. In truth, I had been so captivated by Niles and Charmaine, so into the rough sex I had with Niles with the help of Charmaine, and watching Rowan with Esme, that I had forgotten all about Oliver and Toby. Rowan and Esme, now freed from her beauitful bondage, flopped down on the mattress next to Niles, Charmaine, and me. We all cuddled together, kissed gently, and ran our hands and fingertips over each other, not sure who was touching whom but not caring. The black room, the dark sexy music, the smell of incense and sex in the air, the absolute lack of inhibitions, the voyeurism of Oliver and Toby, and the effects of the E held me and the others in a magical timeless world.

As our ecstatic state mounted we slithered over each other, eliciting moans of pleasure as limbs curled around limbs, breasts rubbed against backs and other breasts, hands roamed, lips met, and tongues licked. The occasional thrust of Niles's hard cock against a belly or back was like a cattle prod. Lucky Niles, the only man among four women. We rolled around for a long time, enjoying each other's bodies and our unbridled displays of affection and sexuality. Then Charmaine whispered to me that Rowan loved to be scratched. Her whisper to me telepathically communicated itself to Esme and Niles. The four of us fell upon Rowan, who, realizing what was about to happen, offered herself to us by kneeling with legs wide and her arms outspread. Eight hands, eight sets of fingernails raked over her whole body, and her screams of euphoria filled the air. When Rowan could stand it no more, she collapsed onto the mattress, still gasping and shivering from the intensity of our attentions.

We collapsed around her and continued our uninhibited explorations of each other's bodies. My hands discovered that Niles's ass felt as lovely as it looked and that Charmaine had small, shy pink labia that concealed a rather generous opening. After some time had passed, I found myself between Rowan and Esme. Laughing and giggling like young girls, we kissed and fondled each other familiarly. Rowan took me in her arms and laid me on my back, then she laid down on one side of me with Esme on the other. Both of them had their hands on me, all over me—four hands touching me and driving me wild. Although I had experimented with enough women to know I am not bisexual, I found this almost innocent girlish intimacy to be delightful and abandoned myself to it.

Esme's hands cupped my breasts and her mouth enclosed one nipple then the other. Gently nibbling each nipple, she drew long, low moans of pleasure from me. My back arched and Rowan's hands moved down my body, over my flat stomach and farther, down to my freshly shaven quim. When Rowan first touched me there, I cried out, releasing a pent-up pleasure I didn't know was hiding inside me. Softly but firmly, Rowan began to explore my folds and clefts. Esme stopped playing with my nipples so I could give myself over entirely to Rowan. Her hands were soft like a woman's, knowing like a woman's, yet she explored me with the stronger touch of a man. No other woman had ever evoked this response from me before and I spread my legs wider, offering myself to her.

I felt Rowan's two prime fingers enter me. When she gently touched my hot spot, the orgasm she gave me almost made me faint. She started using her fingers to thrust into me the same way a man would use his cock, and my hips rose to meet her. As she slipped a third finger into me, the music stopped suddenly. The silence did not quite register in my mind. In a volume that Stentor would have been proud of, into the utter hush I said in a little-girl tone of voice: "I'm sorry my hole is so loose, Mistress, but I fucked Niles and his cock is very big and he stretched me."

Everyone roared with side-splitting laughter, including me.

But in spite of her laughter, Rowan didn't withdraw her fingers from me, she kept thrusting and twisting her fingers into me, smiling the whole time. Then she asked me if I had ever been beaten. I told her no and she asked Esme to get her a flogger. It was then that I explained to Rowan that I wanted Oliver to be the first because I was there to serve him. Rowan understood this, so she asked Oliver to do the "honors." For reasons unknown to me, Oliver's mood had changed or soured, and Rowan had to persuade him to take up the flogger. I was fleetingly puzzled by this but thought no more of it when Oliver accepted the whip.

Taking me by the hand, Rowan led me over to the empty space near the spanking bench. While she did this Oliver tested the flogger against his hand but I barely noticed him, intent as I was on listening to Rowan's instructions. I was to stand facing her back and she would face the wall. When we were in position, she grabbed my hands and pulled them forward so that my elbows were at her shoulders. Then she bent at the waist. She was taller and of a stronger build than I, and when she bent over, I went with her! My feet dangled off the floor and my body was completely supported by hers. She had turned herself into a human spanking bench! This was a wonderful, creative, and exciting position for a beating, but even a strongly built woman like Rowan couldn't hold it for long. And Oliver was fiddling with that flogger for so long you would think he had never seen one before! I had forgotten all about the snit he was in.

Tiring, and tired of waiting for Oliver, Rowan suggested another position on the spanking bench. She laid face up on the bench and I bent over her and rested my head on her midsection, my face up against her belly. Oh, this was just heavenly! Her belly was warm and soft against my cheek, my breasts were pressed between her hips, and her thighs felt strong underneath me. When she held my head in her hands and stroked my hair, the spurt of wetness was so strong it ran down my thighs. I floated timelessly, lost in the warmth and safety of Rowan's flesh until I felt the first stroke of Oliver's flogger. It was a perfect stroke as were the following strokes, but Oliver was unhappy so he stopped. The flogger was not his instrument of choice, so I hugged Rowan and waited for Oliver to return with a cane, his favorite implement of discipline and pain.

Oliver started the caning just the way I had dreamed of it: first many soft taps covering the sweet spots of my buttocks and upper thighs then progressing to medium strokes. He knew by my body language, by the way I thrust my buttocks out to meet each stroke, that I

was ready for the hard ones. There were to be six of them in all: six of
his best, escalating in severity. The sensation of the first stroke, my first
beating with a cane, was intense, electrifying. It started on my buttocks, crept up my spine, then exploded in my brain like a red hot burst
of pleasurable agony. He waited until I had absorbed the first stroke
before administering the second. After each stroke, up until the fourth
stroke, he paused. Before he gave me the final two strokes, Oliver
asked me if I wanted them. He promised me they would be very hard,
and I begged him for them.

He delivered them one right after the other. White-hot fire on my
cheeks, a lightning bolt up my spine, two volcanic eruptions in my brain,
and then it was over.

Rowan hugged me to her and said I had taken my beating very well.
But Oliver didn't say anything, he just walked back to the table and
sat down with Toby. I didn't care. The fire in my brain, the burning of
my buttocks, and the womblike enveloping of Rowan's body became my
whole universe. Rowan and I laid there together on the spanking bench
until the afterglow was gone. Rising, she went to Esme and I went and
knelt at Oliver's feet. I wanted to perform a very special service for
him, one that I thought would truly express my gratitude for my first
caning. I also hoped that the service I was going to offer him would get
him out of the snit he was in. I knelt at his feet until he acknowledged
me. It was several minutes before he decided to tap me on the shoulder so I could speak.

I told him I wished to show my devotion to him by worshipping his
anus. Oliver accepted immediately and positioned himself comfortably on the mattress on his stomach, next to Niles and Charmaine. I
situated myself between Oliver's spread legs, and he raised his hips.
His bum was gorgeous: his cheeks firm and muscular, his hair golden
blond, and his opening looked liked the rosebud opening the Marquis
de Sade wrote of so eloquently, so pink and tender. I stretched out between his legs and taking one cheek in each hand, I spread him wide. I
began with one long "paint brush lick" and was rewarded with a moan
of pleasure. My tongue made tiny circles around his pink puckered
opening many times before I quickly darted my tongue into him, just
once, eliciting another moan of pleasure. As I performed these ac-

tions, I used my thumbs to dig into pressure points on his buttocks, heightening his pleasure.

Everyone was watching me. Their voyeurism skyrocketed my pleasure. I wallowed in the decadence, the lust, and the submission of my actions, and all of this cloaked me in warmth as I worshipped him. Puckering my lips, I placed them on his anus and began to suck it, suck it hard, occasionally darting my tongue deeply into him. From a far away place, I heard Charmaine say that it sounded like a really good rim job. I wrapped my arms under Oliver's hips and raised them higher, sucked harder, and darted my tongue into him more often. Oliver was writhing in pleasure, abandoning himself to me. After too short a lifetime, I came up for air and also to let Oliver catch his breath. Then he asked me to use the binder clips on the pressure point on both sides close to his anus, within the sweet spot. I wasn't strong enough to open the clip, so while I grasped Oliver's flesh between my fingers and pulled it out, Niles applied the binder clips.

After Oliver had absorbed the pain from the application of the binder clips, he asked me to get a clothes pin (the round kind, not the clip kind), which he called a clothes "peg," lubicate it well, and insert it into his anus. Once it was in him, I again began to use my tongue to circle the clothes peg and my hands to massage the flesh of his cheeks near the peg. His groans of pleasure filled the air and he began to pump his hips against the mattress. Several minutes passed before he sated himself and told me to remove the clothes peg and binder clips. Then he rolled onto his back and relaxed for a little while. I was so engrossed in Oliver I had no idea what the others were doing. I stretched out next to him, enjoying the warmth of his body and soaking up his pranic (a source to feed upon, can be sexual, or the thrill of a thunderstorm, the beauty of a sunny day) energy.

With catlike grace, Oliver rose from the mattress, went to the table, and returned with two unused binder clips, lubricant, and a clothes peg. Then he told me that he was going use these things to do to me what I had done to him. Silently, I rolled onto my stomach, raised my hips, and offered myself to him. As I awaited his pleasure, he called out to the others to come and watch. Everyone, except for the usually voyeuristic Toby, gathered round and took turns looking at my exposed anus. Bodies cuddled against me, hands held my legs open, then the flesh of my sweet spots were grabbed by unknown hands. Oliver applied the binder clips and I groaned in pain. The bodies and hands held me down and held me open as Oliver lubricated my anus and inserted the clothes peg.

Hands began to manipulate the flesh around the binder clips, someone pumped the clothes peg in and out of me. Then the hands turned me over onto my back and Rowan thrust her breast in my mouth to muffle my screams and prevent me from seeing who was using me. My lips closed on her nipple and I began to suck it like a nursing babe. The humiliation and pain of it all kindled a passion in me that I didn't know I had, and very soon, instead of fighting them, I was responding to them and releasing that newly discovered passion. Sensing the change in my body, my tormentors renewed their efforts. Rowan removed her breast from my mouth, held my head between her knees and my wrists in her hands. Looking down, I could see that Charmaine and Esme each had a hold of a leg and that Oliver and Niles were using their fingers and the clothes peg in and around my anus. Rowan called everyone's attention to the slender beauty of my body, and as they admired and touched me, Rowan said she wanted to steal my passport so I couldn't go home.

In the timeless environment of the black room, I experienced an exquisite mix of pain, pleasure, and humiliation that washed over me like a wave and cleansed me of the inhibitions, doubts, and taboos society had inflicted upon me. This wave left in its wake nothing but a sexual being, a mindless thing craving more. I willingly abandoned myself to these feelings and concentrated on nothing other than the hands all over me, the legs holding mine open, the bodies pressed against me, the fingers and peg in me, my exposure, and what was being done to my body. My body rocked and shook with orgasms as I let them take their pleasure on me.

I had reached another level and all tension flowed out of me. My captors felt my lack of resistance. Esme and Charmaine pulled my legs closer to my body, which lifted my hips off the mattress. Oliver and Niles withdrew the clothes peg and fingered me deeper and harder, and Rowan leaned over and removed the binder clips, then inserted her fingers into my quim, checking to see if I was wet. Delighted to find me slimy with come, she invited the others to penetrate me. More fingers touched and penetrated me; I could tell the women's touches from the men's but I didn't know who the fingers belonged to, nor did I care. Freed from the bodily bonds of my captors, I reached down and spread my cheeks wider, begging them not to stop, pleading with them to use me more, to touch my breasts, to kiss me or put their fingers in my mouth. I was out of my mind with lust and I would have sucked any cock, any finger, any breast that was offered to me. I would have welcomed any penetration, separately or together.

My wishes were granted but not in any way I expected or could have imagined. Rowan straddled my midsection with her back to me. Her beautiful derriere and her small waist mesmerized me. She whispered something to Niles, then Esme and Charmaine held my legs open. I heard Niles sheath himself then felt him rub the head of his cock against my quim. I thought he was going to penetrate me and I went wild, but he just continued rubbing his head against my quim. Then I felt the tip of his head press up against my anus and realized he had been using my own juices to lubricate the sheath. I begged him to sodomize me, but he only laughed. Rowan started to spank my quim, very gently and concentrating on the area around my clitoris. I groaned when the first blow landed, my body spasmed as I came, and I felt Niles's cock press harder against my anus. Rowan increased the intensity of her slaps, and each time I came, Niles inched more of his head into me, not really penetrating me but just stretching my hole.

As Rowan's blows became harder and faster, as Niles's cock stretched me more, I screamed and thrashed around. But I was completely and inescapably pinned down by Rowan's body and by Esme and Charmaine holding my legs open. I had the use of my arms and hands but I had no desire to stop what was being done to me. I caressed Rowan's derriere while she spanked my quim, and I ran my long fingernails up and down as much of her back as I could reach. This drove her wild and spurred her on to spank me harder. Rowan hit my quim relentlessly, and as she did so Niles began to pop the head of his cock in and out of me. Rowan and Niles fell into a rhythm: She would slap me and he would pop into me. When she hit me again, he would pop out of me. Primal, feral sexuality overtook me as my hips thrust up to meet Rowan's slaps and Niles's thrusts. I stopped screaming and thrashing and began groaning in unrestrained pleasure from deep down in my throat as they amused themselves with me.

Rowan gave me one very hard final slap, and with a growl, Niles pulled out of me completely. Charmaine and Esme let go of my legs. They all flopped down next to me on the mattresses and we curled up together like puppies in a box. I didn't notice until then that Oliver had withdrawn himself back to the table and was talking with Toby. Someone managed to pull a comforter over us because we were suddenly cold after our exertions. I rested for a while, then suddenly, I had to pee. I disengaged myself from the tangle of limbs and bodies, made my way to the shower room, located the drain, and squatted over it. I let loose with a long "ah" of pleasure as I emptied my bladder. Suddenly Oliver was in front of me, asking in a slightly, and puzzlingly, stern voice what I was doing. Still being very high, I giggled and said I was peeing, then asked him if he would like to watch. Everyone started laughing. Oliver shook his head in amusement, refused, but thanked me for my "sweet offer" and told me to go ahead, enjoy myself. My sighs of relief continued to the laughter of all until I was done. Then Esme thoughtfully brought me a napkin so I could wipe myself.

Silly, a little wobbly on my feet, still rolling, my bladder thankfully empty, and sexually satisfied, gratified, and sated, I plopped back down on the mattress, burrowed under the comforter, and snuggled in. At twelve thirty the next afternoon, Oliver woke Rowan, Esme, and me. He said it was time to go to the house and get some sleep. Toby had departed for the house and the comfort of his own bed some time ago. We got up, found our clothes, and stumbled outside to find a bright sunny if crisp day awaiting us. Leaving Niles and Charmaine alone in the dungeon, we ran up the path to the house like vampires afraid of being scalded to death by the sunlight.

Oliver asked me to sleep with him and I immediately accepted, but actually I was much too excited to sleep. I ended up standing guard over him as he slept, but his sleep was restless. He awoke in a few hours and told me he wanted me to worship him again. I did as he commanded until he was relaxed and fell back asleep. Then I slept, too. When we finally awoke, it was about eight in the evening.

We jumped into our clothes and made our way downstairs to the kitchen, where Rowan, Esme, and Toby were lounging at the table. Laughing at how late Oliver and I had slept, Rowan said we all must be as hungry as she was, and she began to cook us a lovely spaghetti dinner. I asked where Niles and Charmaine were, and someone said they had left hours ago because Charmaine had to be home by four when her son got home from school. I was disappointed they weren't there, especially Niles, but a kid is a kid. In short order, Rowan had finished cooking and Esme served each of us a heaping plate of spaghetti. We tore into it like we hadn't eaten in days (maybe we hadn't), then sat around the table amidst the ruins of dinner, smoking and talking. Finally, I cleared the table and washed the mountain of pots and dishes.

Esme made a large pot of tea, "British style." After boiling the water, she swirled a small amount in the tea pot to heat it then spilled it out. She put the tea bags in the tea pot, and poured the boiling water over them. In each tea cup, she spooned in the required amount of sugar, added the milk to sweeten it, then when the tea had brewed sufficiently, she poured it into the tea cups. We helped ourselves and then we all adjourned to our separate bedrooms.

My room was cold but after Toby taught me how to build a coal fire I soon had a warm blaze going in the rather frigid little room. (I later found out that Toby had forgotten to turn on the radiator in there.) Turning the lights up, I stripped and for the first time got a good look at the cane marks. Whatever else Oliver may or may not have been, he was certainly a master of the cane. Looking at my derriere in the mirror, I mentally compared the cane jobs I had seen in the states to the one right before my eyes. I was pretty good with the cane but I had seen a lot of botch jobs. Wild swings, wraps . . . another reason I had sought a master across the ocean. The marks were in a perfect line and perfectly positioned, not one wild stroke could be seen. My outer cheeks were pink to red and the black-and-blue marks were centered exactly around the sweet spot. They were so lovely that the idea floated across my mind to become a cane pain slut.

Holding the image of them in my mind's eye, I dove under the pile of blankets on the bed, plumped up the pillows, and burrowed in. The sugar plum faerie that danced in my head that night was blond and wielded a cane.

SIX

When I awoke the next day, I had no idea what time it was, but the thin sunshine looked like early afternoon. I dressed quickly because I heard Oliver moving around in his room and I wanted to present myself at his door and inquire if I could get him anything. Instead of tea, he asked for coffee. Although the coffee was awfully strong, he drank it anyway and motioned that I take the service away. Something in that gesture told me that he wished to be alone in the privacy of his room for the rest of the afternoon. Toby was in the kitchen when I returned. I asked about Rowan and Esme and he told me they had left in the late morning. Seeing him fiddling with chores, I offered my help. He smiled; he had hosted many maid cross-dressers whose "help" was nothing of the sort. The Manor was large, there had just been a party, there was certainly plenty to be done.

Toby and I went at it for a couple of hours: vacuuming, dusting, washing the dishes, and of course, more laundry. While we worked, Toby amused me with tales of people who came to the house and did things that even we perves thought were hilariously funny. Our laughter wasn't demeaning but that of those who shared an inside joke. One fellow would visit in a full military uniform and do nothing other than march back and forth in front of the Manor as if he were on guard duty. A married couple also came by once in a while. They used an old refurbished pony cart to train the woman as a pony girl, complete with plumed headdress, corset, gloves, shoes, bit, bridle, and reins.

Exchanging these pleasantries made the work go quickly, and soon I had time to go check on Oliver. His door was almost but not quite shut, so I knocked and looked in. He was in bed, smoking. When he saw me he patted the bed. I smiled and laid down next to him. Then he started to complain how late in the day it was, how he hadn't gotten anything done, and that he hadn't even showered yet. Whereupon I said in a sycophant's tone of voice complete with accent, "Oh, effendi! You have done many things today . . ." and listed all the chores I had done with Toby that afternoon. Oliver laughed and rolled me over onto my belly. My dress flopped up and exposed my derriere, calling his attention to my cane marks, my lovely bruises. Then he grabbed one cheek in his hand and squeezed it hard, called me "cheeky," and laughed again.

As he continued to grab my cheeks and squeeze them, I, too, started to laugh. I heard him say something like "cheeky bottom" and "canes," and in a flash he was off the bed. I went after him. He rooted through the wardrobe, took out a very flexible cane, and flicked it against his palm. The sound of it was different from the one he used on me in the dungeon. As it whistled through the air, I ran my hands up through my hair. "What's the matter, darling?" he asked oh-so-sweetly, a smile in his voice. "Nothing, milord," I whispered. My knees almost gave out on me. "Pull your dress up and bend over the bed," he said as he pointed to a corner of the bed. I bent over it. Not happy with the arch in my back, Oliver pressed me into a position more to his liking. He wanted my derriere to stick out farther and to do this, I had to bend my knees and brace them against the box spring. Not a very comfortable or easy position to hold. But when Oliver said, "Yes, like that, darling," the Capricorn goat in me became determined to hold that position, come hell or high water.

Oliver didn't give me the warm-up like he did the first time. This was to be six of his best, straight out. He tapped my derriere two or three times before he landed the first stroke. And what a stroke it was! It landed squarely across my cheeks, right above the last welt of the first set. This cane was different all right! It took longer for the pain to sink in, but when it did, it was red then white hot. It shot, not crept, up my spine and exploded in my brain in a star burst of agony that made my quim cream. I grasped the duvet cover with both hands and buried my head in it until I could absorb it. Oliver waited until I settled back down then he gave me another two or three little taps to let me know where the real stroke would land. Then the second stroke overtook me. Again he waited until I was ready: two or three little taps, then the full swing. I could feel that no one blow overlapped another and that this set was directly above the first. It was going to look beautiful and I was going to be so proud of them.

Wanting to please him, wanting more of this unbelievable pain for myself, greedy for it all, I arched my back and stuck my derriere out farther for the fourth stroke. After I settled down, Oliver, my lord and master, whispered in my ear that it was time for the "last two"—the best of his best. I whimpered. I was deliciously ashamed of how much I wanted them, and at that very moment I decided that when he next caned me, I would ask him for eight strokes, not six. The fifth and sixth strokes were not spaced out like the first four. These landed one right after the other, hot, hard, and heavy, and I had no time to absorb the fifth before the sixth hit. Almost overcome with the explosions in my mind and body, when Oliver told me to remain where I was, I was happy to oblige. I don't think I could have moved anyway.

From behind me I heard the unmistakable and lovely sound of a condom being removed from its wrapper. Oliver pressed himself between my legs and penetrated my quim. He hurt me a little when he entered me but I was wet inside and I savored the slight pain his entry gave me. Encouraged by my moans, Oliver pounded into me, ramming me deep, hard and fast. I cried out in ecstacy at his use of me, thrilled to have him inside me. The extra inch his Prince Albert ring added to his cock was just enough to hit my spot. He shagged me until I came, and then he came.

I was giddy for the rest of the evening but not so out of it that I couldn't go staggering off on my stilettos to find Toby and show him my marks.

SEVEN

Charmaine called the Manor and told Oliver that she had put Oliver and I on the guest list for a mixed off-premises swingers/fetish nightclub, The Cross, in north London. The club was small and intimate with a bar and lounge area and two separate dance floors. The males outnumbered the women by at least two to one and Charmaine and I took advantage of this by flirting outrageously with all and sundry. Everyone there was rolling, including our little entourage of Oliver, Niles, Charmaine, and myself. Our train quickly expanded to include another couple, Leon and Barbie, who were there when we arrived. Leon was a little shorter than I like my men to be, about five-foot-five or so, with dark brown hair held tightly back with a rubber band, and glasses. There was nothing special about his looks other than his sharp fang teeth, but he had great presence. Leon exuded so much confidence that it not only surrounded him but also cast a protective shell around his slave girl, Barbie.

After the introductions and we were well out of hearing distance, Oliver remarked to me that he thought Leon was a real asshole and that he didn't like the way Leon treated his women. "Then why do you speak to him?" I asked naively. Oliver shrugged and added that everyone was nice to Leon because Leon had been around since "before the beginning." He also ran an exclusive club and had his uses. I don't know why I thought that such things would not enter into the scene over there, like they did in New York or Florida, but I did, so this attitude surprised me. (In fact, the British were every bit as political as their US counterparts.)

The coziness of the place, the smoky atmosphere, and the dim lights made it seem that this was a big house party. The clubbers weren't a bunch of strangers there for one night, but people who had known each other for years. Even the purple sofa Charmaine was ensconced on had the look of something one would have in one's home, though perhaps not in that shade. As I shared the sofa with Charmaine, handsome young men would drift up to one or both of us, sit for a while, massage our hands or feet or necks, look into our eyes and tell us we were beautiful, then drift away. Endless bottles of water flowed but not once did Charmaine or I go to the bar. We were like goddesses, the purple sofa our pedestal, and the bottles of water offerings of ambrosia from our devoted followers. When the roll hit and the rush began, the massages felt wonderful and sent chills up and down my spine. My eyes glowed and I believed that I was as beautiful as they said.

Although I arrived with Oliver, once he was confident that I was happy and could handle myself, he drifted back and forth between the lounge and the dance floors. I decided to stay in the lounge area for the evening, enshrined on the purple heart-shaped sofa. It was the perfect vantage point from which to see all the denizens of the dark as they went up to the bar. I took up enough space on the sofa so that whenever Oliver or Niles came back for a rest, there would be enough room for them to sit down. Charmaine was still there but she was flirting heavily with this one guy and not paying attention to us. Each time Oliver or Niles came to sit, I had water or soda there for them, and, as they had left their jackets with Charmaine and me, I also became the Keeper of the Fags and Coats as well as the Water Bearer. It didn't take them long to notice I was playing a game, and they quickly played along. A curled hand extended my way meant a beverage was desired, the smoking gesture meant a cigarette was desired. When through with the beverage, it was simply handed back to me without a word.

Once we had all regrouped at the purple sofa, Niles invited us back to his flat in Maida Vale for a private party. Leon and Barbie declined but we had picked up three other people along the way, a couple named Nate and Anna, and Tony, the single male Charmaine had been flirting with in the club. Tony turned out to be her on-the-side lover. Back at Niles's it was clear the three newcomers were fish out of water, and the core of the group was to be Niles, Charmaine, Oliver, and me. Nate and Anna left almost immediately, but Tony sat and stared and stayed well past the point of courtesy. It was obvious there was no place for him there. He offered nothing and made me quite uncomfortable. Finally, seeing that his presence was holding back not only me but everyone else, I told Charmaine I was going to ask him to leave. I took Tony aside and told him that I was very new at this, that this was my "first" play party, and I really wanted to let go but couldn't with him just sitting there staring. I asked if he would be a gentleman and leave the shy lady to her pleasures.

He proved to be a gentleman, and we all breathed a sigh of relief when he left. We started to roll up hash spliffs and gobble down more E. It was clear Niles wanted to be with me. He had kept me close to him ever since we walked in, so that put Oliver with Charmaine. She didn't seem to mind. Charmaine was such a pleasure and attention slut that I later heard someone say that she would do anything to have people look at her, even take an enema in public. She was so open about it, so empowered by her sexuality that I found her to be quite refreshing. We lit up the spliffs while Niles readied the room for our little foursome.

Quilts and comforters were piled up on the floor in front of the electric heater, the front room door was closed to keep the heat in, music came through the speakers, and the lights were dimmed. Charmaine was the first to undress, but she was undecided whether or not she felt like being with Oliver that night. It was clear I was going to be with Niles, and I had sent her lover Tony home. I knew when Oliver suggested giving her a back massage, he was thinking that the massage would help get her into the mood. Niles and I kissed; his pheromones so overwhelmed me that I was almost senseless. I lay in his arms like a rag doll while his tongue opened, probed, and explored my mouth. He handled my body roughly, being very physical with me, taking my clothes off as he pleased, moving me to where he wanted me, and adjusting my limbs to suit his needs. He pinched my nipples cruelly and became very excited that I could take so much pain there, but he was very gentle with my quim. He drove me wild with his tongue in my mouth and his fingers deep inside me.

Four people in the golden glow of the heater, enhanced by E and hash, the intimacy of the little scene—everything made me very wanton. Niles had shed his clothes and had me in his lap, and I laid back against his chest. He held me in one arm and used that hand to torture and pinch my nipples. My legs were splayed open and the skin of my newly shaved pudendum glowed pale against the skin around it. One of Niles's legs held one of mine down and open, two fingers were buried up to the knuckles in my quim. I squirmed on his fingers until I was so wet my thighs were smeared with my own juices. If Oliver and Charmaine had stopped to watch us, I hadn't noticed. Draping an arm around Niles's neck, I placed the soles of my feet together and arched my back, loving Niles's fingers probing and stretching my quim. Niles had quite a nice body, great legs and butt, and a big pretty circumcised cock. I so wanted to shag him but he was directing the action and it was time for a break.

While we took a rest, we watched Charmaine and Oliver. They were in their own little orbit. Their two blond heads and two pale bodies took on an otherworldly glow in the orange light from the heater. Charmaine was on her belly, her hips up, legs slightly open. Oliver was on his side next to her, propped up on one arm and with one leg nestled in between hers. His free hand disappeared between her cheeks. She was moaning heavily as Oliver worked his gloved fingers into her anus. The more she moaned, the more he renewed his efforts, the more she moaned. . . . turning her head, she saw Niles and me watching her with Oliver. Our hot eyes made her pleasure mount and she began to raise her hips to meet Oliver's thrusts. Our eyes stayed locked as Oliver made Charmaine come. I was a little envious of her. Oliver had not touched me there except to administer a couple or three (excruciatingly painful) slaps. To hide my confusion, I turned to Niles in a welter of passion and opened myself to him. After more kissing and more torture, soon I, too, was in my own orbit.

Sometime later, Charmaine started to dance to this great tape Niles had, called *Pink and Squiggy Bits*. I liked the music and I liked dancing with girls, so I got up to join her. But almost as soon as I did my little step toward her, she sat down, either leaving me to dance for all of them, or wanting all the attention for herself. I danced for my own joy, for the pleasure of Niles and Charmaine, but most of all, for Oliver. As the song neared its end, I assumed the ritual position Oliver had taught me all those months ago. Catching his eye, I reached back and spread my cheeks. I was rewarded with a smile. When the song ended, I sat with him on the sofa and offered my dance to him. He accepted it with a casual nod.

Niles and Charmaine were roughing it up on the quilt-covered floor.

Grabbing Charmaine by the hair, Niles forced her head down onto his cock. Earlier, Niles had wanted me to suck his cock, but I blathered on about Oliver having to be first in everything and that I hadn't sucked Oliver's cock yet. With the exchange of partners, this could now be accomplished. Niles went to work on Charmaine's face while I sucked Oliver. I was surprised his cock tasted so sweet and clean since he was uncut. I enjoyed using my tongue to play with his cock ring, a new toy for me. He gave me some directions but basically let me do what came naturally to me. I had told him over the phone that I didn't give very good head, but that was not quite the truth. The truth was that I didn't give very good head to uncircumsized cocks and Oliver was not cut. A defense mechanism? Certainly. A good thing to have; that and a safe word. But at the end he said that I hadn't done badly, so I was happy he enjoyed it.

Charmaine had rolled away from Niles and was more asleep than awake. Niles's hot eyes on me told me he wanted to play with me some more. Charmaine roused herself at 8 a.m. and decided to go home, leaving me alone with the two men. The closer Charmaine got to the door, the hotter Niles's eyes became. As soon as she was gone, Niles threw what little restraint he had left to the wind. He pulled me off the sofa by the arm and settled me into the quilts and pillows on the floor. He entered me so gently and worked his way in so slowly that I kept having one orgasm after another. Fascinated, Oliver climbed down to the floor to be near us but not touch us (later on he told me he enjoyed feeling the floor vibrate with our rammings). As I became more aroused, Niles took me in several other difficult positions and made me come often. As each wave washed over his cock, he pounded into me harder and maneuvered my limbs for better penetration.

Oliver's back was to us when Niles spooned me and took me in that position. I reached for Oliver and pulled him closer to me. Niles's long arms enclosed Oliver as well as me. In concert with Niles, I pounded my pudendum into Oliver's backside. Oliver began to masturbate and I reached an arm over to help. A loud, "oh, fuck, yeah," from Niles, followed by his come stroke, let Oliver and I know Niles was ready. Niles hit my spot and I came; upon feeling my body jerk, Niles came, then

Oliver. We rolled away from Oliver but none of us really moved. We had pounded and pummeled ourselves into sated exhaustion and we just dozed off where we lay.

It was about ten o'clock when Oliver announced that it was time to make the ride home. Niles took me aside and insisted that I spend a day or two alone with him. As tempting as his offer was, I declined, saying that I had come to the UK to be with Oliver. Little did I know that Niles was going to get his wish. Oliver and I got back to Susing-ham around eleven thirty, went to our separate rooms, and crashed.

EIGHT

Although we awoke around six the next evening, Oliver and I were still a bit high and quite a bit spaced out from the night before. Toby made us a leftover smorgasbord supplemented with bread and fruit, and the three of us picked at that for a while, no one too interested in eating. Then we watched a rented movie, *The Night Porter*, which we'd all seen before. It was a BDSM scene favorite. We were still so burnt that right after the movie, Oliver and I went to bed. I knew he wasn't in a touchy-feely mood, but it would be good to be in the bed with him, to feel his warm pale body next to mine. He fell asleep long before I did and while he was asleep, I observed him in a way that was otherwise impossible. His face looked so soft and vulnerable in the moonlight, and when he threw back the quilt, he revealed the beautiful golden body of a young man.

We slept into the next day, having only a brief moment to ourselves before Toby came in and engaged Oliver in a very animated discussion regarding their feelings about the dominant and submissive relationship. Toby needed a tete-a-tete with Oliver as much as I wanted to be with Oliver, so instead of leaving, I went about serving Oliver as best I could while listening in on their conversation. What I heard surprised me. No matter how hard they played physically, these people were pondering subjects that were explained to me before I turned professional as if they were the greatest revelations in the world. Real basic stuff, but who am I to judge? Hearing this novice-like turn in the conversation and assimilating it into what I knew about their physical intensity drove me downstairs into the kitchen, where I realized they had the cart well out in front of the horse. So to kill time, I made Oliver an American-style breakfast: coffee and bacon and eggs, with the eggs fried in butter rather than in lard. After remarking upon the "delicious" breakfast, Oliver told me that I was doing well. I had been there for several days and he hadn't beaten me once for "correction."

I was pleased by Oliver's compliment, although I was still puzzled by their seemingly backward approach vis-à-vis the mental attachment before the heavy physical stuff. (It was to be many years before I figured it out.) I removed the remains of breakfast and asked to be dismissed to take a bath. Leave was granted, and this time, I built up the fire and let it roar while I gathered up my things. Oliver and Toby couldn't be heard from the bathroom, and once immersed in the hot, foamy water, I floated mind and body to the crackle of the fire and the shwoosh of the water and didn't come back until the water got tepid. I shampooed my hair under a handheld shower nozzle that attached to the dual faucets, one for hot and one for cold, then rinsed off the bubbly remains of the bath. After wrapping one towel around my hair and another around my body, I stretched out like a cat in front of the fire and let its warmth overtake me one side at a time. I had no concept of time and I was in no hurry. I shook my hair out of the towel to let the fire help dry it and lolled around on the rug in front of the fire while turning over the recent happenings in my head. Finally, I harnessed my energy and dried my hair. I don't know how much time had passed.

When I stepped back into Oliver's room, he and Toby were still deep in the same conversation. I made the gesture for "coffee" and got a yes nod. While the coffee percolated, I prepared a snack tray of cheeses, pepperoni, and crackers to take upstairs. Oliver and Toby had been talking for hours and were grateful for this quick bite. But their discussion had progressed so far and had gone off on so many tangents that I couldn't even begin to pick up the thread of what they were saying. So I wandered back to the nice warm bathroom, wiped the vanity mirror dry, and carefully put on makeup. Then I wandered down to the kitchen and made tea just for me, even finding a piece of pound cake.

And when I finally went back upstairs, Oliver and Toby were still at it. I sighed inwardly. I wanted to talk with Oliver, too, and like Toby, I thought this would be the perfect day for it. Day had turned to night, and it was past dinnertime when Toby left Oliver's room. Toby went out for fish and chips and we stuffed ourselves while we watched another movie. About eleven thirty, Oliver and I went upstairs, but he was all talked out and just wanted to read some of his book before retiring. I was disappointed but not surprised and did not press. Wishing him good night, I went about building a nice fire in my little room, laid in supplies to keep it going, and stocked up from the kitchen. I burrowed under the covers and only came out to smoke or get refreshment. It was very late when I fell asleep.

The next morning the bubble burst. Oliver awoke in a good mood but something happened between him and Toby that I wasn't privy to, now his good mood was gone. Toby had passed a remark about "having done enough washing up" and vibes were bad. We had gotten up early because we were going to London but first we had to clean the dungeon. Oliver and I attacked the place like tornadoes and in no time at all, we were finished. Back at the Manor, I went directly to my room. There was a spurt of commotion from downstairs—noise and loud voices—and shortly after Oliver came limping up the stairs. Oliver has kicked a wall and now his ankle was swollen. He announced that he couldn't do London with his ankle in this state, which was quite obvious.

I was dashed on many levels. My disappointment showed in my face, every line of my body. All because Oliver had a temper tantrum. Oliver hadn't played with me for a few days, vibes were getting very strange in the house, and I seemed to be getting caught in the middle. Niles and Charmaine seemed very far away in London and I felt quite alone, even when Toby called me for lunch. We ate together, but as soon as the last forkful was downed, Oliver closed himself in his bedroom and Toby made himself scarce. I washed the dishes and made tea for myself, trying to fill the time. Finally around four o'clock, I could stand it no longer. Taking pillows and blankets from my room, I curled up on the settee at the foot of Oliver's bed. He awoke and found me there. He didn't say anything but I did persuade him to let me look at his ankle. I iced it right away and practically forced two ibuprofen tablets down his throat.

Again I wanted to talk with him and again he wasn't in the mood, but I had to get it out of me. Oliver made it clear that I wasn't the problem and I made it clear that I was the victim of the problem. He told me then that for the last two to three weeks he hadn't felt like playing much and that his moods had been up and down. And tomorrow, he said as an afterthought, "a beautiful couple" named Sonya and Michael were coming for the week and it would be the "five" of us. I groaned inwardly; how I hate "odd numbers," someone always gets left out. Having no idea what effect his words were having on me, he went on to say that the day after that, he would be spending the day in Maida Vale where Niles was organizing a "gang rape" for Charmaine. (At least someone would be getting some.) I had a sinking feeling in my stomach. In an attempt to salvage what looked to be going completely down the drain, I suggested that I spend a night with Niles, and Oliver suggested a night much later in the week. We called Niles.

It was as Oliver had said; with the "rape" happening there and the new arrivals here, later in the week proved to be better for Niles and the day was set up. Oliver continued to chat with Niles. I went down to the kitchen, journal in hand, anxious for them to hang up. I wanted to call Niles back but I didn't know what to say to him. That it wasn't working with Oliver? Or that Oliver himself wasn't "working"? I knew their conversation was over when Oliver came into the kitchen. He saw me writing and peered over my shoulder. Annoyed at this invasion of my privacy, I slammed the book shut. He assured me he wasn't looking then asked if I was angry about the phone call. I dismissed that with a wave of my hand. So what that he spoke to Niles in a warmer, sexier tone than he did to me? Maybe he was more turned on by that little scene on the floor at Niles's the other night than I originally thought.

Back in my cold little room I sat on the edge of the bed, staring at the ash-laden fireplace. My silence must have been disturbing to Oliver. Soon he appeared at the connecting door and looked in on me.

When he asked what I was doing, I told him I was deciding if I wanted to sleep in my room or his. Whatever he thought I was going to say, that was not it. Seeing the expression on his face, I suddenly announced that it was much too cold in my room and that I would be sleeping in his. Oliver kept well away from me in the night, but I was still much warmer than I would have been in the bed in the room next door.

NINE

How did this day start? I haven't got a clue, lost as I was in what Oliver had told me yesterday about his moods and the new arrivals. I wouldn't have been quite so lost if his ideas and mine, as the conversation progressed, had some common ground, but they didn't. Oliver and I wouldn't be playing anymore, even though it was something I could still do to some degree. How devoted does one have to be to serve tea? How enamored does one have to be to drink it? Instead, we spent the day awaiting the arrival of the "beautiful people," Sonya and Michael, a couple who were very much in love, very much into exploring their BDSM desires. By the time they arrived at six o'clock that evening, my head was so full of visions of their beauty that when this rather below-average-looking couple got out of the car, I was somewhat disappointed, maybe even a little dismayed. And I was uncomfortable with them right from the start. Something about Sonya made my hair stand on end. I was greatly relieved when Oliver said it was time to pick up the Ecstacy and invited me along. I couldn't get into the car fast enough.

When we returned I was happy to see that I was suffering from menstrual spotting; it gave me a reason to keep covered up in front of the "beautiful people." I produced a black leather cupless teddy from my bag and paired it off with my black thigh-high boots and single-breasted black wool jacket. I looked sexy enough. After a couple of false starts, we all managed to be in one room and took the E together. I truly hoped things would get better under the influence of the drug.

They didn't. Oliver, Toby, Sonya, and Michael were all so enthralled with each other and talking so animatedly that no one noticed when I withdrew from the conversation. There was no music to offset the chatter. Michael would start to ramble, then Sonya would jump in and ramble on some more. Oliver and Toby awaited her words like they were pearls before swine, but I was bored. It was that same, old, overdiscussed, asked-and-answered question about whether love and beauty can co-exist in a BDSM relationship.

Every time I was just about ready to shut them out and concentrate on the E, one of them would do something clumsy or loud and splat me right back to Earth. Able to stand it no more, I got my Walkman. Plugged in and tuned out, I lay before the fire. Soon I felt like dancing so, Walkman in hand, I tried out a dance step I had seen in *The Night Porter*. Oliver largely ignored me unless Sonya seemed interested, and only paid attention to me when he saw her eyes on me as I did "the Night Porter" step. I moved into a better position for him to see me and did some of my best moves. Doing this showed off what was left of my cane marks and Sonya remarked that it looked like I needed a new set. Finally the silly cow had said something right!

So I was made to show them off again and then to crawl to Oliver and beg for another set. In between audible pleadings, I whispered to Oliver that I preferred to be caned in private because I wasn't entirely comfortable in the present company. Sonya saw me lean my head into Oliver's ear. She called out, "Oh, doesn't she have to say it loud enough so we all can hear?" For some idiotic reason, Oliver agreed but realized the error he had made when he saw the shock and horror on my face. How could I tell his other guests that they made me so uncomfortable I didn't want to be caned in front of them? And how utterly stupid of him, I thought. He whispered, "Don't explain, just beg." So I did, loudly enough for everyone to hear. But after all of that, Oliver only said, "Later, I'm not in the mood right now." I didn't say anything but thought that it was a neat trick and got us off the hook. Oliver realized he needed to create a diversion so he asked me to give him a back rub. Before straddling Oliver, I motioned to Toby to go get the boom box and put some music on. We needed something in the air other than tension.

Sonya and Michael moved off the bed onto the floor in front of the fireplace. Toby left and quickly returned with the boom box and a beautiful, expensive full-length black leather body bag. He set up the music and joined Sonya and Michael in front of the fire, showing them the body bag in detail. I continued to massage Oliver but I could feel under my fingers that he was not relaxed. He kept twisting to look at the other three, so I made fast work of finishing his massage. He couldn't get out from under me soon enough and leaped off the bed. Sonya was slowly putting Michael in the body bag. Staying on the bed, I rolled a joint and smoked it while I observed the goings-on in amusement and annoyance. Amused at the "conversation": "Look how gently she touches him (as Sonya trailed her fingers up Michael's exposed chest)," "She is so sensual with him (as Sonya placed a kiss on Michael's forehead)," "Oh, she *asked* before she blindfolded him," and "Such love, such love . . ." ad nauseam. Each comment was stated in a wondering tone of voice as if it were a revelation or an epiphany. As if one couldn't be tender *and* dominant, or precede sadism with gentleness! For people who played so hard on the physical level, they were really dunderheads otherwise.

I was annoyed that Oliver had left me flat to join these two pear-shaped persons in what appeared to me to be baby-step psychological discussions and newcomer tenderness exercises when he could have been having some real fun (to my mind anyway) with me! Turning on my side, I noticed that Oliver's canes were next to me. I picked one up and started to play with it, then a song came on that I liked so I pretended my body was a cello and the cane its bow. Suddenly, the four of them turned and saw me playing bow and fiddle. Oliver jumped up and left the room and was gone for several minutes. It crossed my mind that perhaps he had gone to prepare a room to cane me in. Toby, after seeing my cane dance, left the room and came back in a few minutes, followed by Oliver. Walking directly over to me, Oliver asked to see me in private. I jumped off the bed and followed him into my stone-cold little room. Still thinking I was going to be caned, I asked to be taken to a warmer room.

So where did he take me? Into Sonya and Michael's room, of course! But I was still game, until I noticed Oliver didn't have his canes. He sat down in front of the fire and I knelt in front of him. Putting his hand to his forehead, he told me that it wasn't working out, that he had hoped it would and that he had given it every chance. He couldn't read me and we just didn't connect. He was going on about it as if it were a lifetime commitment, not a caning. His words were not a total surprise to me. But I was surprised at his vehemence and so I managed to say the exact wrong thing: "I felt it, I felt it last night and knew then that I had to withdraw from you. But at least I was willing to play it through until the time was more appropriate. And you didn't make it clear that even in a social setting, you wouldn't be playing with me." He mistook what I meant and blasted me: "As if things aren't bad enough! (I found out later on that Oliver and Toby were having problems.) I'm not into play-acting! You don't understand! Caning is a religion for me! A religion! And I can't do it with just anyone!"

"Just anyone?" I said. "You selfish, immature fool! I think you're upset that I'm taking this so well, upset that I knew what you were going to say before you told me." Oliver looked shocked. He can dish it out but he can't take it? I thought. "What happens now?" I asked. I meant that night, right then and there. He took it in more general terms and said that I didn't have to leave and that we could still be friends. He was brainless enough to say that I could return to the "party" (and save him a lot of embarrassment explaining my absence, no doubt). Go back in there with Sonya's hot eyes on me? Reading in her mind that as Oliver's slave, Oliver could "command" me to interact with her? Listen to Oliver and Toby coo over Sonya? Perish the thought!

Before anything else could be said, I got up and went into his room. He came in hard on my heels, relieved that I had rejoined the "group." Or so he thought. I entered smiling and marched around the room, gathering up my boots, jackets, bed pillows, whatever. This brought all conversation to a halt as everyone watched me. Taking my possessions, I adjourned to the frigid little room next door. I called for Toby, and as he helped me make a fire, I passed a remark about the cold. Then he decided to check the radiator. It was ice cold; it seems he had turned it off! I looked at him thinking, You're joking, right? Aloud I asked why. He said to save on heat. I was thunderstruck. Here he was the lord of the Manor, a big mucky-muck in the local town, and he turned off the heat in a seven-by-twelve room to save *money*? What, ten pence a day? No dishwasher, no tumble dryer, no hot and cold water out of the same faucet, the heat shut off in a tiny room, what kind of household, or "Manor," was this? You can tell what kind of mood I was in!

Toby left the room. I sat on the edge of the bed and looked at the crackling fire. The door between Oliver's room and mine was open and I was unaware I was being spied upon until I heard that silly cow Sonya say, "She's just sitting on the end of the bed." Annoyed at this, I got up to close the adjoining door. It was then that I noticed I had left some of my blankets in Oliver's room so I walked directly into his room, collected them, and when I crossed the threshold back into my room, I firmly closed the door behind me.

Now everything that had happened set in. I was very high on E and my thoughts and emotions were jumping all over. Bitter disappointment was replaced by righteous anger, which was replaced by insouciance, which was replaced by who knew what. I should have had the presence of mind to take some of the hash to my room with me. Now things were picking up next door. Voices and laughter could be heard through the door and very soon, the sounds of caning. I could hear Oliver tell Sonya how to assume the position, the same position I had assumed for him invisibly for so many months, then I heard the fall of the cane on her backside. Someone had a polaroid and I heard the distinctive sound it made as it spat out the picture. Now I had to listen to the sounds of their play through the door whether I wanted to or not. But after about a half hour had passed, I had had enough.

I went out into the hall and knocked on the main door of Oliver's room. When he came out into the hallway instead of letting me in, I brought him into my room. I told him that I was "over it," but the sound of the party from his room, a party I should have been in on, was hard for me to listen to. Could he kindly move the fun and games someplace else? He had the grace to look embarrassed and mumbled, "Of course." Shortly after I heard them all move into Sonya and Michael's room, which didn't share any connecting walls with mine. I fell into a fitful sleep, dreaming of cane strokes that never landed.

TEN

After a long night came a hellish day. The five of us bundled into Toby's car and drove into London. Sonya and Michael were meeting her father for lunch at the Savoy and Oliver was going to take a cab from there to Niles's, who was hosting Charmaine's "rape" today. Left to ourselves, Toby and I went off to De Vetters, a custom design bondage and leather gear company, to kill time before Sonya and Michael met us there. Enthusiastically Toby pointed out items he would like to have for the dungeon, perhaps recalling that I said I would get him a gift. Well, if he actually thought I was going to buy him a "gift" worth several hundred pounds, he had another think coming. I admired the pieces he pointed out in an oblivious sort of way, as if I didn't know he was "hinting" at getting one as a gift and said, "Oh, yeah, that's nice," then wandered away.

Some of the De Vetters staff broke for lunch and Toby and I went with them. The Indian food smelled delicious but faintly nauseating at the same time, so I decided not to eat. Conversation that I took no interest in whirled around me until it was time to leave. We were back at the shop for only a few minutes when Sonya and Michael walked in. We spent more time there while they fitted and ordered a custom-made leather body bag to accommodate Michael's lack of height but considerable girth and purchased an off-the-rack leather straitjacket. I was bored when I should have been amused or at least entertained by my surroundings. Even when we went to another fetish shop, Restraint, Ltd., where I bought an inflatable latex butt plug and an inflatable latex dildo, I kept fluctuating between anger and disappointment over the Oliver situation and didn't know what to do with myself. I don't think anything would have made me happy right then. I was greatly relieved when we headed back to Susingham.

But my relief was short-lived. It was at least two and a half hours back to the Manor from where we were and here I was, trapped in a car with that silly cow and her fire-plug husband. All Sonya did was talk about how wonderful Oliver was, how skilled Oliver was, how understanding Oliver was. Oliver this and Oliver that; on and on she went. Was she totally stupid or was this malicious? I was doing fine before she started her ode to Oliver, but the more she went on, the more rattled I became. I think I started to believe her lavish praise and began to feel that I had tossed away something, someone oh-so-wonderful without a second glance. I pulled myself together and blocked out her rhapsodizing over the wonders of Oliver.

After a fiasco of a dinner, we all went upstairs for a nap. When everyone was safe in their rooms, I crept back downstairs to call Niles. I had forgotten all about Charmaine's "rape" scene and Oliver being there until Niles answered the phone. Niles said Oliver had already left and should be home shortly. I asked Niles if I could take him up on his offer and spend the next couple of nights at his place. He said yes right away. We chatted then hung up, and for my part, I was greatly relieved that I would be getting out of the Manor. I killed more time by calling Rowan and relating to her the events of the last few days. I recalled her remark "to watch my heart" the first night we met and smiled wryly at her astute assessment. Things were getting better already. And later on, another woman, Fiona, a dear friend of Oliver and Toby's, was due over. I couldn't wait till she got there; maybe her unbiased presence would help alleviate the situation. I sat in the kitchen, smoking, enjoying the big room, the old house, and the short moment of privacy.

About ten o'clock the household began to rouse and people tumbled into the kitchen. Fiona arrived about ten forty-five followed by Oliver just a few minutes later. I had thought that there was going to be a party in the dungeon, but Fiona took off with Toby and then Oliver took off with Sonya, leaving me alone in the kitchen with Michael. So much for that. I bid him good night and went to my room where I rolled a nice fat spliff, smoked it, and fell asleep.

ELEVEN

After an extremely uncomfortable morning in the Manor, the five of us piled into the car for the two-hour drive into London. Fiona had left in the predawn hours. My bag was packed for my stay at Niles's, and after the excruciatingly long silent ride to his house, I couldn't wait to get out of the car and get away from the couple from hell. I bolted from the car, grabbed my bag, and hurried up the walk to Niles's. Oliver followed close behind me, then overtook me. He took my bag, saw me into Niles's, and before leaving gave me a queer, expectant look. Perhaps it was a silent plea for my silence about what had happened at the Manor, but I had no idea what it really meant, nor did I care.

Charmaine was at Niles's and was standing in the front window of the reception room watching the "Susingham Set" rearrange themselves in the car. I joined her at the window to see them off, but "bid them good riddance" would be a more accurate description. Just as I stepped up to the window, Charmaine and I caught that stupid cow Sonya making faces at us! Sticking her tongue out at us, putting her thumb on the end of her nose, and wiggling her fingers . . . you know, all the things adults do to show their maturity. When she saw Charmaine and me, she stopped in obvious embarrassment. And Charmaine saw Sonya, too! Good! I thought, now I have a witness. Charmaine was shocked at Sonya's behavior and then amused by it. We made a show of laughing and kissing in the window as the Susingham Set drove off to go shopping.

Charmaine and I sat and talked for a while and smoked a spliff together, laughing over the silly cow Sonya. Our shrieks and giggles got so loud that Niles looked in on us, saw us laughing it up in a haze of smoke, shook his head in amusement, and walked off into the rear of the apartment. Shortly afterward, Charmaine left to go home and I was alone with Niles. He was being such a gentleman that I started to wish I had gone to him earlier (like when he first asked me to stay) and under better circumstances. Niles was so much more worthy of me than Oliver, and sexier, too. I overheard Oliver tell Niles he believed Niles would be better "at handling me." What kind of experienced master couldn't handle a new (and since I was a working professional domina at the time) but educated slave girl?

After a light supper that Niles cooked, he and I started to play. His green eyes gleamed when he stripped me and ran his strong and well-shaped hands all over me quite possessively. I melted. This was the touch I wanted and this was the man I wanted it from. Forget Oliver and his mood swings! I was supposed to be having fun and now I would have all the fun I deserved. Tossing one of the white comforters on the floor, Niles took me in his arms, tumbled me down onto it, and started to kiss me. His tongue probed my mouth and I felt a sticky wetness between my thighs. One of his hands pulled my legs apart and his two fingers explored my outer quim. He gasped in arousal at my wetness as he plunged his two beautiful fingers into me. I felt the heat rippling off his body and saw fire glowing in his eyes, the eyes of the horned god. With his fingers still in me, he maneuvered us into the same position we were in that earlier night: his back resting against the sofa and me laying back against his chest, our legs spread. One strong arm hugged me to him while the other hand spanked my quim until I came.

When Niles felt me gush, he growled, "Oh, yeah," and pushed me off of him and forced me onto my back. Roughly he grabbed an ankle in each hand, pulled my legs open, and draped them over his shoulders. Then he impaled me on his big, gorgeous, cut cock and shagged me half into oblivion, enjoying not only himself but my multiple orgasms. At some point, Niles put leather wrist and ankle restraints on me but it seemed they were more for decoration than anything else. I didn't care that they were no more than that, I felt almost transported by Niles's attention after the horrible time I had with Oliver and the Sonya and Michael fiasco. We shagged ourselves breathless and finally separated but Niles still had an amazing erection when the doorbell rang.

Wrapping a sarong low around his hips, Niles opened the door to admit Mark. Mark was a handsome, strong-featured, well-dressed man about Niles's age who was also in the scene. I was very excited that a man I never met before was seeing me dressed in nothing but my shoes and the leather restraints, and obviously in Niles's possession. I felt Mark's eyes on me and knew he wanted to play with me even before he said so. Niles told Mark that I was on loan to him from Oliver, and Mark passed a remark about how much "Oliver must be enjoying me," to which I replied, "Oliver was 'enjoying' me so much that I asked

Niles if I could stay here." Mark looked a little shocked at hearing the bald truth, but Niles chuckled at my asperity. Brits aren't accustomed to such directness, but I believe in calling it as I see it and I saw no reason to protect Oliver. He hadn't done the same for me.

An hour or so later, the courteous amount of time for dropping off "party supplies" Mark left. I asked Niles to cane me, softly at first but with no middle warm-up, just followed by single hard strokes. I bent over the arm of the sofa and held on to a chain Niles had attached to a wall hook. I let him beat me and beat me until I cried and sobbed out all the pent up frustration inside of me, a truly cathartic experience. Niles's technique was good but Oliver's was a bit better. Niles tapped me just a little too long before he actually hit me and then he gave me double strokes instead of single ones. But no matter, it worked. I felt much better, cleansed of the smell of Oliver and Toby and Sonya and Michael, and more like myself again. I was still bent over the arm of the sofa when we shagged again, and during the shag, I started to cry anew simply because I was brimming with emotion and Niles felt so good inside me. Niles became very aroused by my crying; he liked to be rough and hard and inflict pain while he shagged. I called it "brute sex" and "savage love" and I loved it; it was one of my favorite games. The "distress" of the woman heightened his excitement and spurred him on to great efforts. Niles was big into rape fantasies, as evidenced by the gang "rape" he had set up for Charmaine. And so was I.

After we had shagged ourselves into exhaustion, Niles lay down on the sofa and I set myself up on the floor next to him. Then a song came on that I liked and I began to dance for Niles, slowly, seductively, and doing only floor work. I danced from the depths of my soul, expressing my pain then my release from it, as tears of sheer emotion rolled down my face. When the song was over, Niles told me I danced beautifully, then thoughtfully added that he understood how one can make great beauty out of pain. I was pleased by his perceptiveness.

It was probably about three in the morning when we went to bed but I couldn't sleep. I got up, rolled a big splift, and smoked the whole thing. When I crept back into bed, I curled up next to Niles. His arm enclosed me and pulled me to his chest. I nestled my head into the crook of his shoulder. From there, I could smell his pheromones, strong, dark, libidinous. We slept until two o'clock the next afternoon. It was the best night's sleep I had gotten since I arrived in England.

TWELVE

Oh, it was heavenly to wake up with Niles between my legs! We shagged long and we shagged hard, and since I knew he hadn't come yet, I begged him to spurt his pearl jam on me, to shoot it all over my splayed body, to drench me in it. My words goaded him on and soon I felt his lovely hot white jism decorate my belly and face in long pearly ropes. Using my hands, I rubbed his come all over my body and face, loving the sticky feel of it on my skin. Niles enjoyed watching me do this so I hammed it up for him.

Niles took a bath then asked me if I wanted the "water." This question was a bit of a surprise because no one I knew in the states ever used another person's bathwater. But in Britain it was common practice because all the household utilities were à la carte. No heat or hot water was included in the rent, so if one hadn't shaved or urinated in the water, it was considered "re-usable" by putting in more hot water. I turned on the hot and climbed into Niles's bathwater, adding more bubble bath to make myself a nice sudsy bed in which to lie. I thought we were just going to hang around the house for the rest of the afternoon, but Niles had other ideas. Realizing that I had been stuck out in the country and had seen nothing of London, he had planned an excursion for us to Portobello Road, then onto Piccadilly Circus.

Being late in the day, there weren't many stalls or tables still open at Portobello Road, but we did much better in Piccadilly Circus where there were four fetish shops to browse. In a shop called Perdition, I found a fantastic pair of PVC pants with a built-in waist clincher and a zipper with three small balls on the end of the toggles. When I saw that the three ball toggles could be arranged to dangle between my legs, I laughed in delight and showed Niles "my balls." He laughed and tweaked them. I put the pants on hold and said I would be back in a couple of days to pick them up. We realized we were hungry and stopped at a restaurant called The Dome for thin yet delicious English sandwiches and drinks before jumping the underground back to Niles's house.

About ten thirty that night Charmaine called and invited us to her house, which was only a short walk away. When she called, I was writing in my journal and Niles was working on a computer program. Niles and I finished up what we were doing and got to Charmaine's around midnight. As soon as I walked in, I was hit with bad vibes. Because of the emotional roller coaster I had been on, I blamed myself for them. As it turned out, they had nothing to do with me and everything to do with undercurrents running between Niles and Charmaine. Charmaine was suspicious of our late arrival, thinking that Niles and I had been "plotting together" and talking about her, suspicious about what Niles and I did together. A totally ridiculous idea that had no basis in reality, only in Charmaine's heretofore undiscovered (by me) deep seated insecurity and her insane jealousy over anyone Niles showed an interest in.

We explained over and over again that we were both busy when she called and that it was unreasonable for her to think that we were going to drop what we were doing and just run out the door. She sent Niles down to the kitchen to make egg salad sandwiches and grilled me alone. When Niles returned with four very well made sandwiches, she questioned him closely based on what I had said to her. Actually, the whole thing was ludicrous especially since Niles didn't behave irrationally when she had the nerve to invite her lover to Niles's party! After much ado, Niles and I were able to persuade the overly insecure and suspicious Charmaine that our delayed arrival was not due to plotting, neither together nor separately. But her suspicions were barely allayed and hardly concealed. I decided that this was her problem, hers and Niles's, and that they would have to work this out on their own. I would speak no more about it.

Niles took my cue and let the subject drop, and paid no more attention to Charmaine's unfounded accusations. Upon finding that we were no longer going to humor her, she, too, let it go. That squared away for the time being, I suggested that she and I pay great attention to Niles's cock. At least she knew how to double! If I was on his head and shaft, she would be licking his balls. Or vice versa. If she was tonguing the left side of his shaft, I would be taking care of his right side. When I withdrew to take a breath, Niles started to get really rough with her, beating her in the face with his cock, ramming it down her throat until her eyes watered and her nose spurted. I laid back to watch. Having an audience excited her more than having "company" to play with, and once, when she came up for air, she asked me if I was aroused by watching "her," not "them." She was utterly astonished when I told her "no," but honestly, watching "her" did not excite me, especially after her earlier paranoid display. She didn't want company, she wanted an audience. (If she had asked me about watching *Niles* that would have received a different answer.)

Niles and I left around four a.m. and went back to his place, where we promptly fell asleep.

THIRTEEN

Waking up at two in the afternoon was turning into a habit. But as soon as Niles and I saw the time, we dressed and literally ran out the door to make the shops before they closed. First we went to Knightsbridge and the wonderful array of shops there. In a department store, I found a beautiful pair of black suede pumps with pointy toes and spike heels, decorated with straps up the arch to the ankle. The shoes were quite fetish-y looking and the straps made my feet look like they were in delicate bondage. Since all my shoes have names, I named these shoes the "Niles pumps." Then, at an indoor upscale flea market, I found a lovely floor length sheer black knit dress with thin shoulder straps that could be worn in a variety of ways. I was very happy with these purchases when we headed off to Piccadilly Circus and Perdition to pick up the PVC pants.

These missions accomplished, we headed back to Maida Vale. Hungry, we ordered in Indian food, which was absolutely delicious, the best I ever had. But all day I had been ignoring the fact that after tonight's party at Vibe Bar, I was supposed to return to the Manor in Susingham with Oliver. I was dreading it. I was so much happier (to say nothing of warmer) at Niles's that I wished I didn't have to leave. Somewhat disheartened when faced by the reality of my return, I was quiet as Niles and I took turns getting ready. While he bathed, I ironed his ruffled shirt, laid out my outfit for the night (a floor-length, halter neck, zip-front black PVC ball gown, black thigh high stockings, and black patent leather stilettos) and packed my bag. He dressed while I bathed and patiently waited for me to get ready. My bag in tow, we took a cab to Charmaine's to pick her up because she was also going to Vibe Bar. Even after the E was passed around, I was quiet on the way there.

But once inside, I perked up. Vibe Bar was part of a museum, and the space was terrific. A large lounge area, well-equipped dungeon, and spacious dance floor made up the party space, and everyone was dressed to thrill. However, there was absolutely no heat on at all, and I just could not understand how all these latex-clad people could be enjoying themselves in the freezing cold environment. Then I remembered that E made one so warm they probably didn't notice. All the same, when I checked my coat and bag, I kept my Turkish woolen shawl with me so at least my shoulders would be covered. Charmaine was wearing a white halter top, matching miniskirt, and open-toed platform shoes and didn't look the least bit cold. The men in their leather pants, long sleeve shirts, and boots fared a bit better in the chilly air.

The three of us were rolling along just fine when Oliver sauntered in with Sonya and Michael. It just so happened that I was standing inside the entrance to the lounge when they arrived. I was surprised, unpleasantly so, by the presence of Sonya and Michael. They were supposed to have left already; that was why I was going back to Susingham with Oliver tonight. Before they could see me, Niles was at my side. He guided me to the far end of the lounge where Charmaine and the sofas were. I guess he didn't want it to seem like I was standing by the door looking for Oliver. After Niles could no longer see Oliver, he found seats for the three of us, saying snidely "let him find us." I laughed at Niles's remark and his somewhat dismissive tone of voice, then forgot about Oliver and the "beautiful people" as I set myself to enjoy the party.

Later on, I spied Oliver leaning against the bar. He was looking straight at me as if I were someone else. I knew I looked very desirable in the PVC gown and I knew he knew it. But what difference did it make? I looked away but unfortunately the next people my eyes fell upon were Sonya and Michael. She was dressed in a military jacket that belonged to Oliver and it did nothing for her thick-waisted figure. Other than the jacket, she wore only pantyhose and boots. Michael wore only a leather straitjacket and some rope around his naked scrotum, his feet bare on the freezing-cold stone floor. I was thoroughly disgruntled that they were still at the Manor. When I looked back to where Oliver had been standing, he was gone. Glancing around the room, I saw him running hither and yon, speaking to one person after another. Niles, following my gaze, said that Oliver was trying to put together enough people for a party back at the Manor's dungeon.

I gathered that Oliver's intention was to assemble a group that would include me. Having me go back to the Manor with no one in particular for me to play with was causing him problems. I was more than a bit insulted by this "have to palm her off on someone" attitude of Oliver's. Niles and Charmaine had been invited but weren't going because they didn't want to bother with the long trip back into London from the countryside. So I asked Niles if I could spend one more night at his place. He agreed but had to run it by Charmaine because she was also spending the night. The stupidly suspicious Charmaine questioned me closely about my "motives," which I assured her over and over again were purely selfish ones: I hadn't been getting along with Oliver; I didn't like Sonya and Michael; I hated being stuck out in the country with nothing to do and no way to get into London. Then I reminded her about Sonya and her immature act in the car. After she was satisfied that there were no head games going on, she agreed to let me stay another night at Niles's.

Niles went off to find Oliver, who was visibly relieved that I was spending another night away from the Manor. Oliver didn't even have the courtesy to say good night to me; he just bolted out of the club after he found out I was going home with Niles and Charmaine.

FOURTEEN

Back at Niles's, I dug out my camera and took pictures of Niles and Charmaine and of Niles alone. Right after I put the camera away, Charmaine and Niles both stepped into the role of "top." First Charmaine stripped me of my elegant dress and opera gloves and donned them. Then she commanded me to kneel and address her as "princess." Donning my dress and gloves did make her look like a princess and she paraded around the room under the admiring eyes of Niles. Niles suggested I wear something of his and handed me a maid's outfit. It was ugly and had obviously not been laundered in a very long time. I put it on to please them but I didn't feel beautiful in it. This was evident to them by the way I kept plucking at the thing and making little faces, so they quickly took it off me and let me be naked. I was much happier naked, being one of those rare people who actually look better unclothed than dressed. I wanted to dance for them, to feel their appreciative and desiring eyes upon me, but Niles had other ideas. Handing another hit of E to each of us, he said he wanted to get "started on me" right away. His words sent frissons through my body.

He tried spanking my quim but I wasn't in the mood for that. Before I lost interest completely, I said, "Oh, Niles, let's get right to it. I want you to sodomize me." Well, if Niles was so eager to start on me right away, why waste time beating around the bush? Charmaine said, "Well, that was quick and to the point." Then both of them laughed.

First they blindfolded me, then they led me into the bathroom and sat me down on the edge of the tub. Charmaine lubed my anus while Niles filled up the enema bucket. I heard the water splash into it and the little sound the hanger made when he attached it to the pipe. Charmaine moved away and next I felt Niles's hands on me, pulling me off the edge of the tub and forcing me to the floor. Once I was on my knees, he pushed my shoulders down and ordered me to hold my hips up and spread my knees. I felt him push the nozzle all the way into me, then I felt the stream of water entering. Someone began to work the nozzle in and out of me, but since no hand touched me, I couldn't tell who it was. I was breathing heavily, steeped in delicious humiliation that both of them were watching me. In my mind's eye, I pictured the tableau: a well-dressed man and a woman standing in a bathroom, with a naked woman on her hands and knees on the floor with an enema nozzle inserted into her anus. I took the whole thing without pause.

Two large fingers, Niles's, were roughly inserted into my anus and checked to see if any of the water remained in my lower passage. Pleased that it was all deep inside me, Niles helped me to my feet and led me around the apartment. We ended up in the reception room, where Charmaine awaited us. She and Niles rubbed my distended belly and she dipped her fingers into my quim. It was dripping wet and she announced this to Niles with great pleasure. Niles led me back into the bathroom, sat me down on the toilet, and commanded me to empty my belly. He left me there and rejoined Charmaine, who was still ensconced on the sofa in my finery. Water exploded from my bottom and I knew they could hear it. I could hear them discussing what was coming out of me, basically nothing since I had hardly eaten, but it was very exciting and humiliating to be talked about like an object. Empty at last, Niles came in and oversaw my ablutions, then guided me back into the front room.

Roughly he pushed me over the arm of the sofa and Charmaine handed me the chain to hold on to. She held my cheeks apart while I waited for Niles's fingers to enter and stretch me. Instead, he plunged his gorgeous cock straight into my anus. Even though I craved the anal pain, he hurt me too much when he did this because I wasn't lubricated. When I said something about it, he pulled out and Charmaine applied the tiniest bit of lube. The next thing I felt were Niles's fingers inside me, working my opening hard, pulling my opening this way and that, driving his fingers deeply into me. Oh yes, he was hurting me, but he was hurting me in a way I needed and wanted to be hurt. I was slippery and his hard probing fingers felt so good! I relaxed and enjoyed the onslaught of his fingers, reveling in this most exquisite of all pain. Abruptly he withdrew his fingers and rammed his cock into me, penetrating deep and hard. I screamed at the sudden invasion, which egged Niles on to greater efforts. He grabbed my hips and nearly lifted me off the floor as he sodomized me into semi-oblivion.

He pulled out of me as quickly as he had entered. I felt him spread my cheeks, then he said to Charmaine, "Her hole is gaping open, I can see way up inside of her." I blushed with shame. Niles was playing a wicked mind game, and the emotional sensation was somewhere between heaven and degradation. I had dreamed of this so many times, of someone saying those exact words, and now, without being told, Niles had said them. I was thrilled when I felt Charmaine get off the sofa and join him behind me. I could feel their hot gazes looking up my passage and I came. His large fingers and her smaller ones diddled in my quim. They laughed at my wetness, which made me wetter. I felt a small whoosh of air as they moved away from me. The next thing I felt was leather wrist restraints being buckled on me, then being attached to the chain I had been holding.

They left me there splayed and on display, ready for the pleasure of either of them, while they sat on the sofa and talked about me, my body, my desire to be sodomized. They rolled a spliff and shared it while they spoke. I was wallowing in shameless burning desire and outright lust, picturing how I looked to them and imaging what the three of us looked like, relishing every second that passed. But I had gotten very quiet, which upset Charmaine. She said something about it and Niles responded by getting up and driving his cock back into my anus, hurting me, making me scream again and glad to be chained to the wall. He rammed and slammed me as he pleased until finally my legs collapsed from under me. Only then was I released from my bonds, seated on the sofa and had my blindfold removed. My anus felt enormous and my pearl jam made a gooey mess between my thighs. I was in heaven!

But I didn't yet know where heaven really was.

Niles had no intention of just letting me sit. He had a new toy and he wanted to play with it. He grabbed my ankles and pulled them toward him until my back was on the sofa's seat cushion, then he held my legs up, roughly located my anus, and hammered into me. Facing me now, his expression was one of sadistic joy, and the more I screamed and struggled, the harder and faster he rammed me. Charmaine tried to hold my upper body down, but at a grunt from Niles, whose shagging had turned almost bestial, she moved back into her corner of the sofa. Being sodomized in this position was very painful but I wanted it and

I was loving it. No one had ever taken me this roughly before and it filled a hunger in me. I turned into a grunting writhing animal and forgot myself as a civilized being. I grasped the cushions in an effort to meet his thrusts, I clenched my muscles to give him a tighter fit, I spread my legs sideways, pulled them up to my chest. I wasn't thinking, I was reacting in a primal, feral way to the sensation of pain and elation. I gave Niles permission to hurt me and hurt me he did, taking me anally over and over.

Niles did everything roughly and it was no different when he pulled out of me and flipped me over onto my side. I felt something cold and enormous being pushed up against my gaping opening and I tried hard to relax to receive it. But it was too large and I felt myself start to tighten up and resist it. Charmaine grabbed the back of my head and held a bottle of nitrous oxide to my nose. I inhaled deeply and felt the familiar falling-off-a-cliff-backward sensation. With frequent sniffs of that drug, Niles was able to work the entire dildo into me, stretching me more than I had ever been stretched in my life. Once it was inside of me, Niles punched the flat base of the dildo into my quim and gave me a screaming, thrashing, exhausting orgasm.

When I was thoroughly sated and almost passing out, Niles made a bed for me on the floor of the reception room in front of the fire. Then he and Charmaine went into the bedroom. Although the door was closed, I could hear the timber of their voices: hers needy and whiny; his deep and assuring. Tired and sated as I was, it was still some time before I could fall asleep.

FIFTEEN

When I woke up the next day, both Niles and Charmaine were gone. They left a note stating that they had gone to Charmaine's house and included her phone number. I felt a little bereft, alone with the thought that I had to go back to the Manor that night. But all good things come to an end. I went into the bathroom, and while I filled the tub, I looked as my backside in the mirror. Niles had sodomized me so brutally that he had left bruises up and down my cheeks. I was thrilled by these bruises and cherished the small tingling pain that sitting down in the hot bath caused me. After that, I called them at Charmaine's house. They weren't coming back and gave me instructions on how to lock up the house and where to leave the keys. Disappointed that I wouldn't be seeing them again, I thanked them for the wonderful time they had shared with me.

Not wanting to go back to the Manor, I took advantage of their absence and took my time washing the dishes and cleaning up the kitchen, folding up the bedding in the reception room, and sweeping the floor. Finally, there was nothing more I could do without invading Niles's privacy, so I called Oliver at the Manor to hit him up for a ride. I was relieved to hear that Sonya and Michael had left that morning, but no ride was forthcoming. Oliver said he didn't feel like making the long round trip into London. He told me what train to take from Waterloo to get to Susingham and said to call him when I knew what time the train would be arriving at the local station. This necessitated another call to Charmaine's, this time for the number of a mini-cab, or car service, to take me to Waterloo. While I waited for the car service, I called Waterloo for the schedule, then called Oliver back. Unfortunately, I had to call Charmaine's yet another time, because, upon hearing a foreign accent, the cab never showed up. Charmaine made the call and eventually the car arrived.

I didn't see much of the surrounding countryside because it was full dark when I boarded the train. It arrived a few minutes early, so I stood there in the English rain smoking a cigarette and waited for Oliver. The ride back to the Manor was a quiet and uncomfortable one. Oliver was still hung over from the big party the night before with Sonya and Michael and who knew who else. As soon as we got back to the Manor, he went right to his room, closed the door, and stayed there. I had no desire to stay in the little room with its adjoining door locked against me, so I found Toby and asked him if I could relocate "for a few hours." I had no intention at all of returning to the cold room with its bitter memories, but I had learned that it wasn't good to tell these people any more than they needed to know. Toby let me into the large room with two double beds in it, located on the other side of

Oliver's room, one that had first housed the lovely Rowan and Esme and had just this morning been vacated by Sonya and her husband Michael.

After Toby had gone downstairs, I brought all of my things into the large room and made a big, roaring fire. Then I went into the sleeping Oliver's room even though the door was closed against me. I wanted the boom box and some of the hash and didn't care in the least if I disturbed him. As far as I was concerned, he was already "disturbed." But he was sleeping very soundly and never even knew I was there. Niles and Charmaine had given me a hit of E and some GHB (a notorious mixture of nail polish remover and industrial cleaner) to take back to the countryside and that went into the big room with me, too. Then I went down into the kitchen and loaded a tray with soda, ice, fruit, cheese, bread, and whatever else I found that appealed to me, including the phone. Toby saw me doing this and smiled, thinking it was for Oliver. I could have let it pass but why? They hadn't cut me any slack. I told him in a pseudo-polite tone that I was going to have a little party by myself and that Oliver was dead asleep. I went upstairs, closed the door, and locked it behind me. I made my own little world and stayed in it.

I got very stoned and changed from my street clothes into one of my fetish outfits, something I did when I was either very happy and wanted to celebrate, or when I was very sad and wanted to feel better. It was around midnight and I decided to call Rowan. We spoke late into the night and I found my initial opinion of her reinforced: she was one very intelligent and perceptive lady. She said that she knew right away Oliver wasn't right for me, then added that he didn't deserve me; that was why she had passed that remark about hiding my heart when she and I first met. I told her about the immature shenanigans of Sonya and Michael, my voluntary "banishment" to Niles's, and the goings-on there. She made another remark about Charmaine and Niles that puzzled me at the time, something about being careful there, too. Changing the subject before I could inquire further, she asked me to describe what I had bought on my shopping expedition.

Upon hearing about the PVC pants with the three little balls, she asked me if I had a camera with me. I did but hadn't used it since I had taken the photos of Niles and Charmaine in Niles's reception room. She giggled and asked to me put on my favorite clothes and take pictures of myself. Then I was to call her back when I was through. My pleasure! This was something I did at home when I was in a good mood or needed to be in one, and I enjoyed setting the camera up, pressing the timer button, and then racing to get into position for the lens. I started to enjoy myself and eventually really got into it, looking for pieces of furniture I could pose on or over and making repeated wardrobe changes. When I called her back, she "ordered" me to sleep in the same bed she slept in, the one farthest away from the fireplace. I assured her that I would do just that and we said good night, promising to speak again on the morrow. Happy at having company and someone to "play" with even if it was over the phone, I did as she bade. Before I fell asleep, I called her again, this time to let the "mistress" know I was in her bed.

SIXTEEN

What a surprise—I was up before noon! I lounged in bed to get the feel of the house, decided it was okay, then donned the dress and shoes I had bought while shopping with Niles and went down into the kitchen. Oliver was already there, sitting at the table. Putting on the kettle for tea, I spoke with him politely. Not because I wanted to per se, but because I had consumed my supply of E and hash the night before and I needed large quantities of mood-altering materials, which he had. He went to his room for them and as soon as he came back I rolled a fat joint and smoked it right there, sharing it with him. I felt his eyes on me—I looked great in that dress—but pretended not to notice. Although I thought that this day would be our last chance to speak about our "encounter," I wasn't going to make it easy for him. He said nothing so I gathered up the mind-altering substances and took them upstairs to the luxurious bedroom I now occupied.

Again I built a roaring fire and made trips back and forth to the kitchen to lay in supplies for the afternoon. First I ate a hit of E, then smoked some hash and got marvelously high. I left the door just the tiniest bit ajar, just in case "someone" wanted to make contact with me. It was after three o'clock and I hadn't received the expected knock. Oliver wasn't in his room, so I left a note on his bed stating that now would be a good time to talk. Returning to my room, I changed into a petticoat, corset, lace-top thigh highs, and pumps. It was, as usual, very cold in the rest of the house, so I donned my black wool blazer. Toby called me at four o'clock for dinner and guess who was in the kitchen? Oliver! Toby complimented me on my outfit and looked over to Oliver, smiling. Oliver, on the other hand, got up and literally ran upstairs, leaving his half-eaten dinner on the table.

That was the final straw. I lost my appetite and picked at what was on my plate, then left the mess to Toby and went to my room. I called Niles and begged him to come out to the country so I wouldn't have to spend my last night there alone. But he had to attend a community board meeting and after that he was going to Charmaine's. Hanging up with Niles, I called Charmaine to thank her and say good-bye. On the phone, I started to cry. I told her that it was my last night in London and that I didn't want to spend it alone. I wanted to be beautiful for someone and *that* certainly wasn't happening out here. She wanted me to pack up my things and go to her place right away, but somewhere inside I was still foolishly hoping that Oliver would soften toward me, come in and talk with me, or, dare I hope, cane me. Of course Oliver did none of these things. Unbeknown to me, Charmaine had called back and spoken sharply to Oliver and told him he was treating me terribly. She insisted to him that he help me pack and send me to her. When she called back to speak to me, she told me he had refused.

But at that point, I didn't want to leave the little world I had made in the big bedroom. I felt that if I left that room I would shatter into a million pieces, most of which would never be found again. I don't know what she said to him but I guess she embarrassed him enough to make him knock on my door. I called out, "Enter," and was surprised in a numb sort of way to find him standing there. I was in one of those weird crying states: Tears were running freely down my face but I was not actually crying or sobbing. Oliver told me I "seemed so much better," to which I replied sarcastically, "in relation to when?"

He sat down on the bed and told me that he had gotten my note but that he didn't feel like talking today; he was planning on speaking to me the next day, the day I was due to depart. I looked him right in the face and said, "If I'm in the mood to talk then . . ." Then things just started to come out of my mouth: "You never tried to make it work with me; you never gave me a chance; you just withdrew from me," and other accusatory, guilt-giving statements. As I said these things I rolled over onto my stomach and he saw the bruises on my derriere. He lowered himself to the floor and ran his hands over my bruises admiringly. I told him the marks weren't only from a caning but also from Niles's brutal sodomizing after the Vibe Bar party. Seeing the stunned look on his face, I went for the jugular. I said glibly, "Good things happen and sometimes they happen to me," and smiled a cold smile. This took him completely off guard. Hurrying to the door, he told me to be careful partying.

I called Niles and Charmaine at Charmaine's house and thanked them for all they had done for me, for allowing me into their lives for those days, and said that they shared something very special. I told them that without them I wouldn't have had a vacation. Getting them on the phone one at a time, I told each of them how much I had enjoyed Niles's brutal use of me, using words and phrases that would best express my gratitude to the one I was speaking with at the time. Hanging up with them, I phoned Rowan and spoke with her for a while before settling in for the remainder of my stay. When I mentioned Oliver, she started to sing "just a gigolo . . ." and trailed off laughing. Asking me if I could keep a "secret," she told me that Oliver was known around town as Toby's procurer, because Toby, in spite of being "the Lord of the Manor," couldn't attract enough people to attend his parties without Oliver's help. When I laughed at this revelation, I have to admit that my laughter was mean and at Toby's expense.

Shortly after I had hung up with Rowan, Oliver appeared at my door. After hearing me talking on the phone, his curiosity had gotten the better of him. He wanted to know what I had talked about with Niles and Charmaine, and with Rowan. I smiled and said "nothing." When a look of relief washed over his face, I added, "nothing other than my vacation." He looked a little nervous after I said that and I laughed to myself. He hung in the doorway for a few seconds, but I ignored him so he went away. Later on, I heard new footfalls in the hall and peeked out. To my great surprise, there stood Esme, Rowan's personal slave girl. The ever-presumptuous Oliver had called her up and invited her over to keep himself entertained!

I continued to get blasted although I was already quite stoned. Might as well leave with a bang, I thought. I built up the fire, laid out an array of outfits to change into over the course of the night, and lined up the CDs for the boom box. Freed of the mental bonds of Oliver, I danced and posed in front of the mirror, and even in my sadness, or because of it, I found myself to be beautiful. From an internal world of confusion and uncertainty, caught in the downward spiral of masochism, I projected an experienced-yet-innocent sexuality that was cleansing and uplifting. My eternal flame of hope grew stronger, and as I danced I touched my body. Not in a sexual way, but in a way to shed the old and embrace the new.

I danced a beautiful ballet to the aria of "Lakshmi," from an opera by Delibes. At the start of it, when the music was light and airy, I became a bird in the sky, floating high above Earth. As the music changed to a fuller orchestral sound, I spread my wings and soared to the sun. My heart beat fast like a bird's and my feathers were warm from my nearness to the bright orb. This was delightful. I turned and banked as I flew upward, the yellow eye of the sun reflected in my own bright black bird's eye. I danced and danced until I exhausted myself and I began to fall from the sky, away from the outstretched arms of the sun, its round pulsating face receding from mine. Down I tumbled, frantically beating my wings to no avail but not really caring. My downward flight became an arching dive, filled with grace and beauty, exploding in my mind to unplumbed depths within. As the music ended I fell back to Earth, no longer a bird but now a petal from a flower tumbling in the wind. My eyes still burnt from the bright sun as I fell to the floor.

SEVENTEEN

It was the final day of something that had in reality ended before I returned to the Manor from Maida Vale. I arose about eleven thirty and went downstairs to find both Oliver and Toby in the kitchen. Esme had left in the wee hours while I was asleep. Little was said other than that Oliver had to go into town to do an errand. I shrugged and made tea. He left and I went to my room to pack. After last night, I didn't know what, if anything, could be done to repair the damage and I wasn't sure I cared. By one thirty I was finished packing, so I took my camera and shot some photos of the Manor, inside and out, but none of Toby or Oliver. I saw the car in the drive and knew Oliver had returned. I walked into his room and said, "It's now or never" and sat down on the end of the bed. Although yesterday my head had been filled with a thousand things to say, I couldn't say a word. We sat in uncomfortable silence until he rolled a spliff for us to share.

After that, we were able to converse a little, but nothing much was said. I suggested that he stay away from Esme because, first of all, she was Rowan's collared slave and it was unethical for him to play with her without Rowan's permission. I had been on the phone with Rowan the night before and I knew that Rowan had no knowledge of Esme being there. He had the grace to look abashed at breaking a cardinal rule of BDSM: *Thou shalt not play with another's collared slave without their owner's express permission.* I continued by saying that he wouldn't understand Esme any better than he understood me, and if all he wanted was a nice disposable toy to play with, he should be sure Esme knew that.

Then I asked him to give me back my letters and stories, the ones I had sent him from the states. He looked disappointed, even a little unhappy, at having to return these things to me, but he said he understood. It took him a few minutes to gather them up and put them in a green folder. I took the folder from him, surprised at how thick it was. He offered to give me back the photos, but I told him he could keep them and added coolly that I had the originals anyway. Suddenly, looking at the stories, I decided I didn't want them. I handed them back to him saying that they were only stories after all, fantasies I had created with no basis in reality, and that the letters were more important. As he took them from me, I went on to say that the day and night before I had done some thinking and had come to the conclusion that the problem we had hadn't been entirely my fault. I felt that in spite of what he had said, that was what he wanted me to believe.

Everyone he had introduced me to, except Sonya and Michael, had liked me and many of them had wanted to play with me and get to know me, so hence, part of the problem must lie with him. Under his breath he muttered something like, "Okay, so now blame the whole thing on me." Angry now, I retorted, "I never said the whole thing was your fault. Is your conscience pricking you?" I emphasized the word "prick." He blushed. To soften my words I said, "Look, it's not all your fault any more than it's all mine. We connected for that short time in the states but in the longer run, we didn't. And the timing was bad." This ruffled his feathers and he said to me stiffly, "You didn't like our other guests." "And some of them didn't like me," I snapped back.

But something occurred to me just then: I had met Sonya and Michael at a fetish event in New York about a year earlier. Without thinking, I said, "You mean Sow Sonya and Buffoon Michael? I met them at a fetish weekend in New York some time ago and didn't like them then. (This was true, I hadn't liked them when I was introduced to them but I had forgotten all about it.) Why should I like them now? And what would you have done if Niles hadn't asked me to his place? What would you have done if you hadn't been able to palm me off on Niles? I would have liked to spend time with Niles under better circumstances. Both he and I deserved it!" Oliver just nodded his head and looked away.

For some reason still unknown to me, I went into my bag and brought out a story I had written with the intention of giving it to him one night when we were playing. But that hadn't happened so it had remained in my bag. Maybe I gave it to him because I just didn't want it around me. It was called "Waiting for the Lord: Corsets and Caning." I told him not to read it until after I had left. There were two more stories I had written for him in the bag but just as impulsively, I decided to keep them for myself.

When he read the title of the story, his eyes lit up. This annoyed me to no end. I said to him, "If caning is your religion and you are its high priest, you should have caned me for my sins, for my infractions." To this he replied that caning was not his religion but that it was "holy." Besides, he went on, in his religion there were no priests or confession. I told him that was a damn shame because what good was the release and relief of penance without having made confession? That without a witness, the shame of humiliation was no shame at all and that penance without a confession was not much more than unreflective violence. He adamantly disagreed, so I said blandly that we agreed to disagree; I then lit a cigarette and blew the smoke in his face.

We talked a bit more but, again, not about anything important. We spoke mostly about mind-altering substances and their side effects, dos and don'ts: no Prozac with E but drink lots of orange juice; not to eat before taking GHB but okay to eat later on; and that with both alcohol should be avoided altogether. The ride to the airport was a silent one and much to my surprise, instead of just dropping me off at the terminal, he parked the car and came inside with me. After checking in and checking my bags, we went to one of Heathrow's many cafes and ordered coffee. Softened up some by his consideration and this new turn of events, I became more talkative.

I said that all day yesterday I had hoped he would relent and spend some time with me, maybe even cane me. He brightened until I said that that hope had gone away when I saw Esme in the hallway. He replied that he had thought about caning me today but he didn't say why he hadn't done so. I didn't ask him but instead said I liked Niles's caning style, so I had let Niles beat me until I had cried and then I had felt a lot better. At least he understood this. I continued by saying that I was pleased to have come so far in my mind to love the cane before I had ever felt it on my flesh. He looked sorry when I said that, perhaps because he hadn't caned me again after all.

His next statement was the very last thing I expected to hear: an explanation and partial acceptance that the "problem" was his fault. He started out by saying that our timing had been bad; he had many other things on his mind when I got there. He told me that when I had arrived he and Toby where having problems within their master/slave relationship. Oliver said he had been on the verge of taking his collar back from Toby, a right every master had when he wanted to end a relationship. (I found out later on that it was Toby who wanted to return the collar to Oliver. This would have been a disaster for Oliver because Toby virtually supported him.) The day he had spent in long conversation with Toby was about exactly that. It was then they had decided to give their relationship another go—that he and Toby loved each other "too much" not to give it another chance after a meeting of the minds. Having to juggle my wants and desires and the needs of the other guests with those of his collared slave had been too much for him and he had withdrawn. He added that in a few months we could "try again." I said, "yes, maybe," in what I hoped was a non-committal and blasé voice. He reassured me that we would meet again.

I took the green folder out of my carry-on bag and placed it on the table. I remarked drily that now that he knew me, perhaps he should read my letters. He insisted that he had read them when they had arrived. I asked him if it bothered him that I had taken them back; he didn't say yes or no but just stared at the thick folder on the table. From underneath downcast eyes, he said the letters contained very good visuals, indeed that I was a talented writer, and then he lifted his head and smiled at me. When I pushed the folder to him and nodded at it, he grabbed it, folded it in half, and jammed it in his jacket pocket.

I finished my coffee and said it was time to go. As I turned to leave for the security line, he said to me, "See, I'm not so bad after all." We laughed and I turned away. But before I got more than a couple of steps away from him, he grabbed me by the arms and hugged me to him. I kissed him on the cheek. When I pulled away from him, he pulled me to him and kissed me on the lips. He let me go and just as I began to turn away he did the same. I boarded the plane without looking to see if he was looking back.

EIGHTEEN

How long is a week spent in darkness? How long is a day without a night? How long is a month without the touch of the master? How long does it take for fantasy to become more real than reality? And what state of mind does one have to be in to do such a thing?

When I turned my back on Oliver, I did not turn my back on England. I returned to New York armed with phone numbers: Niles's, Charmaine's, Rowan's. I knew I would return there, I knew I *had* to return there, that there was something there for me that I couldn't find here. But what do we know, even when we think we know it all? I did return to New York but only long enough to pack up everything I owned and move it eleven hundred miles south to Fort Lauderdale, Florida. This move was not willy-nilly; I knew before I left for London that I would be moving. My lease was up, the rent had skyrocketed, and I had no steady income with which to pay it.

To this day, all of the reasons for the move seem to be the right ones: better living conditions for the income I had, good weather, free parking, cheap medical insurance, beaches, no state or city income taxes—you know the reasons. But there is more to life than that. I left New York at a time when I had finally made inroads into the BDSM community, my phone was ringing off the hook with friends and business, and I had made for myself what anyone could look at and call a "life." I had friends in New York, people I had known for ten to twenty-five years, and a large family. Although I had relatives in Florida, I didn't know anyone else there and I am not the sort that makes friends easily. And there I was, moving an additional eleven hundred–plus miles by plane away from that place I loved so much: London.

So what was I doing? I don't really know. I do know that I cried as we packed my things into the truck and that I sat in silence or in silent tears as the miles blurred by. After three days of this, I arrived at my aunt's house in Hollywood, bleary, weary, and much worse for the wear and tear. But my aunt was happy to have me there, glad for my company and the money I was paying her. The friend who had driven down with me left in four days and I spent a week busying myself with unpacking and settling in before I allowed myself to think about what

I had done. Once that reality began to dawn on me, instead of taking it out and dissecting it, instead of examining it carefully and dealing with it, I firmly slammed the door shut on it and went on my way.

I relived that time in London over and over again in the lovely world I created in my mind. Going back and forth between this world and that one was a very easy thing for me to do. I kept in contact with Charmaine, talking about the nights we had spent together and letting her fill my ears with the life and times of Niles; she had known him for twenty years. They met when he was dating her older sister. I called Rowan and she and I discussed playing together in a very private dominant/submissive scene over at least two or three days when we next met. It was all very exciting and helped to ease the sense of loss I felt when I left New York for Florida.

And of course, I called Niles. I treasured the memories of the time I had spent with Niles, and would recall them one at a time and savor them anew. I had long conversations with him and created a fantasy world that revolved around him. Not that I just sat in the house and did this. My friends in New York had seen to it that I had a few local phone numbers of scene people and I contacted them. Through them I connected with a much younger, prettier, more "London-style" group than the one in New York, or the one my New York friends had turned me on to in Florida. I was Madelaine from New York, I was an author and a former professional domina, I had just returned from London before I moved to Florida, and I had a "British boyfriend/master."

I would call Niles every Monday night and we would stay on the phone for hours. He would tell me what was going on in London, about the club parties and about the private parties he had been to; I would relate my stateside version to him. And then I would shyly bring up the things he and I had done together, speaking hesitantly at first, then more volubly as time went on. I lived for adventure, not for my sake but for the "re-tale" value these outings had as proof of life to Niles. I sent him music, bondage faerie and BDSM comic books, and the occasional letter via US mail. I knew his phone number and address, post code and all, by heart. Then one day, I decided I would like to visit London, or more especially, Niles, again. I found a time frame when there was a big event going on and planned my trip around that, as something we could dress up for and attend together. And, not wanting there to be any confusion over why I was there, I made it clear that I was coming to London to visit *him*, not the city and would that be all right? Great joy when he said yes.

Bursting with the news, I told all my new friends that I was going to London to visit Niles, and that during my stay we would be attending the Sex Fetishists Ball. For weeks before the departure, I walked around in a higher state of consciousness. My phone bills were astronomical, but since I was in orbit, it hardly mattered. What did a few more dollars spent on the phone bill matter when I was going to see the master?

And so it began.

NINETEEN

As the date for my departure approached, Niles fell ill. During one of his wild sexcapades and its acrobatics, he had pulled something in his groin and his bollocks were swollen up to almost twice their normal size. Of course, when we spoke, he downplayed that aspect of it and assured me he wanted me to visit him. It wasn't until I got there that I realized the seriousness of his situation.

The flight was a disaster as well as an hour late landing. Screaming babies, lousier-than-usual food, and lights kept on too late into the flight assured I got as little sleep as possible. All that was blown out of my mind like fog disintegrating in the morning sun when I first spied Niles. Even through his rugged handsomeness, his illness showed in his face, especially after having gotten up very early to meet my eight a.m. flight and then having to stand around the airport for that extra hour. But he was still drop-dead handsome to me, even more handsome than I remembered or his picture had captured. His handsomeness, strength, sense of humor, self-control and awesome pheromones struck me anew and, tired as I was from the long flight from Miami, a smile lit up my face when I saw him and a calmness washed over me. At last I was with the man of my dreams, the master I so desired!

We got to the car as quickly as possible so Niles could sit again and relieve the strain on his bollocks but not after some hugging and kissing. London was starting to come alive as we drove into the city and approached his place in Maida Vale. The sun shed its light through the clouds on the buildings and streets. But I was the clear winner in the shine department.

And then we were at Niles's. As I burst through the door into his flat, I tried to deny the feeling that I had "come home," but with mixed results. Happy to be there, I ran from room to room, bounced on the bed, checked the food supplies, whatever, before I noticed that Niles was sitting on the sofa in a state of exhaustion. Emotionally bludgeoning myself for being selfish, I hurried to see to his needs. Niles was in much worse shape, physically and financially, than he and Charmaine had led me to believe. When the injury first happened, he had to be brought to the hospital, where he stayed for several days because his condition was very serious. In that time, he had charmed the nurses. Self-employed, he had been setting up computer systems for the technologically challenged before his injury and had not been able to ply his trade for many weeks.

After not hearing from Niles for a week, Charmaine went to his flat and let herself in. She found him sprawled out on the floor, half conscious, and called the ambulance. She had visited him in the hospital and had given him a blow job there behind pulled curtains, but since then, she was nowhere to be found. Another friend of Oliver's was visiting from the states, and she had the hots for him, so after Niles had come home from the hospital, Niles was on his own. His house was more than a mess. He was broke and the cupboard was almost bare. This struck me as very odd at the time: Here he was, very sick, no food, no income, and in a dirty house, and no Charmaine or any of his other lady friends looking in on him either. When I asked about this, he shrugged his shoulders and said "Well, you know . . ." and just trailed off. Well, I didn't know so I pressed for more information. What he told me made my mouth drop open, and although I didn't know it at the time, gave me my first clue as to what "relationships" meant to Niles.

No one had "been around" to look in on him or look after him. He didn't need or want that from his girlfriends/lovers/slaves. All he required of them was that they enjoy, or submit to, the brute sex he enjoyed so much. Okay, I understood that but I didn't understand these *women*. What was up with *them*? Where was their humanity? Only in it for the sex or not, I didn't see how anyone could let a sick man, never mind a sick man whom they had sex with, lie in a dirty bed, unfed, with laundry everywhere, and not do anything to help him. But like Charmaine, once he couldn't make the sex magic with them any longer, they were off and running and wouldn't be seen again until he could give them what they wanted. I was aghast. I decided I would be the strong one, the one who was there for him, and take care of him the way he took care of me when I was hurting. Not that our "hurts" were similar in any way: I was suffering emotionally when we had met and his suffering now was physical but he was in need and I would fulfill his needs, all of his needs.

After I relaxed, scrubbed, sloughed off and, most important, shaved my quim in a much-needed hot bath, Niles and I took a midday nap. Niles's bollocks may have been swollen but there are many ways to handle a slave without straining oneself further, or at all. Maybe my excitement communicated itself to him, maybe he was sex starved, too, or maybe he just wanted to quiet me down. He had me on my back and was stretched out on his side next to me in the blink of an eye. One of his large, strong hands held both of mine over my head; almost simultaneously one of his legs kicked mine open and pinned the near one down. At his strong and familiar yet much-missed touch, I relaxed my legs and splayed myself for him. His big warm hands slid up my belly to my breasts. He fondled them roughly and squeezed them hard and I responded wantonly to his touch, loving it that he was teasing me before he penetrated me.

Sliding onto me, using his upper body to pin me down, his roaming hand caressed my neck in an upward motion and came to rest on my cheek. His lips brushed my other cheek and I half moaned, half sobbed in lust. Niles brushed my cheek with the front of his fingers in a delicate, loverlike gesture. He touched me so gently under my chin and on my neck that I was almost completely relaxed when his hand closed on my throat. When I opened my eyes in what I will confess was a small panic, his scarred, handsome face loomed over mine, his gleaming green eyes carefully watching mine. I stopped struggling and let him choke me.

When I ceased to struggle and focused on enjoying the sensation, I found it to be delightful. A floating between here and there, between awareness and void. He slid two fingers into me. He opened his hand in the instant before the world went blank.

I took gasping breaths to fill my lungs. Lovely air! Impaled on his fingers, I tried to put my arms around his neck, to hold him, to hug him after he let me go, but I couldn't move my arms. Niles watched me for a while and made sure I was okay before he withdrew his fingers. Then he turned onto his side and took a nap. I was almost too excited to go to sleep, but somehow I managed.

Niles was up before me. I slept so soundly that I didn't hear or feel him leave the bed or the room. From the kitchen, I heard the sounds of a meal being prepped so I went in that direction when I got up. I was tickled to see Niles in the kitchen; seeing a man who was proficient with the pots and pans always charmed me. And Niles is quite a cook. One of those people who can look at a kitchen that seems bare to you or me and produce a nice meal from it. This was a thrown-together dinner made of food already in the house, but it looked as if someone had spent time planning it: lamb steaks, baked potatoes, and a mix of stir-fried vegetables. And it was mmm mmm good, too! I like a man who knows his way around a kitchen. Over dinner, Niles mentioned that Adam's monthly party was that night and that he would like to go.

I was surprised because I thought he would want to rest instead, but he said that we'd only stay an hour, so I happily agreed. Miss a London party? Not this girl! He wore his usual leathers and ruffles and I planned to wear the PVC pants with the three little balls and teamed them with a sheer black mesh top and my low-top platform boots. A small latex collar shaped like a bat completed my outfit. As I rooted through my suitcases for my clothes, I remembered I had gifts for Niles. What perfect timing! I found the gorgeous black moose-hide heavyweight flogger I had custom-made for him. It was a thing of true beauty and could deliver blows ranging from moderately soft "splashes" to almost savage confined blows. Behind the door in the front room was a long mailer tube and in that was a custom-made cane. I found him in the front room all dressed and ready to go. In the nude, I knelt and presented him with first the cane then the flogger.

The cane, with its crystal ball at the end for balance, handsome red leather grip over-laced with black x's and twenty hand coats of shellac was quite pretty, but there were very slight ripples in the wand that Niles thought would spoil its use. But as soon as he picked it up, he felt the magic of the thing and took to playing with it, first lightly in the air and then very lightly on me. Not hitting me with it, but running it over my body as if I were a cello and it was my bow. Another thought he snatched from my mind—to use it on me the way I played with it myself. I sighed luxuriously; maybe we wouldn't be going out after all! I bent over the arm of the sofa and assumed a position for being caned. Niles played the cane up the back of my thighs to my derriere, then bounced the cane between my upper thighs until they were spread far enough apart to please him. I buried my head in my arms and awaited the blows.

Which did not come. I heard Niles's footfalls around me, smelled his pheromones pervade the air, felt my skin tingle from his nearness, and burned for the blow to land, but all I could feel were Niles's hot eyes on me. Moving to where my head lay buried in my arms, Niles grabbed me by the hair and forced my head between his thighs. I grabbed hold of his thighs to support myself just as the first blow landed on my anus. The pain was stunning; a white hot burning shot through my body and then, suddenly it was gone. Then another blow landed, then another and another. I struggled to remain in position, I struggled not to bounce or wiggle to evade the blows. I was very frightened of bashing my head into Niles's swollen bollocks and doing him more damage, but I was much more concerned about this than Niles was. The blows rained down on my anus.

Then abruptly they stopped. Niles opened his thighs and I almost fell. Using my own impetus, Niles pushed me as I stumbled and I fell to the floor. I landed on my back, Niles loomed over me like a giant. I displayed myself to him as a sign of submission. His eyes lit up and he brought the cane down on my freshly shaven quim. I screamed in genuine pain and fought to maintain my splayed position and accept his will. But my scream had caught him. He heard the genuine pain in it and it turned him on more than any award-winning performance. He ordered me to draw my knees up to my chest and hold them there. Once in position, he caned my quim and my anus as he pleased, and brought the thin whippy reed down on my tender pink labia and puckered opening until I sobbed out, "Please, master, don't hurt my quim and my anus anymore, please . . ."

One more very hard blow to my anus brought me to my feet, facing him. I ran my hands over the ruffles of his shirt and begged him to stop. "What do you say?" "Please, Niles . . ." "You say, 'Mercy, please, master, mercy.'" "Mercy, master, please, show mercy." He hugged me to him with one arm and with his free hand he explored my oozing aching opening. I clung to him, kissing him, licking him, rubbing against him. I was on fire for him and would have done anything, even spread my cheeks for more strokes of the cane, to have him inside me. He ordered me to rise and dress. As I left the room, I looked over my shoulder and saw him admiring the workmanship of the flogger and testing its balance. The look of it fit the look of him and he recognized that as well as the beauty of the piece. What a rare man! Definitely, exceedingly masculine but in touch enough with his feminine side to appreciate an object of beauty. A man who would appreciate a bouquet of flowers.

I was pleased with the outcome of my dressing efforts. The reflection in the mirror didn't look like someone who had spent the better part of the last thirty-six hours in airports or on planes. And the three little balls dangling between my legs tickled me silly. When I returned to the front room, Niles handed me a hit of E and I took it. He showed me a double sided clip hook: He had attached the flogger to one end and the other to one of the belt loops on his leather pants. Tonight would be a night of firsts: the debut of the flogger and christening of the cane, my first time out alone with Niles, and my first appearance in public as a slave.

TWENTY

I was never to know if it was a setup, but when Niles and I got to the club, Rowan and Esme were already there. They were right in the door-way—Rowan holding the collared Esme by a leash. Rowan looked magnificent in a catsuit made of a black shiny material called ciré and over-the-knee black leather stiletto boots. A long curly black wig hid her own medium-brown hair, and nestled in the teased-up crown of the wig sat a high tiara. She looked every inch the "mistress" and I wasn't the only one who noticed. Many cast appreciative glances at Rowan as they walked by. Turning, Rowan saw Niles and I come in and greeted us warmly. When she hugged me, she whispered in my ear that she was "happy to see I was in good hands with Niles." My heart swelled when she said that and I gave her an extra squeeze.

Rowan and I attempted to carry on a conversation, but the noise level and the people pushing back and forth made this impossible. And speaking with Rowan was very awkward under the baleful, watch-ful eye of Esme, who was still attached to Rowan's wrist by the leash. Since Esme was Rowan's collared slave, Rowan had asked Esme for permission to have me as a guest and submissive at Rowan's home in Summerland, as Rowan and I had discussed over the phone. A very re-spectful request, more of a formality really, but Esme had withheld her permission. Esme was feeling very insecure in her relationship with Rowan because Rowan had recently taken up with Gavin, a very nice, somewhat well-to-do submissive man. I guess I was just too much competition in Esme's mind. This is something I never under-stood although I have often "gone without" because of it. The problem here wasn't me, and actually, it wasn't Gavin either, although Gavin may seem to be the immediate cause of Esme's distress.

Esme was the problem, her own worst enemy. To the insecure Esme, Gavin and the financial security he represented certainly could be perceived as a threat to Esme's relationship and monopoly of Rowan. But refusing to give Rowan permission to play with someone who lived five thousand miles away for a mere two or three days was a ridiculous and completely unnecessary show of the power of the submissive and unworthy of Esme. She knew that I knew she had denied her permission and I wanted her to feel small because of it. I let Rowan overhear me casually ask Esme if Esme had enjoyed herself up at the Manor with Oliver all those months ago. I was on the phone with Rowan when Esme was there and I knew damn well that Esme had snuck over there without permission. The look on Rowan's face more than confirmed it. She shot a look at Esme that made Esme blush with shame and hang her head. But even her mistress's anger was not enough to make Esme relent, so my two or three days with Rowan was never to be.

After this, Esme looked even more doleful. I greeted her cordially, even a little more warmly than was necessary, just so I could prolong her agony. But I had already made my point, so I began to take in my surroundings. I'd enough of *woe-Es-me* and the wet blanket her presence threw on things. It wasn't long before my gaze fell on Niles who was deep in an animated conversation with a friend. He looked to be getting quite done in with excitement and exertion. I approached him smiling and suggested we find him a chair. Taking him by the arm, Niles and I wandered off in search of a suitable seat and found him a nice old arm chair off to the side where he could relax comfortably and see everything. And being Niles, everyone would come up to greet him. After he was settled, I went to the bar for drinks.

When I came back Rowan was there, with Esme in tow, speaking with Niles. I hadn't even sat down when Rowan told Niles she wanted to play with me right there in the club. Niles gave his permission, and giggling, I gave mine. I was rolling my brains out but I knew what I was doing. But we weren't in the play area so there was this stir when we dragged Niles's comfy chair and all of our personal stuff into the playroom and set up "shop" in there. We placed Niles's chair at the head of an area rug that was not being used and situated the chair so that it seemed to be a throne. Laughing, he took his place in it and we unloaded the rest of our stuff onto the floor around it. Rowan pulled a flogger out of her bag and signaled to Esme with it. Esme hurried to stand in the middle of the area rug and after I recognized what was happening, I hurried to join her.

Esme moved over so that we each had equal occupancy of the rug.

She spread her feet about eighteen inches apart, I spread mine eighteen inches apart. She clasped her hands behind her neck, elbows out, and looked straight ahead, and so did I. Then we waited for Rowan. We didn't wait long. She circled Esme first, corrected the angle of Esme's elbows, adjusted her center of gravity, and did little things that would have gone unnoticed by someone other than Rowan. By sneaking peeks from the corner of my eye and from under the shield of my hair, I was able to make minor improvements to my stance. Then Rowan turned her attention to me. She was not as picky with me as she was with Esme and I was relieved and disappointed. She placed her lips next to my ear and said in a clear voice, "Watch Esme and do what she does. I am going to run her through her positions."

Being a mistress myself, I knew about "positions" because I had my own set; many mistresses had a "set." What did impress me was the method used to communicate the position number. In a noisy club, a spoken or even (heaven forbid!) shouted command can be lost or become garbled. Rowan had solved this problem by singing one operatic note to attract Esme's attention and then making a hand signal to indicate the position she desired. The right index finger was one, the middle finger was two, and so on, then six was the thumb alone, seven was the thumb and index finger, and so on. When one reached "ten," one switched to the other hand to indicate counting by tens and used the left thumb to mean ten, the index finger to mean twenty, and so on. Hence, "thirteen" would be the index, middle, and ring fingers of the right hand and the thumb of the left. Rowan used thirteen positions.

Singing her operatic note, Rowan held up her index finger: position one. Esme dropped to her knees and assumed my position one: the universal position of homage performed to greet all masters and mistresses. This was the same first position I taught my slaves and I was sure there would be other similarities, if not in position number, but in the positions themselves. I was correct: A good seven of them were positions I used in session, either exactly the same or with slight variations. Position two was for a standing inspection; three was kneeling position; four a variation of three. Position five was almost the same as one, only without the kiss of homage; six was for the very bad slave. In position six, the slave was to lie face down on the floor, feet together, arms outstretched, nose to the floor, and await the displeasure of the dominant. It was very similar to the position Roman Catholic priests assume during ordination. I assumed it when commanded but I was not too happy about lying face down on a filthy public floor. I was happy that I was dressed and Esme was the one wearing only shoes and a g-string.

After penance comes forgiveness and that was what position seven was for. Standing on one's knees, the freshly disciplined and humbled recalcitrant slave hugged the mistress's right thigh, head on her hip, and waited for her touch of forgiveness. Eight was a standing up waiting position similar to one of mine. Position nine was new to me, and a very useful and interesting one. In the hands-around-the harem/pass-me-your-slave/boytoy swinger/fetish parties in London, how did you politely and in context communicate that you had no desire to be "given" to this or that person? You got into position nine! You laid on your back on the floor, drew your closed knees and feet up to your chest, placed your arms stiffly at your sides and stared unblinkingly at the ceiling. Upon seeing this position even the most unconscious, self-centered, unthinking of dominants will recognize this as the slave's refusal.

Position ten was a lap-sitting position, a special treat for the slave. Eleven was another standing position, but twelve and thirteen required that we got down on our knees. Rowan ran through all thirteen positions in numerical order. After we had assumed the position, she would come and inspect us and make little adjustments before singing out and signaling the next one. I tried not to outdo Esme in assuming those positions I already knew, but I also did my very best to memorize the positions. Although I am relating this to you coolly, I was transported by this experience. I have never been played with so publicly before and in such a real "public" place with "real" players in a "real" fetish club, and my experience with Rowan, and, yes even Esme, was my first BDSM encounter with a woman. The onlookers' gazes and the lust I could feel emanating from them embarrassed and excited me and I fervently hoped that my performance for Rowan had heightened Niles's desire for me. It had set me on fire.

My attention drawn away from myself by the high operatic note, I saw Rowan signal for position two. After that, she started to call out the position numbers at random and this was when I was pressed not to outdo Esme. Then I said to myself "screw Esme" and did the very best I could, occasionally remembering and executing the correlating position sooner than she did.

We had executed several positions when Rowan repositioned us near, or actually on, Niles. Esme and I were on our hands and knees facing Niles with our backs to Rowan. Each of us had our head nestled up against one of Niles's thighs and Rowan was flogging us and hand-spanking us. As Rowan beat me, I caressed and kissed Niles's thigh, feeling myself cream into my PVC pants. He smelled so good, his thigh felt so strong and warm under the cool leather, his presence was so re-assuring; I saw no reason to share. Catching Esme's eye, I made a small "no-no" gesture to her, meaning that extending behavior corre-sponding to mine toward Niles would *not* be appreciated. With down-cast eyes, she acknowledged my wishes. *I'm only here on vacation*, I thought to myself with malicious amusement, while you, Esme, can have either Rowan or Niles whenever you want. You denied me my pleasure so now I will deny you yours. Unworthy of me, yes, but since Esme knew what was up, it did feel good.

Rowan turned all of her attention to Esme, leaving me clinging to Niles's thigh. His large warm hand insinuated itself into my hair, close to the scalp, and used my locks to pull my head around. He pulled my head back and ran his free hand up my throat; remembering the night before, he felt more than heard my gasp of lust. Letting go of my hair, he pulled me between his open thighs by the collar. Slowly stiffening his fingers between my throat and the collar, he cut off my air supply until I was weak and almost to the point of fainting. Gone was the crowd, the music, the dirt on the floor; all that existed was Niles and his hand around my throat and the pinwheels projecting themselves on my eyelids. I hung from my neck by the collar in his hand and I loved it. All that mattered was Niles's touch and what he was doing with me, to me, for me.

Suddenly that high note reached my ears and Niles let go of my throat. I whirled around to see Rowan giving the signal for position six, the "ordination" position. I obeyed but I really didn't want to leave Niles's embrace for that of the dirty floor. Reluctantly I crawled to the rug and soon Esme and I were face down, awaiting the pleasure of the mistress. But things don't always turn out as we wish and as soon as I was forced to leave the emotional and physical comfort and security of Niles, to rip my mind away from the beautiful place it had been to make it focus on the filth beneath my nose . . .

I became terribly disoriented and a panic attack ensued. The floor fell out from under me and I was tumbling through blackness. I didn't know where I was or how I had gotten there and a strange roaring silence filled my ears. From that horrid position on the floor I tried to hoist myself onto my hands and knees and crawl away from there. My arms failed me. Again I struggled to rise but Rowan's foot came down on the small of my back. I called out for Niles to help me but either no sound came out at all or it was drowned out by the music. Still trying to crawl, I reached out to try to grab hold of Niles's foot to reconnect myself but I couldn't find it. I tried to shake Rowan's foot off but she pressed down harder. Suddenly Niles recognized my distress, grabbed me up in one fell swoop, and deposited me in his lap.

Rowan left Esme face down on the floor and inquired about me solicitously. After ensuring herself that I was reconnecting and felt safe with Niles, she returned her full attention to Esme. I was more than happy to stay alone with Niles, my master, my lover, my savior once again. I knelt between his thighs and he hugged me to his chest. His pheromones filled my head and chased away the remainder of my earlier panic. His strong hands caressed me gently and stroked my hair while his melted butterscotch voice whispered calming, soothing sounds into my ear. His hair fell around his face like a curtain that was long enough to conceal me also. I hid under there, under this curtain of hair. I buried my face in his chest and sniffed him; I ran my hands over his chest, rubbed my body against his leather-clad crotch, and snuggled in as close as I could. Playing with Rowan was fun but this, this was what I burned for.

After I had returned to Earth guided by Niles's voice and presence, we enjoyed ourselves watching Rowan play with Esme. It was obvious even to a casual observer that Esme was Rowan's personal slave and that she was very well trained. It seemed they read each other's minds and flowed from one action into the next seamlessly. It was almost balletic and this was reinforced by the final position Rowan commanded Esme to assume. Rowan extended one leg and braced herself on the back leg. Esme placed her head on Rowan's foot and a hand on either side of it, then she went into a headstand with both feet completely off the floor and spread open, using Rowan's outstretched leg as a brace against her back. Once Esme was firmly in this position, Rowan began to flog her quim. This was a very erotic beating that mesmerized Niles and I as well as many of the onlookers.

The club had gotten crowded since we had arrived. When we had moved into the play area, we were the only ones playing and none of the equipment was being used. But nothing lasts forever and right next to Niles's seat was a St. Andrew's cross (an X-frame). A new "mistress," and I use "new" to mean the amount of time she'd had to perfect her craft, moved in with her slave. Having no idea of protocol, how to secure a play space, and so on, she carelessly began to flog the slave. And almost caught me in the face with what was fortunately a spent stroke. I tried to say something to her but Niles made a "don't bother" gesture to me and signaled me that we were going to move our stuff someplace else. We found a quieter, less dangerous area and I knelt at his feet. Small as it sounds, this was a very exciting thing for me to do. Experienced as I was as a dominant, I was still a very new, albeit a very willing, slave, and these small public acts thrilled me.

Although I was well occupied with behaving as a proper slave should and being a credit to Niles, the club scene was rather old hat to him and there being nothing much left to look at, he started to get "bouncy." Considering his injury, bouncy was not a good thing and I wanted to get him home. It had been a long day. Not wanting to make it too obvious that he was overdoing it, I waited a few minutes while he bounced up and down in the chair in time to the music. It was approaching two in the morning when I suggested we leave, and after a short hesitation, Niles agreed. I helped him into his coat and scrambled into mine, then, arm in arm, we walked slowly around the club looking for Rowan and Adam to say our good nights. Everyone bade Niles a warm good night and get well as we passed and I was exhilarated to be the one he was with.

We found Adam, Rowan, and the re-leashed Esme and said our good-byes. I hugged Rowan warmly and let my feelings for her flow through me into her. Rowan felt this so strongly that we broke our hug very briefly, looked deeply into each other's eyes, and then hugged again. The melancholy Esme looked on but her woebegone expression annoyed me. To offset this, I made a big fuss of saying good night to Adam, but when it was time to say good night to Esme, I just waved my hand at her a couple of times and said "bye." Arm in arm, Niles and I walked out of the club.

It was probably around two thirty when we got back to Niles's. I thought he would be tired and want to go right to sleep. But I was still rolling hard and so was he and bless his dark desires and enormous amounts of testosterone, he had other ideas. Our play began the "usual" way: Niles rough-handling me and using his body to hold me down and my legs open. He sniffed me loudly, sniffing to smell if I was in heat. It was very erotic. His tongue probed my mouth, his fingers teased my quim and pinched my nipples, and I came alive under his touch. I arched my back to thrust my breasts out and braced my feet to meet his fingers, thrashing my head in passion and calling his name aloud. His beautiful cock, hard and throbbing, was pressed against my thigh, and I tried to rub it with my leg, wanting to give back to him some of the pleasure he gave me.

I said earlier that this night was a night of firsts and Niles had another "first" awaiting me. Depriving me of his fingers and tongue, he pressed my head down on his cock. I opened my mouth eagerly; I loved to suck him, he had the most gorgeous cock and he and it gave me great pleasure. I fell upon him eagerly, using my lips and tongue on his lovely and engorged knob and my hands on his throbbing shaft, making him moan. Suddenly his hands were in my hair, pulling my head up off his delicious member. I fought to have his cock back in my mouth but a sharp yank of my hair stilled me. I laid there docilely, his hands holding my head still, my face only inches from his cock, inhaling his scent and that of our sex, and awaited his pleasure. His hands guided my head back toward his cock but as soon as I opened my mouth to suck him, he pulled my head away.

This happened twice before he wrenched my head back by the hair and said to me, "Let me tell you how it is, Madelaine. This is not a blow job, no. This is a face-fucking. Do you know what that means?" I garbled out some negative sound—I didn't know what a face fucking was but Niles was quick to fill me in. "No lips, Madelaine, no tongue. No pleasure in it for you, only for me." He rose to his knees, still holding me firmly by the hair, and dragged me so that my face was in the proper position to take his cock. "You are to open your mouth, let your jaw fall slack, and take it. No caressing, no making nice, your face is my cock receptacle now. Do you understand, Madelaine?" To emphasize his words, as he spoke he slapped me in the face with his cock. I was making mindless noises, aware only of him, his cock, his uses for me, and my own wetness making my thighs sticky. I moaned, "Yes, Niles, only for your pleasure, only yours."

Giving my hair one more hard yank, he growled at me, "Then do it!" I dropped my jaw and relaxed my throat. Niles's strong hands positioned my face just where he wanted it, then he rammed his cock into my mouth. His hard knob slammed into the back of my throat and his pulsating shaft stretched my lips. The hard probe to the back of my throat made my nose spurt and my eyes tear. My discomfort aroused Niles more and after he got a better grip on my hair and head, he pumped into my mouth like it was nothing but a hole made especially for his amusement and pleasure. I gagged and choked over and over and it was several minutes before he let go of my head just long enough for me to take in a deep gulp of air. And then he was on and in me again, his hands in my hair holding my head steady while he pumped my face.

The more I struggled, the more I incited his sadism. I wallowed in his sadism. I loved that he shared it with me, trusted me with it. I would be a worthy receptacle for his cock and a co-conspirator in his sadistic games. I would become the sex toy he wanted and love every minute of it. It seemed I had waited my whole life to be here, waited to be a slave to just such a master and it was worth the wait. The snot smearing my face and the girl-jam smearing my thighs were badges of honor to me and I wore them proudly. I began to crave the gag and heave at the end of the deep thrust, relish the lack of air because his cock was so far down my throat, and most of all, abandon myself to the feeling of being nothing but a sex object, a thing to be fucked, a life support system for a set of three holes. When he came, I swallowed his spunk, every sweet creamy drop of it. And then he kissed me.

TWENTY-ONE

For creatures of the night, we were early risers. In the cold and dank London weather, where it gets dark so much earlier than in New York or Miami in the winter, two o'clock in the afternoon was getting to be our sunset. Niles was feeling punky and looking knocked out after last night's excursion and exertions. I wrapped him in his robe, put his worn but warm and comfy slippers on his feet, and settled him in on the sofa. I dressed quickly so I could run to the bakery before it closed at three, and after that, I went to the local market. Then we spent a restful day in the house, talking and watching two televisions at once. I established a rule that when we were home, the only things I would allow him to do for himself were things that I couldn't do for him: relieving himself, taking the occasional work call, fiddling with the computer, and well, that was about it. I could see that the more he moved around, the more he strained himself and I confess that my concern wasn't completely selfless. If he was going to strain himself, better he do it fooling around with me than picking up a box!

Niles was in his favorite spot on the sofa and I was on the comforter and pillows on the floor in his favorite spot for me. His cigarettes, lighter, ashtray, bowl of nuts, cup of tea were all within arm's reach when he put his arm almost straight out to the side. When he put his arm out next to the sofa, I was within easy reach of him. We were watching the movie *Chinatown* on one of the local stations, when Niles became curious about the iced tea I was drinking. I told him it was an American thing and handed him the glass. He thought it was just awful and dismissed it as "cold tea with no milk." He couldn't understand why anyone would drink it. Just then the scene playing in *China-town* was of Jake/Jack Nicholson paying a visit to Evelyn/Faye Dun-away. As she invites Jake in, she offers him an iced tea and then they go through the iced tea ritual: "Sugar?" "Please." "Lemon?" "Thank you." The look on Niles's face was just too funny. It was the stereotyp-ical dropped jaw, eyes agoggle, "I heard what they said I just couldn't believe my ears" look, which turned into a double take when Evelyn offers Jake a refill after he gulps down the first glassful. I thrust my arms over my heads in the victory signal and said, "Vindication!" Niles laughed.

After *Chinatown*, we were hungry. I had Indian food delivered, which would give us leftovers for another meal as well. We dove into the spicy aromatic food like we hadn't eaten in days and maybe we hadn't. One loses track of things like that when one lives in a timeless envi-ronment. We lounged about in the reception room, completely un-aware and unconcerned about time. When the reception room curtains were closed, they blocked out all sunlight and one could turn three in the afternoon to three in the morning just by closing them. The elec-tric heater in the wall was on, radiating its warmth and casting a sexy orange glow on the room. The door was closed to keep the warmth in and the world out. I was more than happy at that moment; happiness implies a giddiness I didn't feel. What I felt was content, at peace, like I was finally doing something *I* wanted to do and had found a place for myself to do it.

Niles was very affectionate with me, stroking my head and hair as I sat at his feet, giving me friendly little spanks as I walked by, and fondling my breasts when I leaned forward to rise. Combined with the intimacy of the timeless room, these small caresses made me creamy between my thighs. Niles didn't fail to notice this and started to play with my nether lips, calling me "his hot little bitch," "a slimy little thing," "his slave girl," "his she-bitch," and "his pet." The first three made me pant with lust, the latter two made me pant like a doggie and giggle. "Now be a good little bitch . . ." he said as he gestured to the dishes. I cleared up the remains and while I was in the kitchen, Niles rooted through the piles of outerwear and things on the reception room floor. When I went back into the front room, he had the new black moosehide flogger in his hand. I flung myself into my spot and began to rub my head and hands on his legs, looking up at him with hopeful, willing eyes, eyes that said, "Yes, me! Please, I want you to use that on me."

Over the evening and late into the night he used the flogger on my derriere and upper back, my breasts and my belly, and it felt wonderful everywhere it touched. Its thirty or so lashes, which were soft suede on one side and moosehide on the other, smacked into my flesh and I offered up to it every body part it desired on demand. But as much as I loved and reveled in the feel of the flogger, it was Niles's touch that I craved. His hands mesmerized me. Their very beauty belied the pain they could cause and this was a big part of their fascination. I loved to watch Niles's hand travel down my body and spread my lips. I loved to see his fingers enter me. I loved to see *and* feel as his fingers entered me at the same time because it doubled the feeling of being penetrated. And the contrast between his pale hands and my suntanned skin heightened my pleasure. His two large fingers felt like a small cock inside of me and he used them much more effectively.

When Niles forced the first two fingers of one hand then the first two fingers of the other hand into my creamy quim, it was very hard for me to remain in my spread knee position. Four massive fingers stretching my small opening! Quickly Niles began to tap the spot inside and gave me several almost violent orgasms. I felt my girl-slime gush and it flowed over his fingers. I could feel the cooler air of the room tickle me just inside as Niles spread his fingers to the four corners, making my opening bigger. He kept touching that spot so I was having frequent orgasms while he was hurting me and this was having the desired effect. Associate the pain with the pleasure until they become one and the same. Then at some point the pain alone will elicit the same response. I knew this. I begged him for more and fantasized about him doing the same thing to my anus.

Four massive fingers were withdrawn from me all at once. I lurched and grabbed at them but the imaginative and indefatigable Niles had dreamed up a new pastime. Sitting up suddenly, he grabbed my long hair up into a ponytail on the very top of my head, twisted it tightly, and then made a loop. He used one of his own ponytail holders to secure the looped ponytail and this made a leash handle out of my hair. I smiled. Niles grabbed a hold of it and used it to pull my head around. Satisfied with the results, he rose and led me around the room by my ponytail handle. I closed my eyes and let myself be guided by him; at the quick pace he was setting, my eyes were confusing me, I did better without them. He stopped and used his knee to topple me to the floor and his foot to nudge me onto my back. Getting a fresh grip on my ponytail holder, he dragged me around the room, caveman-style. Being pulled by the hair was very painful but that didn't stop me from coming.

After we came to a stop, I got into the formal leash position I had seen on many dog shows I had watched on TV. Niles picked up on this immediately, and laughing, put me through my paces. I heeled with my shoulder and arm pressed against his calf, just like the doggies did in the show; I sat, rolled over, played dead, came when called, and fetched a dildo, just like a good dog. As a reward I was stroked, petted, caressed, and made to come. When Niles needed to empty his bladder, he pulled me on all fours into the bathroom by the hair at quick-time march. Once at the bowl, he communicated to me by nudging with his knee and pointing with his nose. First I had to put the seat up and hold it up. (It had a nasty habit of flopping down.) After I did that, Niles pulled my head by the ponytail down to his thighs and smashed my face into his balls. He held my head there as he urinated. My back and shoulder were close enough to the bowl that little droplets bouncing back up from his stream dotted my skin. When he finished his stream, my face and mouth were used as toilet paper then he marched back into the reception room holding me by the hair.

Then things began to happen so fast! Niles forced my mouth open, shoved two fingers halfway down my throat, and held me there gagging. Each time I heaved, he'd shove a little more of his fingers down my throat. My nose streamed snot and my eyes watered and smeared my makeup but my eyes said, yes, more. One final thrust and abruptly he withdrew his fingers and used that same hand to slap my face. I fell to the side a little before I caught my balance and went back for more. He sat on the edge of the sofa and pulled me to kneel between his wide-spread thighs. His massive hands squeezed my breasts and mashed them into my chest, then letting them spring free, he slapped them. I clasped my hands behind my waist and arched my back to present him with a more inviting target. Grasping a nipple between each thumb and index finger, Niles began a slow, steady squeeze.

His face was very close to mine and as the pinch got more intense, he started to make another sound I would come to know well. This sound was the querying sound. It was a whisper, a breath that sounded positive; it began and ended with an up-note "em" or an "aitch" albeit there was only that one note. It asked if you liked what was happening, if you wanted more; it asked so many things in that one syllable, all meaning "do you what me to go on?" Besides Niles's overwhelming pheromones, the querying sound and his loud sniffing were the two things I began to associate most strongly with him.

Niles made the querying sound and I whimpered out, "Yes, yes," although I didn't know how much more I could stand. I changed position slightly and that helped me to bear a little more but soon I was calling for mercy. The last syllable wasn't out of my mouth before he freed my nipples. I learned then that calling for mercy meant he would stop whatever he was doing, not that he would stop entirely.

He placed his foot squarely on my shoulder and pushed. I fell over backward but since I had time to prepare for what he was going to do, I fell backward in a graceful arch and landed in an open and inviting position amidst the pillows and comforters. I looked up at him seductively from between my spread knees and slightly extended my arms like I was welcoming him into them. Looking down at me and not breaking eye contact, Niles arose and stood between my open legs. With his soft slippered foot, he kicked me in my quim. A medium kick, the kind you would give someone who was already aroused. I gasped in lovely agony and drew my knees up to my chest. He kicked me a few more times, pausing between each kick to observe me absorb the pain and ready myself for harder ones. After one particularly hard kick, I held onto my knees and rolled over onto my side.

In doing so, I unwittingly presented Niles with a new target: my anus. My quim was on overload and in this new position, my anus was very exposed, stretched, and very inviting. Niles took advantage of all of this before I even realized what I had done. His slippered toe crashed into my opening with a deep thud that rippled up my rectum. My sexy moan changed into a guttural noise when he kicked me again. This was a very different sensation than the quim kicking and produced an equally different psychological effect. Niles knew this and picked up on the change in me immediately. It was time for another petal to fall from my flower and explore the feelings of offering him my anus for such use as that would evoke. He kicked me again, very hard. While I groaned from deep in my throat, I repositioned myself so that my lower buttock would be slightly off the floor. I let go of my knees and reached back. I spread my cheeks for him and growled out, "more, more . . ."

Another kick landed and the pain rocked me. "Faster, kick me faster, harder and faster, please," I groveled and pleaded with him and spread myself more. And dear Niles, in his wonderful sadism, obliged me. He kicked my anus hard and fast. I was a co-conspirator and willing recipient of the pain and humiliation he was dishing out and I let him turn me into a mindless moaning thing. The only coherent words I said were, "Yes, kick it, kick the hole" and other dirtily worded terms of endearment and encouragement. Time stopped or raced, I could never tell which when I was with Niles, and whatever demons had driven me had been driven out of me by Niles. I covered my anus with my hands and rolled over onto my back. I stretched my legs out in front of me. "Mercy" had been called and recognized although it had been unspoken.

Mercy for my anus, I meant. For the creative, romantic sadist there are so many other parts of a woman's body to explore and exploit that when one wears out or needs a rest, there are still other goodies to play with. Niles bent at the knee, got one arm under me, then crammed three fingers of his other hand inside me. Before I could protest at the sudden and painful invasion, Niles picked me up, carried me the few short steps to the sofa, and threw me down on it. His action stunned me into silence. I had never had my quim used as a handle before and the shame of it, my sweet wet hole, being used to move me from one place to another made me cream.

Niles knelt next to me, his head level with mine, and placed his hand on my throat. He made the querying sound and searched my face with his eyes. I made my whole body go limp under just that one hand on my throat in response. I said yes with my eyes and stretching my neck forward, I made his hand "tighter" by pressing my neck against it. I blew him kisses and mouthed "Yes, yes, do it," between them. Then his fingers were bearing down on my throat, cutting off my air. I struggled, not against him, but to keep my eyes open and gazing into his. His other hand covered my mouth and nose when I opened them and soon the velvet blackness fell. When I came to, the first thing I saw when I opened my eyes was Niles's rugged face above mine. When I smiled, he made another sound I was to come to know well: the pleased brute grunt. Niles made this sound after he had committed some new abuse on your body and you liked it. I liked when he made this sound; it was incendiary to me and made my blood boil.

He flung himself down next to me and rough-handled me into a new position. He was nice and comfy laying on the sofa while I was somewhat less comfortably astraddle him and sitting low on his rib cage. I was still a bit lightheaded and quite malleable from our previous escapade. I sat docilely while he ran his hands all over me, squeezing and pinching and slapping whatever appealed to him at the moment. Then he grabbed both of my small wrists in his large left hand, forced them behind my back and held them there. I was breathing very heavily and every inch of me felt alive, tingling with sensation and on fire with lust. When his hand went to my face, I winced but his touch was a caress and I calmed down a little. Niles and I had talked about the face-slapping problems left over from my childhood and I knew that in spite of the knots in the pit of my stomach, I would allow him to do this to me. He let my wrists go.

His lovely warm hand caressed my face for a few more seconds and then withdrew. I could tell by the angle that the arm was withdrawn at that it was preparing to land a blow. I was so excited I was almost hyperventilating but somehow I managed to sit there quietly and wait for the blow to land. I heard the whoosh of the air before the blow landed and I don't know how I kept still. But I did. The blow landed squarely across my cheek and had enough force behind it to knock me to the side. I pressed my hand to my face and leaned forward to place my head on Niles's chest while I absorbed this feeling, outside and in.

Niles waited patiently, exuding pheromones, more certain of the outcome of the battle going on inside of me than I was. I had gotten very
wet when he slapped me and I could smell the scent of my own sex. I
lifted myself up and got back into as close a facsimile of the original
position as I could.

I lifted my head and met Niles's eyes. "I think you need an anchor,
my dear," he said. He shoved me down on his body then pulled my
chest down onto his. He held me there with one hand while the other
grabbed for his cock. I felt its hard knob against my lips, lips that were
still red and tender from being kicked, and felt the now-familiar spurt
Niles could induce at will. He rammed his cock up into me and sat me
up. Impaled upon his cock with my opening stretched wide, I was
suitably anchored and subdued. I lifted my head to signal my readiness. My warm brown eyes met and held his jade green ones. A dark
hard glint of sadism flashed in them before the next blow landed
across my face. His cock proved to be a most effective anchor. Although the second blow has harder than the first, it took me less time
to absorb and metamorphosize than the first and I was back in position very quickly.

A great one for drama and taking advantage of the moment, Niles
caressed my face and turned my head this way and that, looking at it
from different angles as if he were sizing it up for the next slap. I knew
this, it was called creating anticipation, and it worked on me as well as
it did on every slave I had ever had. I was on the verge of begging him
to slap me when he did. And it was the mother of all blows. Anchored
to him by his cock in my quim or not, the impact sent me reeling and
Niles had to reach out and catch me. But when the blow first landed,
when the white hot palm first crashed into my face, I'd had an intense,
body-wrenching orgasm. My shame over enjoying the slap and the
subsequent orgasm caused by it made the delicious burn of humiliation sweeter. Like an animal, I began to bounce up and down on his
cock, as mindless of him and his injury as I was of myself; of myself as
a thinking human, not as a set of wanton holes craving sex, or of him
as a pole to dance on. It was the first time we had sex since I had arrived and I was starved for it.

That night when we went to bed, I slept with my head in the crook of his shoulder, just like I would do every night after that. It was a perfect fit for my head. He would curl his arm around me; I would stretch out full length next to him and press my body against his. Some nights we would lie quietly in each other's embrace and on other nights we would talk; sexy nighttime intimate talk, talk of fantasies and sensations and of dreams fulfilled and of those yet to come. Whether we were lying quietly or talking, Niles continued to fondle me, as if to calm me for bed or reassure me by his nearness yet keep me a little sexually aroused, too.

TWENTY-TWO

Another lovely, lazy day spent lounging around the flat with Niles. He was feeling a little perkier today and spent some time sitting at the computer. About six he came into the reception room and asked if I wanted to go out for a little while. His eyes gleamed and he tried to hide his smile. Something was up. It was just another overcast evening. What was so special about tonight? He wouldn't tell me.

We were dressed and out by seven p.m., which seemed to be some "magic time." The ride wasn't long but it was through a pretty area of London where I hadn't been previously. A lovely park with gently sloping hills was ahead on the left. Niles told me it was called "Primrose Hill," although no roses, prim or otherwise, grew there, and that was where we were going. How romantic, I thought, he's taking me for an evening walk in the park and in his condition, too! My girlish heart knocked against my rib cage. As we drove around looking for a parking space, Niles told me that tonight was one of the very few nights that the comet Hale-Bopp would be visible in our hemisphere and Primrose Park was the best spot in London from which to view it. Tonight it was overcast but since rain was predicted for the next few days, this would be our best chance.

The park was lovely even if there weren't any roses to be found. Many other skywatchers had come out for the event and they were scattered around on benches and blankets on the grass and on the foot paths. Niles chose a spot which faced the right direction and had no obstacles blocking our view and we set to raking the sky with our eyes. He seemed to be looking all over the place at once while I divided the sky into grids and scanned a grid at a time. The sky was a pretty dark pink deepening to purple and as the sun went down further, the sky turned to its first shade of overcast night blue. Out of the corner of my eye, I saw something that didn't belong there. When I turned to face it and pinpoint its location, I knew from the knot in my stomach it was the comet. I pulled on Niles's arm in agitation. I was afraid to take my eye off the comet for one New York nanosecond. Finally I got his attention and after much "follow-my-finger" pointing, and "comet at two thirty," I was able to focus his gaze on the royal Hale-Bopp, too.

We saw it streak across the sky, Hale-Bopp's head visible to us for maybe only ten or fifteen seconds, but it was unmistakable. There, right before my eyes, was what we are all made of: stardust. Hale-Bopp was the most wondrous, unearthly thing I had even seen in my life. Seeing it made me feel different inside, a little enchanted and a little enlightened, and I curled my arm tightly through Niles's. When he smiled back at me, I realized he was shuffling from foot to foot and that his face was a little pale. It had gotten damper and the wind had picked up since we left the flat. I decided it was time to go home. The walk back to the car tired Niles out more and by the time he got us back to Maida Vale in his manual transmission car, moving his arms and legs all at the same time, he was quite done in. I got him into his robe then I made us a thrown together dinner of Chinese-style chicken and stir-fried veggies. I let him rest while I cleaned up.

Every time I went in the kitchen on a "regular" errand like making tea or coffee, I always waited in there until the water boiled, because these few minutes several times a day gave me extra time to clean. Little by little it was shaping up in there and soon Niles would notice. I knew he wanted and appreciated a clean house but had no compunction to do the work himself. And I already knew that any "service" of this sort was not expected of his "lady friends," or nor did they offer it. So I did it. It was part of the romanticism of being his slave and something I had been thinking about before I fell asleep each night. I was so very content looking after Niles and thinking of nothing and no one except for him. I found joy in looking after him, especially now when he needed someone. I discovered since he had only penetrated my quim once with his cock because of his injury my joy did not come entirely from sex. I can assure you that when I reached behind the toilet bowl in my rubber gloved hands to clean out the whatevers, I was not thinking of sex!

Niles had dozed off while I was in the kitchen. I lolled in my favorite spot on the floor at his feet, amidst the pillows and fluffy white comforter, lost in my memories and dreams. It was probably around ten p.m. when he roused and began to show an interest in his "slave-girl." The short nap had revived him nicely and he called for his new cane to be brought to him and the box of E. He said in a velvet growl that tonight he would break the cane in on me and he beat me often and hard. I extended my tongue and he placed the pill on it. Without breaking eye contact, I brought the glass to my lips and swallowed it. This evoked strong feelings of surrender and I offered my power to him.

Sometimes I was bent over the arm of the sofa to be caned. Other times I was made to stand in the middle of the floor, feet wide, knees slightly bent, hands braced on my thighs, and bent over at the waist. I took as many strokes as I could each time he caned me, for his benefit and for mine. I wanted to know how far down I could reach into the depths of my masochism and still love it. On his behalf, I wanted to please him and that meant bearing as much pain as I could. I knew my pain excited him in a way that sometimes drifted outside of the romantic and consensual and this scared me. But then I do find fear to be delicious sometimes and I like to live dangerously. Images of the Marquis de Sade, made over in the likeness of Niles, danced in my head.

Managing to look not only handsome but majestic in his robe, Niles used the cane on my buttocks at will. But then he wore himself out and laid down on the sofa, leaving me standing in the middle of the room with my red welted derriere sticking out. I cast surreptitious glances at him over my shoulder but he wasn't paying attention to me. I sub-spaced out until his voice brought me back. He ordered me to come and straddle him. Eagerly I obeyed, smiling down at him. From under the sofa, he pulled out a pair of leather wrist restraints and slapped them on me. Then he tied them together with a very short length of rope and tied the rope to one of the large eye hooks in the wall over the sofa. I couldn't remain on my knees in this position because the hook was too far over my head so I had to stand on my feet in a low squat. From his prone position, Niles could cane me or use his fingers on me as he pleased.

I had some difficulty retaining my balance in my high heels on the soft sofa cushions and swung around more wildly as the blows from the cane rained down on me. I arched and stretched, or strained, then hung limply from the restraints, to abandon myself and make myself look beautiful to Niles. I wanted to make him want to touch me, play with me, hurt me, explore me, beat me, caress me and I got my wish. My quim took the worst of it. But dear Niles was reading me very well tonight and knew when the last stroke was the last stroke. He knew which scream meant "more" and which one meant to stop. He was masterful and I reveled in the bright white pain he gave me, especially when he landed a blow directly on my clit. I came so much that my thighs were creamy and still I couldn't stop coming. After about an hour of this, I dangled limply from the wrist restraints and needed a rest. Niles cut me down but left the cuffs on my wrists. I collapsed onto his chest and we rested together and shared a spliff in our timeless environment.

Sensing that even my slight weight on him was a burden, I lifted myself off him and got into my position at his feet on the floor. My neck was right near his hand and when I nuzzled it, he began to stroke it. Full of guile, I mentioned that I had brought a corset with me, among other things, and no sooner were the words out of my mouth than I was ordered to put it on. I returned to the reception room wearing lace-top thigh stockings, high-heeled shoes, and a very poorly laced corset. Niles took one look at it, laughed, and soon his strong fingers were plucking at the laces to right them. Getting them all lined up properly, in one long strong pull Niles laced the corset all the way closed, giving me a slim twenty two inch waist. He made me stand and model for him and made sexy growls of approval.

When I resumed my place on the floor, his massive hand immediately went to my throat. Slowly but surely he cut off my air supply, and trusting him, I relaxed into his grip. I was completely unprepared for what happened next. On the other occasion he had strangled me until I passed out, I was lying comfortably and safely in the bed. That was a gentle kind of choking, his face close to mine, his eyes looking to mine, until I drifted off into darkness. Now the more I relaxed into his grip, the more brutal his grip upon my throat became. His face loomed over mine and I saw amusement in his eyes as he applied more pressure to my windpipe. I struggled against him fruitlessly, seeing brightly colored spots before the room went dark. As the blackness fell, silence roared in my ears, all feeling and coordination deserted me and I felt like I was floating, or high on the kind of drugs the gods kept for themselves.

I came to on the floor, sprawled out among the bowl of nuts, ashtray, cigarettes, and such, with my head just a few inches from the raised tile piece in front of the electric heater. I felt like I had done way too much E and all the rushes had hit me at once. The room spun into focus but I was unsure where I was. A small part of me wondered how many brain cells had just been killed off. I called out to Niles and as soon as I saw his face, as soon as his hands touched me, I became re-oriented and crawled back to the sofa. But I still wanted to know what had happened because I was a little distressed at having come to on the floor. Niles calmly told me that he had choked me until I passed out then he had let me go. I slid off the sofa (where my upper body had been resting) onto the floor, kind of flopped onto my side, and then rolled onto my back. That was how I had landed in the nut bowl with my head so near something that could have cracked it open: namely, the sharp-raised edge of the tile in front of the heater.

As giddy and hot and sexually crazed as I was, a little voice started in my head that I chose to ignore. He let you fall, it said, he let you fall and you could have gotten hurt. Yes, I could have, I replied angrily, but I didn't so shut up and leave me alone! Little voice will not spoil my fun! I turned the volume off on the little voice and went on my merry way. I was very excited about having been sexually asphyxiated in such a rough way and my quim was dripping wet. I begged him to touch me between my legs and feel how wet his slave had gotten for him. He reached down and ever-so-lightly ran his fingers over my outer lips. I shuddered at his touch and moaned without realizing I was doing so. When he withdrew his fingers from between my legs, they were slick and wet so he wiped them off on my back and belly. I bemoaned their loss but Niles shoved me away roughly and used his feet to kick me into a footstool position.

I curled up in a comfortable little ball and positioned myself beneath his feet. This small lesson in objectification was emotionally exhilarating to me. Becoming his footstool and subjugating my personality to provide a service where the reward was the service itself, not sexual gratification, opened new paths in my mind. I became a footstool by thinking about what a good footstool does: It provides a warm, soft surface on which the master can rest his feet, it is silent and does not intrude into the master's thoughts, and it does not wiggle around. I thought of how his feet looked on my naked back and concentrated on feeling their warmth and giving them mine. His feet were long and narrow and as beautifully shaped and delicately boned as his massive hands. There were clearly the most beautiful feet I had ever seen on a man in my life. And that longer second toe drove me wild! It just cried out to be sucked. But footstools do not have mouths so I crouched there silently, floating on the breezes of my thoughts.

It was much later when we awoke. Niles had gotten cold and wanted to go to bed. I was so stiff he practically had to unfold me so I could walk to the bedroom. Once in bed, my head in the crook of his shoulder, I snuggled in close and breathed in his delicious scent. My dreams were sweet and peopled by handsome sadistic masters and willing, wanton slave girls.

TWENTY-THREE

Niles and I spent the next day as we had spent the days before: lounging around the house, smoking, talking, sharing jokes and memories, and just being together. When he wanted to rest or work at the computer, I made myself scarce by doing more housework and laundry, or writing in my journal. As I moved from task to task, I felt as if I had "come home" and that this was where I belonged, doing what I wanted to do, freeing the "me" hidden deep inside. Me, who roamed the earth like a gypsy! Me, the lady-without-a-land! I felt I had found a home keeping house, doing laundry, grocery shopping, and cooking in Niles's funny little flat in Maida Vale. I hoped against hope that this place *would,* in some way, become my home.

Although the cupboard was almost bare and no income was being earned to run the house, Niles's sex drive had not suffered at all. Injured bollocks or not, his testosterone levels were still on maximum overdrive, a very normal state for Niles. Having me there at his beck and call, ready, eager, and willing to do anything for him/to him/with him was very pleasurable for him and he took as much advantage of the situation as he could. When I was kneeling on the floor in my spot with my head on the sofa next to him, or resting my chin in my fisted hands so I could look at him when we spoke, he was very affectionate, stroking my hair and touching my face. I melted when Niles touched my face. I don't know why this small gesture always had such an effect on me, but it did. Maybe it was because Niles's hand was so large he could spread his fingers and cover my entire face with it. Maybe it was because he was very strong and I knew the same hand that was caressing me could also hurt me. Maybe it was because his hands were so beautiful, or that they made me feel so good even when he hurt me . . . or maybe, just maybe, I was falling in love with him.

Even in our timeless environment, when darkness fell, the power of the moon held us in thrall. This was a night that started out like many other nights but turned into a magical night of new discoveries. We spent some time lounging around in the front room smoking hash and laughing over the differences between American English and British English. When I said that my "bangs" needed to be trimmed, he asked me why I wanted to cut up sausages. There was no garbage can in the house; that was called the dust bin. Grilled meant broiled and "New York–style deli" bore no resemblance whatsoever to anything any deli in New York served. "Porky pies" meant telling lies, "dog and bone" meant your cell phone. Silly as it seems, this went on for several hours until Niles said he would be more comfortable lounging around in bed instead. I readily agreed.

We climbed in, stuck our heads under the quilt, and cuddled until we were warm. Having his strong arms around me, his lean hairless body pressed close to mine, and our legs intertwined made my quim wet and his gorgeous cock hard. I felt it press against my belly and I began to rub myself on it, loving the feel of it on my flesh and the thought of it being inside me. Niles made the best sex magic I had ever had and I wanted more. But dear, cruel, creative Niles had other things in mind.

Taking me in his arms and holding me like a lover, he began to kiss me slowly and deeply. I responded to his kiss like I'd never been kissed before and wrapped my arms around his neck to keep him close. He sniffed me and goose bumps grew on my skin. He growled at me and I whimpered in pretend fear. His hand closed on my breast and I arched my back as if saying, "more, more." And he gave it to me. Holding me in one arm, he used his free hand to explore my body, touching me everywhere, even behind my knees and in the crooks of my elbows, looking for hidden or previously undiscovered erogenous spots. He found several and time proved that he was the only one who those spots responded to. But he did not penetrate me, not even with his fingers. He continued to play my body like a violin until I begged him to enter me, to shag me, to take me for his pleasure.

Growling, he clamped his mouth down over mine and silenced me. I succumbed to his kiss and laid there, a receptive vessel for his lust and passion, and let him do as he pleased. Gently his fingers stroked me but only on the outer labia. Questing fingertips sought my clit and teased it until I came. His leg held my two open as he touched me and I shamelessly splayed myself for him. His caresses made me come again and again and soon there was a big wet spot under me. My moaning was constant and mindless and my hands gripped him tightly. The first slap to my quim surprised me but in the blink of an eye, this, too, made me come. Slaps accelerated to punches and I came as much from the punches as I did from the gentle caresses and hard slaps. I was crazy-hot for him, whimpering and begging him to penetrate me, please penetrate me, and to make it cruel.

"So it's penetration you want, is it?" Niles growled in my ear, I thought of a tiger in the jungle. "Want something inside that hot slimy cunt of yours, do you? Something big and hard to stretch that tiny hole of yours?" "Oh yes, please, Niles, please, do it to me, do it hard, hurt me, pound me, I don't care, please, please enter me . . ." I pleaded on the verge of tears. I wanted him so badly I was in physical pain. But instead of entering me, he rolled onto his back and took me with him. He man-handled me until I was straddling him then he picked me up, my knees still tucked under me, and sat me down on his face. I don't enjoy receiving oral sex. I find it boring. Immediately I tried to climb off of him because I was very uncomfortable with the thought that he was going to eat me. But he said, "where do you think you're going?" and very roughly held me to him. I wanted to tell him I didn't enjoy this and didn't want him to do it, but I didn't get the chance.

Instead of lips and tongue, the next thing I felt on my nether lips were his teeth. He used them on my outer and inner labia and the fleshy fold atop my clit, sometimes biting me gently and other times quite hard. My reaction surprised me. This was nothing like that insipid licking and worshipful tonguing that bored me so much. This was electrifying and delightfully painful and oh-so-enjoyable. It drove me totally out of my mind; when I wasn't screaming in ecstacy, it took my breath away. I pulled my hair and mauled my breasts as Niles bit into me. I called out his name over and over but he was relentless. Reduced to a mindless sex thing, I gabbled out that I was his toy, that I belonged to him, that my holes were his to do with as he wished.

Incited by my words, he increased the intensity of his bite. I cried out at this new pain, lost my balance, and fell forward into the wall. My hand found an oddly placed eye hook and I clung to it, still moaning wantonly. I tossed my head, clutched his shoulder, and gasped in pain but I didn't try to get away from him and this fantastically thrilling and humiliating new thing he was doing to me.

I don't know how long Niles gnawed on me but I loved every minute of it. The satyr Niles had other things in mind for me and once I was dripping wet, he pushed me off him in that rough-gentle way of his. I toppled onto the bed beside him, my mouth dry from panting heavily and my quim wet and super-sensitized from his less than tender attentions to it. Grabbing my hair in his massive hand, he pushed my head down onto his cock. I eagerly, gratefully, hungrily fell on it; he tasted so very good and his skin was silky against my tongue and lips. I loved sucking his cock. After I had swallowed as much as I could, I held him in my mouth and down my throat. When I began to gag, he held my head down on his shaft and started to thrust. I came many times. I counted sixty thrusts before I gagged again and then heaved hard.

This final heave caused his cock to pop out of my mouth and unfortunately for me, once I had lost it, he would not let me have it back again no matter how much I begged for it. Then he took me in his arms and cuddled me, my head in the familiar crook of his shoulder. We started talking, sexy talk, talk meant to excite both of us. I asked him in my slave's voice why he liked to hurt me and humiliate me. Had I done something wrong or displeased him in some way? I already knew the answers to these questions but I wanted to hear them from him. He told me that I had been very good and that he was quite pleased with me. "I understand, Niles," I replied quietly. "What do you understand, Madelaine?"

"I understand that you beat me because you enjoy hurting me, not because I have been bad or displeased you. I understand that I don't have to do anything to deserve a beating; I understand that you beat me and humiliate me for your pleasure . . . and mine. Please hurt me, Niles, please. Make me come from the pain you give me, make me love the pain. I want it, I crave it." I burrowed my head into his armpit and began to lick it; his sweat tasted even better than it smelled and I licked harder. Drugged by his taste on my tongue and his scent filling my head, I gave his armpit a tongue bath. After a little while, Niles put his arm over his head. I grasped him as best I could and applied my mouth in earnest, licking, tonguing, sucking. In my mind, he had become the king man-beast. I was one of his animal-like bitch body slaves and it was my duty to lick clean the long silken hair under his arms.

I was well out of this world when he grabbed a lock of my hair and tried to pull my head away. I fought to stay there and he had to get rougher with me. He lifted my head up enough to get his arm down and force me aside some. When I tried to dig my way back into his armpit, growling, "no . . . more, more . . . ," he used my hair to yank my head up and slapped my face. The slap shocked me back to Earth. "Enough, Madelaine." His voice was deep and carried just a hint of menace. "Yes, Niles . . . ?" I whispered. "I'm sorry, Niles, please forgive me." I was as docile now as I was bestial a minute before. He laughed and called me a silly girl. Then his arm encircled me and my head was once again in the crook of his shoulder, our bodies close. Niles fell asleep before I did and while he slept, I gazed upon his ruggedly handsome face, illuminated by the pale moonlight coming through the window. I held him in my eyes until I fell asleep, looking forward to tomorrow.

TWENTY-FOUR

Niles was feeling poorly when we awoke today and I attributed this to last night's exertions. I felt a little guilty about this for obvious reasons so I set my sights on doing more for him. He rested in bed most of the day, with occasional trips to the reception room sofa for a change of scenery. I stayed close at hand so I could cater to his needs and keep him lying down. Late in the afternoon he said he was very tired, so I helped him back into bed. I decided that he was doing way too much on my behalf and that this was my chance to give back to him the care and attention he had lavished on me when I was unwell because of the Oliver situation. Rooting through the food supplies in the kitchen, I discovered things that with just a little supplementing from the local store would make a very nice dinner. I left very quietly so as not to wake him and went to the market, list in hand.

I returned pleased with my purchases, happy to take the cooking off his hands. Niles was up and about when I came in. He said he had heard me leave but had no idea where I could be going. Seeing all the grocery bags, he became most curious about what I had been up to. I guess the sight of all those bags made him hungry and he wanted to dig through them right away and start dinner. When I told him I had dinner well under control, he offered to stay in the kitchen and keep me company while I cooked. I told him that his only job was to relax and let me take care of everything, then I chased him, literally, back onto the sofa and set him up with a bowl of nuts, a pot of tea, and the hash. As I was leaving for the kitchen, Niles asked me what I was making for dinner. Chicken Parmigiana and spaghetti, I replied smiling. He asked how I would prepare it and when I answered "on the stove with love and care," he laughed.

After I served him his dinner, I returned to the kitchen to prepare my own plate. From the front room came the sound of metal cutlery against the glass plate, followed by a loud, sincere, and somewhat surprised "mmm." Being a very good cook himself, that "mmm" was the biggest compliment he could have paid me. I smiled from ear to ear and thought I would burst with joy. When I sat at his feet with my own plate, Niles was generous with praise, saying that the dinner was quite good, excellent in fact, and thanked me over and over. His praise and appreciation made my heart soar and spurred me on to greater efforts. I decided on the spot that as well as the housework and laundry, I would take over the shopping and cooking as well. The museums and palaces I had wanted to see would still be there when Niles was well. We could see those places together.

We had the customary after-dinner cigarette together amid the demolished remains of dinner. Then I gathered up the dishes, dropped them off in the kitchen, and returned to the reception room to keep Niles company. Upon my return, Niles "ordered" me to sit on the sofa with him and relax. In a "stern" voice, he told me he "knew" what I was doing, meaning the laundry and housework, and continued to say how much he appreciated it. Faking the vapors, I put my arm over my forehead and teased him by saying, "Ah! What is this? A new form of torture? Ordering me to sit and relax when there is all this cleaning and laundry to be done? Oh, the cruelty of it! The inhumanity of it!" We both laughed at my silly dramatics but I "obeyed" him and stayed where I was. I knew from many years of experience that the dishes would still be there later on and that I could wash them when Niles was asleep. Dinner had perked him up and his company was so much more enjoyable than that of dirty dishes!

An hour or so later, I suggested that it would be very nice, very nice indeed, to have a little in-house party. Niles agreed and I broke out the E, which was an effective painkiller. We each did a half and sat around talking until the E kicked in. I decided to play dress up and went into the bedroom to dig into my suitcases. I fixed my hair and put on makeup and emerged wearing my favorite nightgown, a short black jacquard see-through number with spaghetti straps, a g-string, and the "Niles pumps." His broad face split into a big smile when he saw me and soon began to play with me. Pulling the comforter to the floor, we nested on it together, laughing and touching each other but for the satyr Niles, things had to go much farther than that. Not that I minded!

Niles loved to improvise and was very clever using whatever was at hand for his amusement. Tonight he stripped a pillow of its case and used the pillowcase to imprison me. He pulled it down over my head and body, covering my upper torso to the waist. I was exposed only from the waist down and he freely had his way with my quim without the burden of seeing my face and the pleading and passion in my eyes. He slapped it until it was hot and very pink. He used his fingers to make me come until my g-string was soaked. Roughly he pulled the g-string off me and crammed it, wet end first, up under the pillowcase and into my mouth. It made an effective gag which I could not remove because the pillowcase held my arms trapped at my sides. I was going wild in there and loved the way I felt: with only my sex organs exposed for Niles's pleasure I was bound yet so very free to guiltlessly enjoy the pain and humiliation he was giving me.

Timing was one of Niles's gifts and he perceived that I'd had enough of being in the pillowcase a second before I did. He sat me up and freed me from my cotton prison, then pulled the g-string out of my mouth. Growling, he tossed me into a prone position and fell upon my nipples and breasts, the parts that had been unavailable to him when I was "under wraps." His large hands cruelly squeezed and manipulated my breasts, eliciting moans of pain and delight, then begging and pleading when he intensified the pain. But no matter how much he hurt me, I planted kisses on any part of his body I could reach.

Niles used my breasts to pull me up into a sitting position. Now I could hold him in my eyes *and* see my own torture. His grip tightened on my left breast and kept tightening until I almost said my word. But just at that instant, milk or something squirted out that nipple and landed on Niles's chest. He let go of my breast and when I looked down, I saw the milk dribbling out. I freaked. "Niles, what is that? What is that stuff?" I could hear the near panic in my voice. Calmly he replied that it was breast milk. But instead of calming me, this freaked me out even more. "Milk?" I shrieked. "How can I have milk, Niles? I've never been pregnant!" Seeing my consternation, he gently took me in his arms and told me that there was always some fluid in a woman's breasts and that his rough squeezing had made it flow. I wondered to myself how he knew that when I, the owner of the breasts, didn't. My consternation changed into sexual arousal and I began to have more deeply submissive feelings toward him.

Overcome by his patience and the experience, I bent my head to his chest and began to lick the milk off of it. But consternation set in again when I got a real taste of the stuff! It was horrible! Absolutely disgusting, even if it came out of me. I think that made it worse. It was so very sour and unpleasant that I started to gag and heave. In a state of agitation I choked out, "Niles, that can't be milk! Babies would die if they drank that!" Then I made a face and tried to spit out what I had already swallowed, punctuated by the occasional "blick" or "yuck." He guffawed and hugged me then pointed out in a calm voice that the E would greatly affect the taste of my breast milk. This rang true and I swigged some soda to wash away the taste. Reassured, I nuzzled up against him to show him I was ready to continue with whatever game he wanted to play.

Growling his approval at my acceptance, he threw me down on the comforter and climbed on me in the sixty-nine position. He thrust two fingers up my quim and fingered me hard, working on the magic spot inside. My back arched, my legs flopped open, and my juices drenched his fingers. As soon as he felt the thick ooze, he reached back, spread his own cheeks and sat on my face. His anus was right on my lips and I knew what he wanted. I was eager to give it to him. With no hesitation or second thoughts, I extended my tongue and licked his anus. He ground into my face, rubbing his anus all over it. He tasted so good even there that I licked and sucked and used my tongue to enter him until he climbed off of me. He slapped my quim, hitting it just right and I came for him on every fourth slap. After each fourth slap, he rammed his fingers into me to check for wetness and he was not disappointed.

We played like this for too short a time before he laid down beside me. He looked all done in even though now we were resting quietly on the comforter. When I suggested we move into the bedroom where he would be more comfortable, he readily agreed. I brought him a couple of painkillers then joined him in bed. Bless the testosterone god because in spite of his pain, he continued to manhandle me until finally he forced my head down onto his lovely cock. I sucked him with all my heart and when he'd had enough, he pulled my head up by the hair. To my great delight, he kissed me on the lips and I felt his tongue enter my mouth ever so briefly. Then he extended his arm and I nestled into the crook of his shoulder, sighing with pleasure at being with him. I licked my lips over and over to savor the sweet taste of his genitals and then we slept.

TWENTY-FIVE

Another glorious morning waking up at Niles's side. He was feeling quite perky and was suffering from the stay-at-home blues so he drove off to service a couple of his computer accounts. After he left, I attacked the never-ending housework. From the looks of things, the house had never been cleaned to anywhere near this extent until I got there. Cleaning up one mess just revealed another. With Niles gone, I could go at it like the white tornado. He was gone for almost four hours.

While he was gone and I was attacking a particularly obnoxious cleaning job, more than just another mess was revealed. It was a revelation about myself, the kind I had come to London to explore. As I knelt on the bathroom floor scrubbing Niles's toilet bowl, clutching a scrubby in my bare hand, I realized how happy I was doing these mundane, and sometimes quite messy, chores. I realized that my joy had very little to do with penetration sex because Niles and I hadn't been doing much of that because of his injury. We did play hard and I loved it but I realized that I wanted to do these things simply to do something nice for someone else. The gift of giving, especially an unexpected gift at an unexpected time made me forget myself and think of nothing except how it would make the receiver of the gift happy. I smiled as a tear of pure emotion ran down my face and knew I had turned a new corner in my life.

When Niles returned, he looked just terrible. He had definitely overdone it; one is always strongest in the morning after a good sleep but the burst of energy wears off quickly. Part of the problem was due to the car: It was, as most British cars, a standard shift. A standard shift means one has to put a great deal of effort into driving in a traffic-jammed city at midday. Both arms are needed to drive: one to hold the wheel, the other to shift. Both legs are needed: one to accelerate and brake and the other to operate the clutch. In traffic, one never gets out of second gear for very long so most of the time all four limbs are in use. Not good for someone with swollen bollocks. We were supposed to go to the bank then to the supermarket when Niles got home but we skipped the bank and did the food shopping instead. It was a good thing I had made a list of what we needed so we didn't have to wander the many aisles. I could see the pain and tiredness in his face.

Parking in London being pretty much the same as in Manhattan, of course we had to park blocks away from the flat. I carried everything except one bag of window cleaner. I don't know why it didn't occur to us to drop me off with the groceries and let him park the car alone and then no one would have had to carry anything. Or maybe I did think of it but was afraid to leave him alone. Once inside, I made him strip off his pants and shirt and wrapped him in a warm, soft robe, then I put his slippers on his feet. Once he was settled comfortably on the sofa, I rolled him a spliff, and I let him smoke it alone. While he smoked, I made tea and gave him a painkiller. Then I dragged the bags into the kitchen to store the food and give him some privacy.

After an hour or so had passed, Niles called out that he was hungry. Although we had just gone shopping, I didn't want to take the time to prepare a meal from scratch, so I made a big fresh salad and reheated last night's Chicken Parmigiana and spaghetti. Repeat or not, he ate it with relish and cleaned his plate.

But all this time, Master Niles's mind was busy thinking about how he would like to play with his toy this night. This man was starved not only for food, companionship, and a little TLC, but also for sex during his illness. That said a lot to me about the people he associated with: there was no emotional attachment or succoring, there was no friend-in-need ethic present here. It was simply: "Oh, you can't shag me so I'm off someplace else until you can." The phone hardly rang since I arrived. It was likely that almost all his friends knew he was incapacitated but it was highly unlikely that they knew I was there. So from my point of view, they weren't bothering to make even a perfunctory call to ask how he was doing, or see if he needed anything. I didn't understand but if it meant he was mine and mine alone, goody for me.

When the plates had been cleared away and I had returned to my spot on the floor, Niles asked me if I had an enema bag with me. When I replied that I did, he wanted to see it. Quivering inside, I brought it to him, the standard red rubber bag used in the United States for douching and enemas, and waited while he took his time looking it over. My mind raced. Dear Niles! He knows how I like, rather love, to be sodomized. I even love the very word "sodomy," a real action verb leaving no doubt about the action itself. And he knows that I know that he will not sodomize me unless he cleans me out. Inspecting the bag for so long and asking me questions about it escalated my arousal, deepened my humiliation, and began to drain me of any lingering pride or resistance hidden inside. I knew he was going to fill my belly with water and make me hold it until it exploded out of my bottom. I knew he would be standing in the doorway watching me expel the water. We both knew that this would humiliate me further and make me more malleable. Softly, he commanded me to strip.

Niles cuffed my wrists together and used them to drag me into the bathroom. He ordered me to kneel on the floor in front of the toilet bowl, with my derriere toward the bowl. I waited there listening to the sounds of the enema bag being filled and watching what I could see of his feet moving back and forth. When the bag was ready, Niles sat on the toilet bowl like it was his throne. Without being told, I spread my knees wide and dropped my head and shoulders to the floor, hoping my back was in a pleasing arch and that my anus was fully exposed. Simultaneously, four large, strong fingers on one cheek and a strong determined thumb on the other pulled my cheeks apart even farther than I had spread them. I felt the cold lubed nozzle slowly enter my anus and tried to relax by breathing deeply. I felt the water flow into me and like a tidal wave, it knocked down another wall inside of me.

Niles stopped immediately when I called for a pause and waited until I was ready before he resumed the flow. It was the only pause I needed to take the rest of the bag and Niles was pleased with me. Being given enemas and the light, floating feeling that followed after the release, sometimes accompanied by a slight giddiness, put me into a head space all its own. When the dirt and water came out of me, it took with it almost all of my inhibitions and left in their place a willingness to go further, to release all sense of self and wallow in abandon, to see how far down the spiral into masochism and submission I would go. Pain did not do this for me, neither did face-fucking, ass worship, verbal or physical humiliation, or even my beloved sodomy. This feeling was a coalescence of many aspects: the physical sensation of feeling the water fill my belly, the expulsion of it, the humiliating position, the full exposure of my genitalia, my consent to the enema, the preknowledge of the release, the anticipation of the exquisite pain of sodomy that was to come, but most of all, the intensely pleasurable shame of wanting it so much.

My retention time was about ten minutes. Niles stepped over me, pulled me up by the hair, and from the direction of the yanking, I knew he wanted me to sit on the toilet. I was ready to release and thought that he would stand in the doorway to watch. Instead, he stayed with me and positioned himself on the edge of the tub. As soon as I sat down, water exploded from my bottom. Niles was watching my face closely, and when I tried to put my head down, he held it up by the chin. He made me look into his eyes as I emptied my belly, holding me in place while my body struggled and contorted to rid itself of its cargo. There wasn't much waste matter but the smell was awful, so Niles put the fan on and sprayed with air freshener. As he sat back down, another explosion erupted from my bottom and again he held my chin and made me look into his eyes as I expelled. My privacy denied me, like an animal having to do its "business" in front of its master, I came hard.

Judging by the odor, Niles deemed I still wasn't clean. He knocked me to the floor and commanded me into the same position, kicking me for emphasis. Again, I waited as he filled up the red bag and lubed the nozzle. Unlike the previous slow entry, he quickly slipped the nozzle into my anus right up to the hilt. He held it in place with one hand and the other opened the tube full flow. He held it in me and feeling his fingers against the tender pink skin of my anus caused me to moan and groan in ecstacy, which we were both on. Somehow I focused enough on my breathing to take the whole bag on full flow in one go, no pauses. This pleased Niles greatly and he let me release immediately. This time I voluntarily held my head up and looked into his eyes as the water spurted out of me. When the water stopped coming out, Niles slapped me across the face and the water would start again. It took me several electrifying minutes under Niles's watchful eye and quick hand to empty myself.

When I was empty, I knelt at his feet, took off his slippers, and began to kiss his feet. Niles allowed this to go on for a few minutes and I became more submissive as he sat there like the lord and accepted his homage without sparing a glance for or reacting to the worshipper. When he'd had enough, he raised his toes a couple of times and I lifted my head. I rested my head on his thigh and he rewarded me by stroking my hair very gently. I asked if I could have a bath, but before I was given permission, Niles asked me to bring him the soap. I stood to hand it to him and he grabbed me by the waist. He quickly dipped his hand in the toilet bowl to wet it, then he twirled the soap in his hand to make a lather. He shoved two soapy fingers up my anus and stroked me a few times. When the soap stung and made my muscle spasm, I whimpered at the sensation. Only then were the cuffs taken off me and I was given permission to wash. I bathed as quickly as I could and while I was in the tub, the soap caused the last stray drops to squirt out of me.

When I returned to the front room, I found that Niles had been busy in my brief absence. The only light in the room was the heater, which was glowing orange. The music was on, a duvet was laid out on the floor, covered by a large piece of gold velvet cloth. As I stepped into the room, he knocked me onto this gilded cloud, face down. He grabbed my legs, spread them, and held them open with his body. Then he gripped my cheeks and pulled them apart. He told me he wanted to fuck me front and back with a beer bottle. I feigned distress and begged him not to, whimpered to him that I was afraid and blah, blah, blah. But when he fingered my long lips open, I arched my back and used my vaginal muscles to squeeze and massage his fingers. I was so wet it was as if someone had dropped an open bottle of lube on me.

I made no protest when he sent me to the kitchen for the beer bottle, and when I returned, I knelt when I handed it to him. He placed his foot on my shoulder and kicked me over. Then he fell on me. Roughly he flipped me over onto my belly and made sure that I was well positioned over his bent knee. Pretending to struggle, I was in reality cooperating with him by elevating my hips over his leg, arching my back and holding my hands behind my back. He rammed his huge thumb up my anus to the knuckle and fingered it very hard, thrusting and probing me deeply. He spread my cheeks again and was able to ram more of his finger into me. He used me so hard I was sobbing into the duvet. But my own consent to this emotional and physical subjugation and the pain of it was so stunningly divine that I didn't try to stop him or get away from him. Prone across his lap, I let him do as he wished. I knew this was only the beginning and I was entranced by it.

Suddenly the thumb was withdrawn and I grabbed at it blindly to capture and reinsert it. One big hand easily restrained both of mine. Something cold and steely was pressed against my anus. I fought to close my cheeks but to no avail. He knuckled my anus with the second joints of his index and middle fingers until I stopped fighting. Then he began to push something into me but I knew it wasn't the wicked beer bottle with its sharp steely teeth. Dear Niles had traded in the beer bottle for a big ugly butt plug and set about working my anus over. He pulled the plug out and rammed it back in, fucked me with it, worked it in gently then twisted it cruelly, popped the head in and out of me; he did whatever struck his fancy and I ate it up. I blew him kisses, moaned and squirmed, called his name over and over, and encouraged him by begging "yes, yes, oh, yes," and crying out for more.

After positioning me so he could see my genitalia and plugged anus, he left me alone on the floor and he seated himself on the sofa. He sat there for a few minutes smoking a cigarette and observing me, a few minutes which to me may well have been a long, lovely hour because I loved it so much. Niles, the fanciful sovereign, was doing with me everything I ever dreamed of and he was doing it by reading my mind.

Niles commanded me to put my high heels on and serve him tea while plugged. As I walked to the kitchen, the big plug up my anus ground into me with each step I took. It was humiliating, the sensation shot shocks into me, and my thighs were thickly smeared with my own ooze. When I returned with Niles's tea, he ordered me to bring him the toy basket from the bedroom. Once again I savored the sensations of walking plugged in high heels. Placing the basket within easy reach, I awaited his next pleasure. He selected a small length of rope, tied my ankles together, and removed my shoes. Then I was sent to make him another cup of tea. My first couple of steps were flat footed and ungainly but I quickly learned that if I walked on tippy-toe I could make progress and still look sexy. When Niles saw this, a smile lit his broad, handsome face.

I knelt gracefully at his feet and lifted the cup of sweet, milky tea to him as if it were an offering from a supplicant to her god. He took a few sips then reached into the toy basket and brought out another piece of rope. He used this piece to tie my upper thighs together. This made it much more difficult to walk as he sent me off on a few more "missions": bring another pillow, make him another cup of tea, turn down the heat. These things didn't really matter in or of themselves; to him, it was watching me teeter around that was amusing and to me it was the challenge of it that was fun. A chance to walk seductively before his twinkling green eyes, to show off my slender body and my grace-fulness; another chance to please the lord and be desirable to him. After my "errands," I sat on the floor at his feet while he finished his tea.

The insatiable satyr in Niles soon grew bored with this game (I think it was only employed to give him a rest) and he unbound my ankles and thighs. Then he slapped the leather wrist and ankle restraints on me and knocked me to the duvet. I landed on my back and in a flash he was on me. Just as quickly, he clipped each wrist to the corresponding ankle. He pulled my legs toward my head, bent my knees at different angles, and finally settled on a position he liked. My knees were bent up to my chest and rested on the outside of each breast. My lower legs and re-shod feet were perpendicular to my thighs and my hands grabbed my ankles from the outside and held me wide. Even my breasts were somewhat squeezed together and my knees could be used to manipulate them a bit. Niles stood up and surveyed his hand-iwork. He kicked the plug into me and didn't pull the kick.

The moan from the pit of my stomach told him he hit home. His beautiful green eyes changed, they glinted harder and become preda-tory. The pain was intense but it was over so quickly I didn't have time to cry out. He kicked me again and the intensity of the pain did not di-minish with the second kick nor the third nor the fourth.

I lost count of how many times he kicked the plug into me, each kick delivering its own separate yet similar pain. I do know that when I broke position, but still left Niles full access to my anus and its plug, he didn't punish me or try to put me back into the old position. Niles kicked me in any position I offered, and I found myself displaying my-self to him in positions that were more exposed and humiliating. It was the pain, the humiliation, the surrender of control over my most sacred opening combined with the willing sacrifice of it, and the aban-donment of ego that made me crave his anal abuse. And he did it so very well. When one particularly angled kick pushed the plug into that spot in my quim that made me ejaculate, girl-juice squirted out of me.

Niles stopped kicking the plug into me when I ejaculated and al-lowed me to rest for a short time while he left the room. He returned with a camera and from the toy basket he took a collar and leash. After putting them on me, he carefully arranged them on my belly, pulled my legs wide, and took a picture of my shaven quim and my butt-plugged ass, still sporting its marks from the beating he had given me a few nights earlier.

But unfortunately he was still a sick man and the amount of energy and creativity spent on our play tired him. I don't think any other man I knew would have lasted that long to begin with, on E or not. I could see the strain in his face so after we quieted down, I suggested that we move into the bedroom where he would be more comfortable. We cuddled together under the duvet and soon Niles was roughly handling my breasts and quim. I waited for him to force my head down on his cock and he didn't disappoint me. I sucked and licked him and held him as far down my throat as I could for as long as he would let me. His cock felt and tasted so wonderful in my mouth, it filled my mouth and part of my throat so completely that I gagged and heaved and my mouth filled with saliva, making it all the better to suck him. When Niles forced my head down on his cock, it cut off part of my breathing. I loved every minute of it.

Wanting something harder, more savage than I was giving him, he held my head in his strong hands and pumped into my mouth and down my throat at his own pace and depth. He was making that little "huh? huh?" sound that asked if I wanted more. Of course I did! I could think of nothing but his cock in my mouth and I caressed it with my lips and tongue. I felt his cock jerk slightly and I knew he had almost come. I don't know why he didn't. I would have loved to swallow his sweet nectar, to have it wash over my teeth and gums and tongue, then slide deliciously down my throat on its way to my stomach. What a sweet snack before bed! Niles remarked that I had almost gotten a mouthful and all I could do was giggle in response. Then he got on up his knees, straddled me, and stroked himself to a growling finish. Pearly ropes of spunk decorated my breasts and I looked in his eyes as I smeared his spunk all over my belly and face.

Falling to the bed next to me, his arm went out, inviting me to curl up next to him. I rested my head in the crook of his shoulder and pressed my legs and belly against the warmth and strength of his lean, sexy body. I was gigglishly delighted that I had not washed before going to bed.

TWENTY-SIX

Today we finally managed to get to a money changers and I was solvent in the local lucre at last. I gave Niles one hundred and fifty pounds to cover the groceries he had bought, the take-out we ordered, the tickets to the Sex Fetishists Ball (which was just a couple of nights away), cabs, and incidentals. I knew it was way over what had been spent but I didn't care. Niles had no income at that point and was still ill. He was very appreciative of my gesture and expressed this to me warmly. Did he read my mind? There were no games as such shoving the money back at me saying, "oh, no, I couldn't," or "take this back"; just acceptance of the gesture for what it was. He was in need and I was in a position to give.

Part of giving was cooking a lovely dinner of broiled lamb chops, baked potatoes, and fresh steamed broccoli. Insisting he rest and relax, I cleared and washed the dishes and made more progress cleaning the kitchen. Niles was finally getting comfortable with being waited on hand and foot. I did everything I could: took out the trash, brought in the mail, cleaned, cooked, shopped, did laundry, made the bed, swept, mopped and I loved every minute of it. I gave him his baths and shampoos, which he began to truly enjoy. I always did his hair first and after a good scalp-massaging shampoo, I would bathe him. I used my fingers more than my eyes to "see" what I was doing and combined a massage technique with a lathering one. I started at the neck, worked my way down to the toes, reserving the genitals for last.

Last but not least, there was the towel ritual. While he was still in the tub, I would wrap his long hair in a towel, turban-style. As he rose, I draped another towel over his shoulders and as he stood up full height, a third towel was wrapped around his waist sarong-style. But wait! There were more towels yet to come. Bathroom rugs or even bath mats are not in abundance in London and I so hated to stand on a cold bare floor. A fourth towel was draped longways over the toilet seat and pooled onto the floor. He would step out of the tub onto this towel and then sit on the towel-covered toilet while I dried him completely, even between his toes and the crack of his buttocks. After that, I re-draped his shoulders in another clean towel and brushed out his hair, long and flowing over his shoulders. The sixth and final towel was draped over the sofa so he could recline there like a lord without wetting the upholstery. This became one of our favorite pastimes.

While I was occupying my mind and hands with bathing Niles, his mind was busy dreaming up what new spasm of lust he could indulge tonight. Pagan sex god that he was, he never ceased to surprise me. Once I was in the front room again, Niles knelt me on the sofa and bent me over its arm, head down, hips high, and knees open. He produced two of the biggest ropes I had ever seen, except in school gyms. One was a good five and a half inches in circumference and the other was six and a half inches! One end of each rope had a large heavy D-clip braided into it; the other end had an ugly black rubber cover on it, with a seam. After he attached the ropes to the same hooks he had used for the chains, I heard him tear open two condom packets and heard the squeaky snappy noises of the condoms being put on the rubber ends of the rope.

He crammed his fingers into my mouth to wet them but there was no need to. I was already dripping from lust and that mindless involuntary moaning had started. First he draped the condom-covered rope end over my back so I would fear and desire what he was going to do to me. He roughly spread my labia and jammed his two saliva-moistened fingers into my quim. His entry hurt me but his fingers went right for that spot so I came, loving the pain it gave me. He used his fingers mercilessly to stretch my small hole enough to accept a third large finger, mostly hurting me but always giving me an orgasm right after the worst pain. He worked me with three fingers until I could feel the colder air of the room gathering around my hot opening.

I gasped when he withdrew from me, but a second later I felt something cold and hard and very large being pressed into my hole. I whimpered in real fear at the size of the thing and with his predator instincts, Niles smelled my fear and it inflamed him. He pressed the rope harder against my opening, then thrust it into me. I screamed and tried to bury my head in the armrest to muffle the sound. I breathed deeply to relax and this helped some, enough for him to ram another inch into me. Again I cried out and this encouraged Niles to twist the thing around inside of me. The pain from being so stretched was incredible, but Niles was very careful to hit that spot and give me a screaming, smashing orgasm right before I was ready to call my word.

After that, of course I didn't want to call my word. If such intense pain was accompanied by even more intense pleasure then I would willingly accept the one to have the other. That was one of the things I had come here to explore about myself. Niles was doing his work well; he was brilliant at conditioning me and I was a receptive vehicle. Spreading myself wider, I rocked back and forth on the rope end Niles was working inside of me as eagerly as if it were his own sweet cock. Relentlessly he plunged the big ugly thing in and out of me and used just the end of the rope to torment my opening by repeated withdrawal and re-entry. My quim hurt badly but those smashing orgasms kept hitting me in waves and I didn't want them to stop.

After I had taken all Niles wanted to give me, he pulled the rope out of me. I groaned with relief when he removed it. Two fingers entered me, checking for wetness. They came out of me covered in slime. Devilishly delighted at this, Niles began to torture me inside by twisting his fingers, entwining them, spreading them apart in a V, curling them and using his knuckles in me, always careful to touch that spot right after he hurt me badly. I raised my hips and leaned into his fingers and spread myself wider for his violation of my opening. Abruptly the invading fingers were pulled out of me and I gasped his name and begged him to violate me more. To further entice him, I thrust out my bottom and wiggled it at him, arched my back, and held my labia open to show him how much he had stretched me.

Very soon I felt him trailing the rope end back and forth across my back, between my legs, and against my labia. I begged, "yes, yes, please" in my softest, and most seductive voice of submission. Finally, thankfully, Niles ungently located my hole and drove the rope inside of me. I screamed in agony: it was the larger of the two ropes that was now in me, the rope with the six-and-a-half-inch circumference. Despite my earlier and very thorough stretching, this rope was agonizingly painful. By sheer willpower, I did my very best to settle down over the arm of the sofa and concentrate on breathing and relaxing but the pain was too great. In spite of all my efforts and my deep desire to be violated like this, I couldn't bear it. As I lifted my head to word up, Niles yanked the thing out of me. My opening felt like it was on fire and I couldn't close my legs.

Niles grabbed me by the hair and turned me around to face him. He pushed me into a half-squatting half-sitting position with my knees splayed open and the soles of my feet together. He shoved my back and shoulders against the armrest and if I tilted my head back, I could lay it over the top of the armrest. I tried to imagine not how I saw myself but how Niles saw me. I wanted to become the most beautiful visual I could, not a person but a piece of sex art with motion but no mind. I arched my back to give myself a longer torso and make my rib cage protrude. Then I spread my hair out over the arm rest in the sexy way I had seen in countless movies. I settled down further into the squat to display my bruises and shaven quim more prominently for his abuse and pleasure. As a last act of submission, I put my arms over my head and grasped my wrists together. My chest heaving with passion, I stretched and splayed myself. I felt beautiful, so very beautiful as I awaited his pleasure.

He gasped in appreciation. I soared the heights when I heard that gasp. Niles gently teased the smaller rope over my clit and lips, making me comfortable with it, making me want it. Electric jolts shot through me when he pushed it against my clit and I came. I felt him gently seek out my opening with it and equally gently, begin to work the rope into me. He gave me time to breathe and relax as he entered me and went slowly with me. As large as the rope was, because of Niles's gentle treatment, it began to feel good inside of me and I wanted more. This was different from the first time he had violated me with the same rope; his second, carefully considered use of gentleness had provoked me into wanting the very thing that had given me such pain the first time.

When I began a slow grind, Niles caught on quickly and held the rope in place. He let me enjoy myself a bit, watching my face carefully as I wiggled and danced on the rope and got a little more of it inside of me. Then he commanded me to open my eyes and watch him fuck me with the rope. I obeyed. The vision of his fine shaped large hand working the rope into my shaven pink quim sent me whirling off into space. The rope, dangling from a hook ten feet up the wall, hung down behind him. Because of the way he was seated, it ran between his legs and the excess was curled up between them, giving the impression that the rope was his cock. Then the rope snaked up into me.

The image was horrifyingly beautiful and hauntingly erotic and I couldn't tear my eyes away from it. As I watched, Niles worked the rope in deeper and deeper; the combination of feeling what was happening at the same time I saw it happening was an extraordinary mix of sensations. I felt him maneuver the rope toward the glowing spot and with just one touch, he gave me a violent, rocking orgasm and my juices flowed. I reached down and held the rope, my hands over his, not wanting these contrary feelings of floating and being impaled to end.

Niles threw off my hands and slowly withdrew the rope from me, driving me wild with this slow deprivation of what had come to be an extension of his own beautiful cock. I begged him to let me keep it in me, almost cried real tears but he continued with his slow pull out. When the last of it was out of me, I rose to my knees and rubbed my body against his, ran my hands and nails up and down his back, kissed his body, rubbed my pudendum against his erect cock, and in general tried to induce him to continue. He sat there unresponsive to my wiles and pleadings but allowed me to persist. This inflamed me even more: worshipping a stone god who could come to life as he pleased and right now it pleased him to accept my worship but ignore me.

Tiring of being worshipped, he pushed me to the floor so he could recline full length on the sofa. I crawled to where his head was and knelt as close to him as I could get. His aroma was overpowering and I got lost in the smell of it. It worked on me like a highly addictive drug and after I fell in love with its high, I had to have more of it. I needed my next fix. Niles gestured for a cigarette so I lit one and handed it to him. He held it in his right hand and when he put his right arm over his head, I crept in closer and rested my head on the edge of the sofa, as close to his armpit as I could get. Niles realized what I was doing and clamped his arm down, imprisoning my face and head in his armpit. "So, you like the smell, do you? Have it fresh from the font." His arm held my head in place and it seemed as if by will alone he made his sweat flow. It covered my face; it was on my lips and up my nose. I became drunk on it, then paralyzed by it.

When he lifted my head by the hair, I was so far into sub-space that Niles had to help me into bed. He laid on his back and offered me the crook of his shoulder, which I immediately nestled into, feeling safe, secure, and sated. His arm encircled my shoulder and I stretched my body out full length against his side. Regulating my heaving breath with his calmer one, I began to come back to Earth, pulled in by the invisible cord that connected me to Niles.

But this entire evening I had done nothing to service his needs; he had spent all his time playing with me. Keeping my hand on top of the duvet, I ran it down his torso and when I met with his erection, I stroked and rubbed it through the duvet. I begged him to let me suck it, please let me suck it, I promise to swallow as much of you as I can, please, Niles, please, let me suck you, I love having your cock in my mouth . . .

Two rough hands grabbed my head and shoved it under the blanket, then forced it down on his throbbing rod. I opened my saliva-filled mouth eagerly and fell on his cock like an animal. I sucked him savagely, not only mouthing and tonguing him but using my teeth, too. I forced my head down on his cock to make myself gag and keep the saliva flowing. I loved to hear him gasp with pleasure over my willingness to choke myself on him. I licked his ball sack and then took one ball at a time into my mouth and sucked it. My arms were wrapped around his thighs, holding them open (an unnecessary action but a sexy one to me) and I buried my head in his genitals. There was no method to what I was doing, I was like a dog with a juicy bone and no one was going to take it away from me.

Niles grabbed my head and lifted it slightly higher up his shaft. He gave my mouth a couple of pumps then readjusted the angle of my head. A couple of more pumps assured him that this was the correct angle and his grip on my head tightened. He started to thrust into my mouth deep and hard, looking for the spot in the back of my throat that would make me gag. Once he found it he hit it every fourth or fifth stroke, giving me just a couple of seconds to swallow the saliva all the gagging had produced. Snot mingled with saliva on my face and on his cock. I didn't care I was eating snot, all that mattered was Niles's gorgeous cock in my mouth. This communicated itself to him and he pumped my face harder. He made me gag and heave with every other stroke and the strokes became deeper and faster. Every time I gagged, my quim got wetter.

In that instant, something inside of me changed: I had taken a further step into submission and objectification. I turned myself into a life support system for the hole in my face and let Niles do want he wanted with it. I didn't care about the snot, the smeared makeup, or my disheveled hair. I didn't care about the dribble from my mouth that was running down my neck onto my chest, or about the steady ooze of come from my quim. He hit that gag spot whenever he pleased and I let him. I let him because I loved the way it felt, because I loved his silken skin and the sweet taste of him, but most of all, because I loved feeling this way emotionally and physically.

The intuitive Niles sensed this and pumped himself into a frenzy. Tightening his already vise-like grip on my head, he began to growl at me. Between growls, he told me he was going to come, and because I had been such a very good girl my reward was to take his come in the face. He pulled my head off his cock by my hair and flung me on my back onto the bed. I opened my legs and held my lips open, I squeezed my breasts and offered them to him. I opened my mouth wide to show I was ready to swallow his sweet nectar if he so desired. How I begged him to come on me! How I pleaded with him to reward my lowly face with his pearl juice! How I humiliated myself before him, calling out to him to shoot his spunk into my face.

He knee-walked up to my face and began to stroke himself hard and fast. I cupped his balls in one hand and squeezed them the way he liked while filthy words of encouragement poured from my mouth. His moans of "oh, yeah" from above me, his feral growls, and almost bestial silhouette in the moonlight drove me to a renewed frenzy. My begging and pleading got louder, my words got filthier and I beseeched him to humiliate me by coming in my face; to come in my face because no hole on my body was worthy of accepting his spunk. Right before he came, he grabbed my head and positioned it so that when he did come, his spunk would splatter all over my face. His aim was spot on. My face was dripping with jism and some drops were in my hair. After Niles came, he tossed me aside like a used condom. I landed on my back to see him still kneeling over me, his eyes glinting. Getting into a sexy pose, I slowly and deliberately rubbed his come into my face and neck and smiled at him wickedly until it was all rubbed in.

Niles laughed and laid down next to me then offered me the crook of his shoulder. I snuggled up next to him and luxuriated in the smell and feel of him. Before I fell asleep, I told him that Messalina, the wife of the Roman emperor Claudius I, had used the collected jism of her personal guard as a moisturizer, swearing it was the best in the world. He laughed again and gave me a squeeze. My last thought before I fell asleep was that I was so very lucky to have found myself at the hands of a real master, a man who could bring out all those secret perversities hiding in me.

TWENTY-SEVEN

We woke up very late today, around three thirty, worn out a bit by last night's amusements. After I looked outside and saw a dismally gray, chill, rainy day, I decided that the warm snuggly bed was the best place for us to be. I brought Niles his tea and smokes and returned to the kitchen. I saw him in the hallway on his way to the bathroom and hoped he returned to bed directly after he was finished with his business. I didn't realize I was holding my breath until I expelled a big lungful when he went back to the bedroom. He needed more rest and there were many ways to make a sick man stay in bed. I made him a very un-English breakfast consisting of a ham, cheese, and broccoli omelette, some concoction of the leftover baked potatoes from last night, and a small cluster of grapes. I arranged the plate as appetizingly as I could.

Loading it onto a serving tray with cutlery, the post (which I had stepped out for while the omelette cooked), and a fresh cup of tea, I served him breakfast in bed. A heartfelt "Thank you, Madelaine!" tickled my girlish heart and I smiled so broadly that it was hard to say, "My pleasure, sir." I excused myself then returned with a miniature version of his plate for myself. I sat on the end of the bed and ate him up with my eyes as he dug into his meal with relish. I asked him if he liked it but I already knew the answer, I just wanted to hear him say it. In between mouthfuls, he gulped out, "It's very good, different. I like it." I smiled and said, "Good," but inside I was dancing and singing. Most men are of the "if you're cooking, I'm eating" variety but then, Niles wasn't most men.

Seeing that Niles was very relaxed and comfortable lounging in bed, I decided a couple more hours of it wouldn't hurt. I put the remains on the tray and dumped it in the kitchen. I grabbed the hash tray and quickly ran back into the bedroom. I gave it to him to roll us a spliff and then I jumped under the covers and snuggled up very close to him, pretending to be cold. We smoked the spliff, got very stoned, then cuddled together. When we woke up, it was about nine; full darkness had fallen.

Both of us had gotten a second wind, almost like our long nap had been a full night's sleep and this was a new day. We moved out into the reception room and I wondered if Niles had planned any pleasures for this evening or if he would just do whatever came to him. Whatever it was, I was sure that it would be new and exciting and exactly what I wanted whether I knew it or not. Because of the tone I had set when we woke up, Niles decided to continue playing in that vein. After reclining in his favorite spot on the sofa, I was made to strip then put on lace top thigh highs and high-heel shoes. I was sent on a variety of errands, one at a time: put the music on, bring a bowl of nuts, fresh cup of tea, cigarettes, hash tray, ash tray, another pillow, another duvet. When I brought each item to him, I knelt to present it and he accepted it in numerous ways: casually, appreciatively, expectantly, and roughly.

After I had presented everything he wanted, I knelt on the floor next to the sofa. I watched in curiosity as he carefully positioned the tea, nuts, cigarettes, ash tray, and hash tray within arm's reach. Niles extended his arm, hand up, toward me; I was several inches out of his reach. He diddled his fingers at me and I moved in closer, closer, closer until my quim was right under his fingers. He dipped them in me and using them to steer me, he moved me a couple inches closer to him. He roughly tested the new position for depth and pain inflection and was satisfied. Now my quim, like one of the objects so carefully arranged on the floor, was within arm's reach, too.

Although he did alternate among the tea, cigarettes, and other items, I was the item on the floor he paid the most attention to. Ungentle fingers invaded my quim, pinched and pulled my labia, and a thumb was used to torture my clitoris. A couple of minutes of cruel attention, then withdrawal for a sip of tea followed by more quim torture. He pushed me over backward and spanked my quim until one slap short of my word. He used my hair to reposition me on my knees near him and calmly rolled another spliff. I was unneeded at the moment but he shared the spliff with me and we ended up taking a little break. After the spliff, Niles gestured to me to take away the tea cup and nuts, generally tidy the area, and bring a capped bottle of water. I rushed to do his bidding then raced back into the reception room.

Niles was full of surprises. In the very short time I had been gone, he had piled all the duvets in the room onto the floor and had strewn pillows around on them. Although the lights were much dimmer now, the low lighting in the room was not low enough to conceal the sadistic pleasure in his face. Wrapped in his dark robe, his long hair streaming over his shoulders, he was stretched on his side on the far end of the duvet arrangement, looking every bit the Romantic Sadist. He patted the duvet and I dove into the spot. I lay down on my side facing him and put my arms around him. I pressed my lips to his and as he kissed me, he tongued a hit of E to me and passed me the water. Then he kissed me again and rolled me over onto my back. Niles's kisses were heavenly. He had a whole range of them and everyone of them made me wet. He sniffed me softly between kisses and made that "do you want more/do you like that 'huh, huh?'" sound I had come to know. My answer was reflected in the renewed passion of my kiss and my arms held him more tightly to me.

Untwining my outer arm from around his neck, he placed it over my head and I knew to keep it there. His warm strong hand moved to my breast and began to tease my nipple. He used his fingers on my nipples in concert with his tongue in my mouth. When he kissed me hard and deeply, he pinched my nipple cruelly; when he kissed me gently, his fingers were light breezes over my erect nipple. Sometimes he would kiss me gently and pinch my nipple mercilessly; sometimes a cruel invading kiss would be accompanied by a gentle pinch. And then sometimes, he would grasp my nipple between his thumb and index finger and looking intently at me he would begin a slow squeeze, kissing me only when discomfort showed in my face. Then he would plant dozens of gentle little kisses all over my face and neck and make the "huh, huh?" sound very softly right next to my ear until I accepted the new level of pain. Although my quim was working overtime and I was still wet from being used as one of the objects on the floor, not once as he kissed me did his hand trail below my waist.

He let go of my nipple after an extremely prolonged and painful pinch and kissed me in a deep soulful way as feeling and blood returned to my nipple. As the pins and needles set in, Niles gently played his fingers over it and intensified the sensation tenfold but did not break the kiss. I cannot describe this kiss to you; a kiss is more than a physical sensation and like most of you, I can tell if a man will be a good lover for me just by the way he kisses. Niles's kisses could have been from a hundred different lovers and this kiss in particular was from all of those lovers rolled into one.

When feeling returned to my nipple, Niles caressed my neck and shoulders with his hand and brushed his fingers across my cheek. Do you know how each one of us has one special secret silly sexy little action that just melts you, blows you away, or tickles your fancy? Mine was tender fingers caressing my face. I had never told anyone this and for the second time Niles was doing it perfectly. I sighed deeply and relaxed even more, trusting him, confident in his capabilities. He played his hand up and down my throat; his lips were on my face; I was floating in his smell and overcome by it. When he tightened his grip on my throat, I lay very still but made sure he saw the consent in my eyes, which belied the frightened whimper that involuntarily escaped my lips.

His grip on my throat tightened and very briefly bright-colored spots danced in front of my eyes. I could almost have giggled at the sight of them, but then I was struggling for breath. As soon as I started to struggle, Niles let my throat go. I took in deep gulps of air and curled up next to him. He hugged me to him and I was soon calm, or as calm as one can be when out of one's mind with lust. I kissed him to show him I was ready for more. Again and again he choked me until I was almost unconscious, but every time I started to struggle, he stopped. Again and again, I kissed him to show my readiness. Until once I took his hand and put it to my throat. His strong presence, the smell of him, my natural arousal heightened twenty-fold by the E, took me to a place I hadn't thought of before. I don't know why I did this, maybe I thought it was a sexy thing to do, maybe I wanted to see how far we would go to feed our hunger.

I placed his hand on my throat and covered it with my own. I looked deeply into Niles's eyes, pressed my hand down onto his and projected "yes" over and over. When he tightened his grip, I stroked his hand in encouragement. He gripped my throat harder and harder and this time when I began to struggle, he didn't stop. My whole body began to shake and the brightly colored spots kaleidoscoped. Even though I knew what was happening, I was very frightened. In a panic, I sought out his eyes. Niles's face was calm and as he tightened his hold on my neck, his eyes held mine. He was smilingly slightly when the whole world went black.

My head was on his chest and his arms were wrapped reassuringly around me when I came to. I started to kiss him and whisper his name, and to trail my hand up and down his chest. He gave me a squeeze and in a lover's voice said, "Did you like that? Huh, huh? Did you?" Still overcome by the experience and trembling a little, I managed to gasp out, "Oh, yes, Niles! It was like dreaming of blackness!" I buried my nose in his armpit and began to breathe. As I soaked up his scent, an odd thought occurred to me. When I first came around and saw Niles's face, his expression was one of curious detachment, as if he had just had an ice cream cone, not throttled me until I passed out. Then there had been the "nut incident." Because his face didn't show that he was scared and I didn't smell or sense any fear in his demeanor or aura either time, I thought it odd that later on he told me that he was "scared" too when I blacked out. I was the first person he had choked unconscious; I had been the first willing victim of his new sadistic desire. All of his previous play, except with me, had stopped just short of that. I agreed that it was a scary but very sexy and transcendental experience. Wet as I was, this new development made my quim ooze and I felt the sticky wetness smearing my thighs.

When Niles suggested we move to the bed, I readily agreed. I begged him to choke me into unconsciousness one more time before we went to sleep. But it was much too soon for him to grant my request, so instead he shoved my face down on his cock and face-fucked me. I gagged and wretched and heaved as he rammed his cock down my throat but I kept going back for more. As much as I loved what he was doing, I wanted to do something more, something else, something that was as much an act of devotion as it was of humiliation. Lifting my mouth from his delicious cock, I begged him to allow me to worship his anus. At first he denied me and face-fucked me deeper and harder as punishment for asking. After an extremely hard heave that made dinner rise in my throat, he lifted my head by the hair, slapped me, and said in a nasty tone of voice, "Do you still want to eat out my asshole?"

"Oh, yes, Niles, yes, please, let me worship you." He slapped me. "You want to do *what*?" Again I begged him to allow me to worship him. Again he slapped me then repeated the question. "Worship you, please let me worship you." Another slap and then he said, "I expect you to say what you mean. 'Let me worship you' means nothing. You are a slut and a slut says, 'Let me eat out your asshole.'" "Yes, Niles." He slapped me again and demanded to know why I was making him wait. I babbled out, "Oh, Niles, oh, master, please let me eat out your asshole! Please let your slut eat you out, please, master, don't deny me." He let me continue to beg him in the most foul language I could think of, allowed me to continue to humiliate myself for several minutes before he granted my request on the condition that I stuck my tongue "as far up his asshole as it could reach."

"Yes, master, yes, thank you, master, thank you . . ." my words trailed off when he lifted his legs and spread his cheeks for my tongue. Then they were cut off entirely when I spread his cheeks with my hands and eagerly thrust my tongue up his asshole. I discovered that just sticking my tongue out of my mouth into his asshole wasn't enough; I wanted to penetrate him more deeply. I found that if I made my tongue stick straight out and then tightened my tongue muscle, I could make an effective little penis out of it. By thrusting my face and head between his cheeks the way one would thrust their hips against a pudendum while fucking, I was able to simulate a small fuck-stroke on his asshole. Niles moaned and held his legs open wider to give me better access to his sweet passage.

I became a slave to his asshole. My mind focused on that tiny opening into his body and pleasuring it became my world. Unembarrassed by my own slurping noises and the animal-like groans I was making, unashamed of my desire to taste his waste if there was any, I licked and kissed and sucked his asshole as well as obeyed his command to stick my tongue up it as far as I could. I let all of the passion and desire I felt for him flow through my tongue as I performed an act that I still considered to be "worship."

All too soon he stopped me. I melted when he kissed me, not minding in the least the taste of his anus on my tongue and face. He extended his arm and offered me the crook of his shoulder. It was time to go to sleep. I tilted my head so that the overpowering scent emitting from his armpits would waft up into my nose as I drifted off, ensuring that he would be in my dreams that night.

TWENTY-EIGHT

I was the early riser this afternoon and spent several minutes gazing at Niles's face from under the shelter of the duvet so my eyes upon him wouldn't wake him. His face was still ruggedly handsome and hardly softened by sleep, so unlike the sometimes goofy, sometimes baby-faced sleep of some men. I slipped out of bed so he could enjoy the fullness of the bed alone and did some of the quieter chores in the never-ending round of house cleaning. As I cleaned, round and round in my head like a siren, went the thought, "tonight is the Sex Fetishists Ball, tonight is the Sex Fetishists Ball!" I was so excited! I was going to wear a custom-made floor-length black leather halter dress with a plunging back open to below the waist and an equally low cut front that laced up from my pudendum to midcleavage. Black leather stilet- toes and below-the-elbow black leather gloves completed my look. Not particularly submissive but sexy and eye-catching all the same. I couldn't wait to wear it!

My chores done, I slipped quietly back into bed and curled up next to Niles. We slept for maybe an hour before he awoke. It was obvious he was feeling perky today because as soon as he had his tea, he told me to bring him the canes. I raced off and returned with them, hold- ing them out to him like an offering. Without further ado, he bent me over the bed and gave me a very slight warm-up before four very hard rapid strokes. The pain blasted through me and when it reached my brain, I came. After taking the four, I hugged and kissed him. Then, pulling away from him so he could see my face, I looked deeply into his green eyes. Parting from him, I bent over the bed and asked him for two more, just two more strokes, please. Niles was very pleased with this request and gave me the two very hard blows I had asked for. And to think that I used to like Oliver's style better than Niles's!

Knowing tonight was The Big Event, I wanted to keep Niles from overexerting himself this afternoon so he could save up all his energy for later on. I encouraged him to rest all day and let me "tend to his needs like a good slave," which I said with a shy smile. He agreed so I settled him comfortably into his spot on the sofa, I brought him tea and a bowl of nuts then went about on my mission to search out and destroy household dirt. I looked in on him once in a while to see if he needed anything and was greeted with a smile and maybe a request for tea. When I had done enough cleaning for two people in one day, I joined him in the reception room and we shared a spliff in comfortable silence.

To my delight, Niles asked me to give him a bath. I loved to bathe him and wash his hair. While I filled the tub, I lit candles and incense, dimmed the lights, and made the room atmospheric. All of the half dozen towels needed for the towel ritual were at the ready when I brought him into the bathroom and disrobed him. Sitting him down on the toilet seat, I removed his worn slippers and helped him into the tub. Then I slowly and seductively stripped myself to bathe him. As I did this, the grungy bathroom turned into the bath chambers of ancient Babylon, with its sea blue tiles and mosaics of dolphins in the tub and on the walls. I felt like the slave of the heir to an ancient throne; a slave who knew that her place in the lord's life was to submit to him and only through acceptance of that submission would the slave be at peace. I knelt next to the tub and began the ritual.

Although I was in general a good bath attendant, with Niles I exceeded myself. As usual, I began by washing and rinsing his long, straight hair first then wrapping it in a towel before I began the very personal bath ritual I designed just for Niles. I washed him with my eyes closed, only opening them when I needed to find the soap or reposition him. Each pass of the soap and my hands on his skin was a caress and I took my time, savoring every minute. And Niles responded like a royal prince who was accustomed to being bathed his whole life. He let me manipulate his limbs with just the least amount of cooperation necessary from him for me to handle his greater weight and size. The added effort I had to exert to bathe him thoroughly yet gracefully aroused very submissive feelings in me. I bathed him humbly but with all the pride of a good slave pleasing her master. The bath over, I helped him to rise and performed the towel ritual with love and devotion. When I was finished, I kissed his feet and rested my head on them until he gave me the toe signal to rise.

After a very nice dinner of Chicken Cordon Bleu, roasted potatoes, and sauteed broccoli, we dressed for the ball. Niles looked so sexy in his soft leather pants with the silver studded belt, a very tight black turtle neck, and his black leather boots. A paddle hung from a clip hook on his belt loop as a master's toy and his silver topped walking stick completed his look as well as gave him something to lean on if he tired. For anyone else, the paddle and walking stick would have been a requirement to meet the dress code; however, Niles being Niles, paddle or not, walking stick or not, he would have been let in right away. Niles was one of the first players in the scene and even people he hardly knew recognized him and his perveratti status and gave him the according respect. I got into my dress with a great deal of help from Niles, who thankfully took over the lacing of the thing. His wolf whistle when I modeled it for him was accompanied by a mischievous twinkle in his eyes and I smiled smugly to myself. I knew I looked good but it was divine to have it confirmed!

When I suggested that we take a cab there and arrive right in front of the venue "in style," he readily agreed. Good! Mission accomplished. All that shifting and clutching was hard on him, the venue far away, parking scarce, then there was the inevitable walk. I had my vacation money to spend; it seemed so much more civilized to be "chauffeured" there and back even if it was only in a mini-cab. Right before the cab was due to arrive, we each popped an E in celebration of my first big fetish event. The venue, "The Powerhouse," was a very long ride from Niles's and the driver was unfamiliar with where we were going or how to get there. Niles knew we weren't going the right way and pointed this out to the driver. The driver refused to look at the A-to-Zed (the local map) then he admitted he couldn't read! So Niles took the map from him and plotted out the route.

Finally we arrived and made our way upstairs. Once out of the smallish entranceway, my eyes opened wide like saucers. The place was immense; I had been in old movie theaters that were smaller. This huge space included a large apron stage on which several awards were to be presented to those who had made major contributions to the scene by their work: photographer, clothing designer, erotic dancer, promoter, and many other categories, including one for "lifetime achievement," which was given to Adam, the one and same Adam who ran Whiplash, which I had been to earlier with Niles, and the Fetish Flea Market, which I had yet to attend. To make this enormous space welcoming and interesting, it had been spilt up into "rooms" by the clever use of chain-link fence intertwined with camouflage net, movable walls, sofa arrangements, grope boxes, and corners meant to be particularly dark. At the very rear, there was a large area devoted to displaying the works of the award winners and some vendors. Mixed in among these were large round tables with comfortable chairs.

The venue, massive as it was, was packed to the rafters. People jammed the hallways and corridors. Sometimes the ebb and flow of the crowd took you off in a direction you did not wish to go. The only way to cross the dance floor was to bop your way across to the music. I had never seen so many well dressed, good looking, happy partygoers in one place at one time. There were probably twenty five hundred people there, each and everyone of them was dressed to thrill and kill. In my leather gown, with my hair in its usual long and straight style, I felt like something of a wallflower compared to these outrageous and flamboyant dressers! Even the men wore more than just the usual leather clothing. Men in latex uniforms or genuine World War II uniforms, men painted and dressed as fawns, half-naked well-muscled subs, latex fetishists, some in latex skirts, seventeenth- and eighteenth-century attire with ruffs and ruffles and lace, pirates, devils, costumes rented from costume houses. Nothing like this was happening in the States! As I walked around trying to take it all in I clung to Niles's hand, afraid that if I were to become separated from him, I would never find him again in the press of the crowd.

I could see the effort it was taking Niles to make his way through the seething mass while greeting people he knew. It was taking its toll on him and he needed to sit down. As we made our way to the exhibition area in the rear where there were seats to be had, we ran into Leon and Barbie. Leon looked quite the famous master decked out in full leather, including accoutrement, part of which was Barbie. When she complimented me on my dress, I thanked her and looked at her outfit to return the compliment. But I was hard pressed to do so. Her long rather pendulous breasts were bare; her tightly laced corset held up her stockings; and her cleanly shaven quim was completely exposed. At a loss for words, I raved about her corset, which was lovely, and smiled a lot; after all, what else could I have said? Nice quim? How often do you shave? Thankfully, the crowd surged and we two couples were pushed in opposite directions. Niles mentioned to Leon that we would be in the back then we were swept away by the impetus of the crowd.

To get to the exhibition area, we had to make our way through the main room, the VIP lounge, and the chill zone. Niles was looking a little pale and I was greatly relieved when we finally reached the quieter area in the back. I was even more relieved to find that Niles's friend Paul had a temporary tattoo vending table and a couple of extra chairs. After making Niles comfy, I went to look at the tattoo designs; I had wanted a tattoo for many years but I couldn't decide what I wanted or where I wanted it. These temporary tattoos were the answer to every undecided woman's prayer: if you didn't like it, it would fade in five days, if you really hated it, you could rub it off with oil immediately after it dried. To my delight, I found a tattoo of a woman wearing a corset with her hands tied over her head. I brought it to Niles and asked if I could have it. His formal reply, "Yes, Madelaine, you may," belied his broad smile and the twinkle in his green eyes.

Now, where to put it? I had a hankering to have it on my right buttock and Niles agreed. I knelt on a chair with Niles standing in front of me, looking in to my eyes. Then I hoisted my floor-length gown up to my waist, all a-tingle inside and held his hands. By bending over the chair and raising my dress, I had exposed my quim and anus to anyone who cared to walk by and have a look. Looking into Niles's eyes and holding his hands made this feeling more intense as I imagined eyes on me and comments being made. Not that anyone was looking or commenting but it was lovely to pretend. Paul dabbed some alcohol on my buttock inside my tan lines and applied the tattoo. I had some strange idea that it was going to "hurt," so I gripped Niles's hand tighter when I felt the tattoo paper against my skin. But of course it didn't hurt, it was the power of my mind taking over. I was very proud of it so I climbed off the chair to show Niles. I arched my back seductively to make my nice round derriere more prominent. He smiled and gave me a friendly spank of approval then looked on as I rearranged my dress.

No sooner had I done that when a sudden urge to pee came over me. I excused myself and hastily made my way to the ladies room. At least fifteen people were ahead of me and it was evident from the noises emitting from the stalls that a lot of them were not being used for their intended purpose but rather as a more private place to shag than the outer rooms. Although the temperature in the club was comfortable, the toilets were completely unheated and I was freezing just standing in line. I had to go and go a lot sooner than the line would allow. I remembered that I had seen several tall plastic neon-colored drink glasses around and found myself an empty one. I slid into a dark corner behind an empty table, quickly pulled the yards of leather prison out of my way and let loose into the glass. When it was full, I carefully placed it on the empty table so I wouldn't accidently kick it over as I redressed myself.

While I was rearranging my dress an elderly man, obviously submissive, approached me very respectfully. He addressed me as "mistress" and said that many men there would be "honoured" to drink the mistress's sweet, fresh nectar; would he like me to find someone to bestow this honour upon? Not caring in the least and wanting to get back to Niles, I waved my hand in his general direction and said regally, "That would please me," and strode off to the exhibition area. Happy to see that Niles was still seated and had more color in his face, I told him this little tale, which he thought was funny, and quite typical of the London scene. We sat for a few minutes and watched the crowd go by. Although all of this was "old hat" to him, it was completely new and very exciting to me and I ate it up like I had been starved for years, which I had.

Offering me his arm, Niles took me on a tour of the exhibitions, especially of the photographs. My favorites were the very sexy black and white shots taken by Quinn Stuart, another friend of Niles's. As we admired them, the photographer himself came over to greet Niles. Niles introduced me to Quinn and I became so shy and uncomfortable that it took a great deal of willpower to hold my ground and not hide behind Niles. Quinn said hello politely enough but he had given me the once-over and in his mind he dismissed me as a potential fetish model. I was greatly relieved when Quinn drifted off to greet someone else. Years later I got to know him better and found him to be a fun, intelligent man.

Having seen enough, we walked back over to Paul's table and made ourselves comfortable. Paul's table was next to another photo exhibit and I saw Leon and Barbie on the other side of the movable walls through the small space between them. Leon called out to Niles; Niles told Leon that I had gotten a tattoo. Leon immediately wanted to see it, gleaning from the amount of my undecorated exposed skin that the tattoo had to be someplace much more interesting. Niles commanded me to show it to Leon and I replied, "Yes, Niles" with a giggle. Immediately I pulled up my dress and, still giggling, I tried to angle my cheek up against the slit in the wall. But alas! I was too low and I had to stand on a chair and adjust my height by bending my knees.

Asking "Can you see it yet?" as I bobbed up and down on the chair was a source of some amusement to all and I didn't mind that this little game was lengthened for our mutual pleasure until, at last, the angle was correct. Barbie said it was "nice" but Leon's compliments were much warmer than hers, probably because my performance, my girlish delight in it, and my nice round derriere pleased him more than it did her. Leon came around the wall to have a better look and gave my derriere a nice hard squeeze then a slap in appreciation. Barbie hung back and looked at the floor. When I pulled down my dress and returned my attention to Niles, Leon and Barbie said good night and made their way off into the crowd, not to be seen again that night.

It was a week night and as it was getting late, the crowd was thinning out. Because the Powerhouse was so far out into the boonies, there were no cabs to be found. When we went back inside to try to find a ride into the city, we ran into Paul again who was in the process of packing up his wares. Upon hearing our plight and knowing about Niles's incapacitation, he kindly offered us a ride into a more central London location where we would be able to hail a black cab easily. While Paul packed up the van, Niles and I stayed inside where Niles could remain seated. To keep him entertained, I performed the positions Rowan had taught me at Whiplash and in no time Niles began calling out position numbers at random. There were still some stragglers around and I was exhilarated when a group of them looked on from a polite distance as I made my devotions to Niles.

Soon Paul was finished loading the van and said "we're off." Niles was all done in by this time and seeing the strain and paleness in his face, I was happy to leave. We bounced along in Paul's van until we reached a more central location. Upon seeing several cruising cabs, Paul slammed on the brakes and, leaving Niles in the relative comfort of the van, I went running off to hail one. We said our thanks and good nights to Paul. It was still a very long trip to Maida Vale but the driver made good time because of the late hour and lack of traffic.

Inside, I undressed Niles and put his robe and slippers on him and made him rest on the sofa. Still in my dress, I made tea and rolled a spliff, knowing it would help him relax. When I returned, he looked preoccupied so I asked him what was on his mind. In a society where politeness and discretion is the norm, I was very surprised by his answer. He replied that his ex-girlfriend, Lilly, had started calling him again and sending him "love" via friends. He wondered what she could want from him because the reason they broke up was "sexual incompatibility." I vaguely recalled Charmaine mentioning this to me, along with the reason they had broken up: Lilly wanted to "top" Niles! Topping the exceedingly masculine Niles, who was also one of the most skilled and respected doms in London, defied the imagination. This struck me as very funny so I laughed. I just couldn't, in the wildest depths of my imagination, envision anyone topping the strong and manly Niles.

But if there ever was information that he should have kept to himself, this would have been it. I really didn't need to know that, did I? A polite "I overdid it tonight and I'm tired" would have been a better answer. In some cases, like this one, lying is an underrated social grace. And where was his darling Lilly now, when he was ill and needed tending? But I kept these thoughts to myself and I said nothing.

I decided that now was the time to have the conversation with him that had been in the back of my mind for days. Curling up on the floor close enough to the sofa to rest my head on it, I told Niles in a soft, sweet voice that I would like to be one of his girlfriends. He laughed and pulled me onto his lap then he hugged me. But his joking reply was, "You live five thousand miles away, Madelaine! What good would you be to me at so great a distance?" I hugged him, giggling, and said,

"But Niles, what harm would it do you?" Then I pressed on and added, "There are plenty of empty flats in Maida Vale!" Looking at me seriously, he gently took my face in his large warm hand. His voice was as gentle as his hand on my cheek when he said simply, "It wouldn't work." "If you say so, Niles," I said but his answer stayed in my mind.

It was almost dawn when we went to bed. As I laid there in the shelter of his arms, my head in the crook of his shoulder and my body pressed full length against the warmth and security of his, I couldn't stop myself from asking, "Why wouldn't it work, Niles?" "Because I'm not the person I appear to be," was his response. "No one is, Niles. Everyone shows different people different faces," I replied quietly. "We play very rough here, Madelaine, maybe you wouldn't like it," he said. "But, Niles, I would excuse myself from any situation I didn't like. That's not a real reason." He said nothing; instead he hugged me compassionately. His hands felt wonderful on my flesh, his body warmth radiated through me and softened the impact of his words so I let the subject drop.

Then the oddest thought popped into my head. In all the time I had been here, although he had kissed me, not once had Niles had a prolonged "make-out" session with me like we had when we first met. The ones that made me so wet. Hard on the heels of the odd thought came a psychic blast: the knowledge of why he hadn't. It was because of Charmaine! (Later on, I found out I was right.) At her demand, Niles had been made to promise that his make-out kisses would be reserved for her and her alone. Charmaine the absent, Charmaine the off-shagging-someone-else, had forbidden it! And it was obvious he intended to keep that promise. She doesn't deserve him, I thought angrily, she doesn't! *I* could love him and take care of him the way he deserves! But I didn't say this to Niles because I knew he loved her. I was beginning to understand something about Niles. He and I were alike in one very major way: We both were moths whose flames were the emotionally unavailable! Instead I changed tactics and asked if we could be friends forever. He smiled at me with his mouth and his eyes and replied, "Yes, friends forever." Happy with this, I buried my nose in his armpit and drifted off to sleep.

TWENTY-NINE

I would have loved to sleep in late after our dawn bedding but I had made plans to see Rowan that day. As it was, I was already an hour late in calling her, but she giggled and said she understood. We met at Esme's flat on College Road and I wasn't surprised to find myself relieved that Esme wasn't there. Rowan had been staying there for the last few days and now she was packing up to go to another place in Camdentown before returning to her own home in Summerland. Her things were in the reception room and we talked as she, seemingly out of long habit, packed with maximum efficiency. One of the last things still out was her "Relaxed One," a back-massaging device and a most excellent vibrator built for two! This apparatus was a good-size fully cushioned rectangle with a small round steering wheel in the middle, which controlled the speed.

She sat on one end and I on the other and she took over the controls. Usually the noise of a vibrator distracted me so much from its intended purpose that nothing happened; my preferred, and quieter, method of masturbation was to lay under the faucet in the bathtub with my legs up, hold my lips open, and let the water do all the work. But the Relaxed One emitted only a low bass-like hum and once I had positioned myself on it just right, it sent jolts through me. Rowan's lovely smiling face, her obvious enjoyment at sharing the vibrator with me, and my memories of playing with her at Whiplash heightened my arousal considerably. Soon we were leaning into each other's arms, hugging and kissing and nibbling, and rubbing our breasts against each other. Slowly Rowan increased the intensity of the vibrator as we embraced and we came together. Laughing, we toppled off the mighty "Relaxed One" and tumbled on the sofa until we caught our breath. How lovely it felt to come so soon after waking up!

After we had recovered, Rowan finished packing and we headed off to Camdentown. We moved her things into a cute duplex with a bathroom that was really a *room* then we headed back to the car for my first trip to the famous Camdentown Market. It turned out to be the weirdest shopping trip of my life. Since there was no parking to be found anywhere, she would run in while I sat in the car. Then she would come out, move the car, and I would go in. One out, one in, one out, one in. Because the car sitter couldn't sit for long without being moved along by the bobbies, I didn't get to see much of the market but at least she got the new satchel she needed and I was able to buy some bubble bath for Niles. This proved more difficult than I thought because of the plethora of "daisy," "watermelon," "rose," and other sweet scents but finally I bought four scents called Earth, Water, Fire, and Air, which weren't noticeably feminine.

We went back to the charming duplex after our alone-together shopping trip. Rowan was spending the weekend with Gavin and we talked and laughed as she packed her new satchel. We were all going to meet at "The Engineers," the restaurant where Esme worked as a waitress. Esme did not look happy to see me. I understood; here was Rowan going off to spend the weekend with a man, and on top of that I was there. Rowan and I arrived long before Gavin did; so long that I started to get anxious about Niles. After about an hour or so, although Gavin had yet to arrive, I bade a warm good-bye to Rowan and a cooler one to Esme (who was definitely happy to see the back of me) and took a cab to Maida Vale.

Relief washed over me when I got there and found Niles resting on the sofa. He didn't look like he had been up and about during the day, or had been doing anything strenuous. I served him tea and biscuits to tide him over until I could prepare dinner, which I started on right away. I made Penne à la Vodka, rich with diced ham, broccoli florets, peas, and the obligatory splash of vodka. This was when I found out that Niles preferred meat as his main meal; hearty as the pasta was, it didn't quite satisfy his appetite. A mere hour later, I was back in the kitchen, making him a fresh green salad and reheating the leftover Chicken Cordon Bleu and roasted potatoes. When I brought the tray into him, he was very pleasantly surprised that I had made him such a delicious snack in just a few minutes. An hour after that, he wanted dessert: a piece of apple strudel, baked of course, with vanilla ice cream on top. If he continued to eat at this rate, he'd get as big as a house! But it smelled and looked so good, I had a piece, too.

By the time we had finished eating and I had cleared the dishes away, it was almost two in the morning. He had slept for a few more hours after I left for Rowan's but we were both still tired from the previous night's festivities and exertions. We toddled off to bed and did our nightly nestling before Niles turned out the bedside lamp. Knowing he was often uncomfortable, if not in outright pain especially late in the day, I didn't push him to play with me. If he wanted me, he knew where I was! I snuggled into the crook of his shoulder and almost immediately started to drift off.

Right before I dropped into a deep sleep, Niles buried his hand in my hair and used it to roughly push my head down to his cock, saying as he did so, "Madelaine, I love the way you suck my dick." I made fake noises of protest but went willingly. As he twisted my face into position, he said in a sadistic tone of voice, "So how about a little dick licking before bed, huh, huh? Open that mouth!" "Yes, Niles," I whispered, too overcome with passion and lust to speak any louder, but my mouth was already open and drooling for him. I fell upon him and rubbed my lips and tongue over his knob and up and down his shaft. I thanked the goddess again for his beautiful cock and fed my deliciously depraved hunger.

"Greedy little dick licker, aren't you?" came his voice from above me. I made gobbling yes noises although my mouth was full. I heard Niles say, "Oh, yeah" at the same time I felt his grip tighten on my head. Then he held my head down and used his hips to thrust more of his cock into my mouth. Because Niles was only half hard, he was able to cram the entire length of it down my throat. Gripping my head more firmly, he repositioned himself until he found a comfortable position then he repositioned my head for maximum access. And then he allowed himself to grow, to get bigger and harder while all of his cock was buried in my face. As it stiffened and lengthened, it filled my mouth completely. The bigger and harder he got, the more difficult it was for me to breathe. Relentlessly, his knob with its large deep slit snaked its way down my throat.

I opened my mouth as wide as I could and tried to relax my throat under his onslaught. I let my jaw drop and stretched out my tongue to protect him from my bottom teeth and give him more room in my mouth. I struggled to control my breathing: inhale on the out stroke and exhale on the in stroke, but Niles kept pumping my head up and down in rhythm with his hip thrusts. I realized my efforts were useless and resistance was futile. Feeling brutish myself, I abandoned myself to his brute desires. My hands caressed his legs and balls, I laid gentle and tender hands over his huge controlling ones. Feeling my release, he pumped harder and deeper until my nose filled with snot and my eyes watered profusely. I felt light-headed from lack of air and tried to beg for mercy. Sensing I was about to go tilt, Niles thrust down my throat three more times, each thrust harder and deeper than the last. These three final thrusts made me heave from deep down in my stomach, then suddenly, he pulled out of my mouth, leaving it gaping open and drooling. I felt vacated, empty; blindly I sought out his hands and attempted to place my head in them to show him I was ready for more.

Niles slipped out from under me, leaving me cold and alone on the bed. A few seconds later he returned and strode up to the bed. I cringed a little when he lunged at me and grabbed me by the hair. I was face down and his grip on my hair was very tight when he dragged me to the edge of the bed. Cruelly, he twisted my head up to his face and continued twisting until I had flipped over onto my back. One hand let go of my hair to knock my knees open then returned to my head and dug in. Niles pulled my head and neck off the bed, then he stepped up to me. My mouth was still too high for his comfort so he pulled my shoulders off the bed, too. With my arms dangling limply and my head hanging down, I started to slide off the bed. Quickly I wrapped my arms around his legs to support myself.

Suddenly, he drove his index and middle fingers into my quim and spread me wide. I was dripping and my lips and thighs were smeared and sticky. Another guttural, "oh, yeah," came from above then he used my quim as a handle to adjust my position. In doing so, he dug his fingers into the magic spot and a deep, almost painful orgasm rocked my body. As soon as I came, Niles jammed his cock down my throat. His hard knob assaulted the soft tissue behind my palette and my face was buried in his balls. I gagged repeatedly as he hit the back of my throat and my whole body jerked and spasmed each time he connected. He never missed. My knees were still spread wide because his two big fingers were deep in me. He used them to hurt me and often he touched that spot after he had caused me much pain, and when I came I was almost ashamed at the pleasure I felt.

Niles was part man, part satyr, and part sex machine with a lively, quick imagination. I gasped when he withdrew his cock and fingers at the same time, and felt vacated and deprived. Then simultaneously he plunged his fingers back into my quim and jammed his cock back into my mouth after I had drawn the smallest of breaths. But soon he tired of this sport and again, my openings were suddenly empty. He commanded me not to use my mouth on him and after burying my face in his balls, he squeezed his thighs together to keep my head there. Ripping my knees open, he began spanking my clitoris in increasingly harder slaps. Niles spanked me until I came then he pinched and pulled on my lips and clit until I came again. He hit me so hard that the blows vibrated up my body and I fought against the pain to keep my knees open under this cruel attack.

Opening his thighs, my head fell free and taking his cock in one hand, he began to face slap me with it. Hand-slap to the quim, cock-smack in the face, sometimes alternating them and at others, a simultaneous slap-smack. I was moaning and writhing wantonly, reveling in the new pain and humiliation I was turning into joy and a freeing of the spirit when one particularly cruel blow made me curl up in a ball to protect myself. Niles made no attempt to stop me or re-spread me. Instead he pulled me by the arm until I was lying in a normal position on the bed. He propelled himself onto the bed with menacing grace and ungently pushed me over onto my side until we were in a side-by-side sixty-nine position. A small sob escaped me when he took my head in his hands and held it in place. "Open your mouth," he growled at me and when I did, I stuck out my tongue and dropped my jaw to welcome him. He sighed, "Oh, fuck, yes," and plunged his big hard cock back into my mouth.

After he fell into a hard face-pumping rhythm, he used one hand to spread the cheeks of my derriere. I drew my knees up the second he touched me to show him my willingness and to give him better access. He dug two fingers into my quim and inhaled audibly when his fingers met with oozing slime. Abruptly he yanked his fingers out of my quim and brutally shoved them up my anus. He had used my own pussy juice as lubrication and a new feeling came over me. Half crazed with lust, I began to massage his fingers by doing "kegels" and spread my cheeks with my own hands so he could get his fingers deeper inside me. Then he started to hurt me. I buried my face in his balls to muffle my screams as he twisted his fingers inside me, spread them at the muscle to stretch the hole, and knuckled me. When he jammed a third large finger up my anus, I screamed and writhed. But the pain was exquisite and I gave in to it completely. I loved to be violated this way and Niles did it perfectly.

Involuntarily I made little sucking and crying noises because I wanted his cock in my mouth while his fingers were so cruelly working over my anus. "Now you want dick down your throat as well as fingers up your ass, do you? Do you?" Niles taunted me. "Say it, say it!" I gasped out, "Yes, yes, fingers up my ass and dick down my throat, please, please," using the coarser words he used. "Then open that hole in your face and I'll put it to good use." My mouth was open and ready for him before he finished speaking. When he forced his cock in my orifice, incoherent noises and little sobs escaped me but he knew I was loving this. He rolled me onto my back with his fingers still deep in my anus and his cock in my mouth then suspended himself over me. Like this he was able to keep my head in place and just by leaning forward, continue his attack on my anus. I kept my knees up and cheeks open for him and gobbled hungrily at his cock. I was coming every few seconds.

Seeking to expand his knowledge of the workings of my body, he drove his fingers deeper up my anus and pushed and pressed inside of me. I knew what he was doing and I wanted it as much as I feared it. Niles was searching for the magic spot in my quim through the thin wall between my anus and my vagina. An anally induced orgasm was the most painful and humiliating orgasm I could have. When I came, the come literally squirted from my quim and the mind-blowing, body-quaking intensity of it made me crave it. My whole body squirmed and shook, impaled at either end on cock and fingers. I could think of nothing else; one of my most enduring fantasies was to have my anus violated while a cock was deep down my throat, and now it was happening to me! Hard fingers passed over that spot through the thin wall and, judging from my reaction to this briefest of touches, dug into it painfully. I turned into a mindless writhing thing as a violent anally induced orgasm rocked my body, leaving me limp and breathless.

Niles withdrew his cock and fingers at the same. He pulled me to my knees by the hair and shoved the three fingers that had been up my anus into my mouth. "Suck your ass juice off me," he snarled. I gently covered his invading hands with mine, my touch a caressing one. I sucked on his fingers greedily and licked under his nails, not caring where they had been. My abandonment to his dark will and sadism excited him more. He spun me around so that my back was to his front, then drove his fingers deeper into my mouth. Roughly, his other hand squeezed and slapped my breasts and pinched my nipples. I tongued and sucked his fingers and rubbed my derriere on his cock, hoping he would penetrate my loosened anus. I became less like a human and more like a forest animal in heat, craving his brutal sex and begging him to fuck me.

Feeling one less inhibition, that one more taboo had been broken, Niles pulled me off the bed and pushed me down on the floor. I landed on my hands and knees, doggie-style. I begged him to penetrate me. Instead I felt his hands in my hair and he half-dragged me (and I half-crawled) to a particular spot on the floor. As he pulled me along, he yanked on my hair and jerked my head around even though I wasn't resisting. Embracing his sadism, I closed my eyes against the darkness and followed where he led. When he pulled my head up sharply, I thought he wanted me to stand. I rose into a half-squat and managed to settle one buttock on a box under the bed that I had bumped into accidentally.

Niles pulled my head back and snarled, "Open your mouth" then plowed into it. I had to bend my neck into an awkward position to suck him because I was too high up and this displeased him. Letting go of my head, he slapped me to the floor. Being only eighteen or so inches off of it, I fell gracefully at his feet and kissed them fervently. Niles took this opportunity to nudge-kick me into a new pinioned position: a nook formed by the platform of the bed behind my head, the box I had been squatting on to my left, storage containers to the right, and the floor underneath me. He kicked my feet apart and held them open with his own. Niles grabbed for my hands but in the dark couldn't find them so he commanded me to put them on the bed above me.

There was a full moon that night and the bedroom faced south. The heavy curtains were open and only sheer yellow curtains covered the window. I looked up at him from my lowly position on the floor and his moonlit silhouette filled my eyes to the exclusion of all else. His hair streamed over his shoulders and down his back and when he turned slightly to the side, I saw the silhouette of his cock. The sight of it became my whole world, it and only it. A delicious fear filled me. He was one of Bacchus's satyrs reborn and he was with me in this very room. He would take me savagely for his pleasure in honor of his god. I reveled in our personal Bacchanalia, delirious with desire for him. All resistance was long gone. I thought nothing of myself and only of what I could do for the raging god of the woodlands, and of what use I could be to him.

As soon as my hands were on the bed, he grabbed them and spread my arms as if I were to be crucified. This made me lean my head and shoulders forward. Niles was standing so close to me now that all I could see was his engorged cock and his balls. My mouth fell open to receive him. Inhaling sharply, he positioned his cock in front of my gaping, drooling mouth and out-stretched tongue and forced it down my throat. I caressed him with my tongue as he violated my mouth. Deeper and harder he rocked into my face until I began to struggle against him. He took his cock out of my mouth and smacked my face with it. In a nasty voice, he said, "just open your mouth." I dropped my jaw, and awaited the satyr's pleasure.

A satisfied "uh-huh" from above was followed by his cock pounding into my face. His pumping was hard and fast but occasionally he paused to hold my head down when my mouth was stuffed with his cock. This loosened my throat further but made breathing almost impossible. Soon I was gagging and heaving again. I felt him grow harder each time I gagged; his cock raged in my mouth and I gloried in it. Nothing mattered except that gorgeous organ in my mouth as he raped my face. Having said the word "rape" to myself was a revelation. Once said, I felt free, floating, weightless; another taboo had been broken and I reveled in the lovely debauchery of it.

I knew in that instant that Niles was going to face-fuck me until I vomited. Another orgasm racked my body as I admitted and accepted this. I lost myself in this thought and opened my mind and body to Niles's will and power over me. This, too, communicated itself to Niles and I felt him change his stroke to one he used when he bent me over the bed and shagged me. He was pumping his cock into my face the same way he would pump it into my quim. Harder, faster, deeper, he was savage in his use of my face. I gagged with every stroke until snot exploded from my nose in a futile effort to breathe. Roaring bestially, "Oh, yeah, fuck, yeah," he squeezed my head between his massive hands and ground his hips into my face. My gagging turned to heaving, then to retching, and still Niles hammered his cock down my throat.

After two more cruelly deep thrusts of his cock, I felt it coming up. I tried to swallow it back down but Niles wouldn't let me. He found the retch spot in the back of my throat and worked it mercilessly. Like clicking the heels of my ruby slippers together, I found myself tranported to another place, another dimension. All I wanted to do was let him use me as sadistically and humiliatingly as he pleased. My mind blanked out everything but his cock down my throat. My quim spurted and oozed. I heaved again and vomited on his cock. He continued to pump me, his arousal as animalistic as mine. My vomit surrounded his cock then ran down it and his balls. The vomit ran down my chin, neck, and belly as each new thrust forced up more of it. It snaked its way down between my spread open legs and over the lips of my quim. Soon a steaming little heap of it was on the floor between my legs. My mind was long gone and I started to rub and smear myself with my own vomit.

Niles withdrew from my mouth, bent down to lift up my face, and he asked me if I was all right. I nodded "yes," too overcome to speak. "Stay right there. Don't move," he said, then padded off to the bathroom in his bare feet and returned with a towel and a washcloth. Very gently, he tried to clean me off but I had vomited a great deal and made a big mess. His valiant attempts were useless. I needed a bath and asked in a sweet submissive voice if I could take one. He agreed, laughing, "Of course!" I used the washcloth to mop up the floor a bit, then Niles helped me to my feet and supported me as we made our way down the hall to the bathroom. When we passed the kitchen, he propped me up against the wall and threw the nasty washcloth away. In the bathroom at last, I liberally poured one of the bubble bath essences I had bought for him that same day under the running water. While the tub filled, Niles washed up in the sink.

Casting a quick glance at the foamy, steaming tub, he turned off the sink faucets, tested the bath with his foot, and climbed in. My heart pounded in my chest, threatening to break a rib. I knew he didn't want me to draw a new bath when he was finished; his intention was for me to bathe in his dirty water. Eagerly, I reached for the soap and gave him a shortened version of the bathing ritual. He declined the towel ritual but accepted a towel from me when I offered it. He dried himself off and before he left the bathroom, he turned and smiled at me with that mischievous twinkle in his eyes. As I stepped into the tub of dirty water and sat down, I smiled at him and said, "Nice touch, Niles." His smile broadened, deepening his dimples, then he left me alone in the bathroom.

I bathed quickly and hurried back into the bedroom. I vaulted onto the bed and pulled the duvet up with me. I nestled into the familiar crook of his shoulder. He swiped his hand under his arm, wet it with his sweat, and wiped it across my face. His arm curled more tightly around me and I pressed my body against his. Then he shut off the light. I laid there in the dark, happy with what I had experienced with him and learned about myself. I kissed his shoulder and armpit with a raging fire burning inside me. Soon the darkness in the room and the closeness of Niles's body lulled me into a deep sleep.

THIRTY

When I woke up in the morning, my head was filled with memories and physical reminders of the previous night. I remembered how I surrendered myself to Niles's brutal desires, only caring about our pleasure, not others' perceptions. I remembered how hot my vomit was as it ran down my body and pooled under my shaven, swollen quim. The back of my throat was sore from the continuous pounding, both nether holes were throbbing, and a few stomach muscles were strained from gagging and heaving, the grand finale, and encore. I delighted in this and knew that more inner walls had been knocked down last night. Once inside, the conqueror was met with cheers and flowers, not resistance.

The conqueror himself stirred beside me and opened his eyes. Looking at the clock, he exclaimed, "Bloody hell! It's four fifteen!" It was that time of day in London when four in the afternoon could easily be mistaken for four in the morning and today was one of those grim misty days. Then I guess he thought, What the hell? and lay back against the pillows. I curled up next to him for a couple of minutes, his arm around me, and kissed his neck and face, getting all warm and muzzy because my head was swimming with memories. While I was out with Rowan, the full day of rest he had gotten before the night's activities seemed to have done him a world of good. So I decided that resting all afternoon was to be the order of the day; then he would be full of lust and vigor later on when it mattered.

"May I bring you breakfast in bed, Niles?" I asked sweetly, already knowing the answer. "Yes, my dear Madelaine, you may." Perfect! Other than a trip to the bathroom, he would stay in bed while I prepared a hot meal, which would take longer. I brought him tea with chocolate-covered biscuits first, then went back to the kitchen and rattled those pots and pans. I knew he would be wondering what I was cooking for him, having already proven myself to be more than capable in the kitchen. It was to be one of my famous fluffy omelettes: three eggs whipped with milk, filled with sliced ham, broccoli florets, and Swiss cheese. Two slices of buttered toast and a small salad on the side completed the meal. I arranged the plates, napkin, and cutlery on the tray in an attractive and appetizing way and brought it to Niles. Re-ensconced in the bed and propped up on pillows, his appetite whetted by the sounds and smells from the kitchen, a broad smile lit his face when I came in with the tray. When he thanked me for making him such a delicious meal, I could hear genuine appreciation in his voice. Sweet music! Then he cleaned his plate.

I brought the rolling tray to him before I cleaned the kitchen; a ha!

another way to keep him resting! But he was finished before I was and went into the reception room. On the pretense of bringing him another cup of tea, I was relieved to find him lounging comfortably on the sofa listening to music. He had started smoking the spliff so I hurried back to the kitchen to finish up in there. I joined him in the reception room and took my usual spot on the floor. We passed the spliff back and forth while we enjoyed the music and the comfortable silence. I felt that we were alone together in our own galaxy, that there was no world outside of the confines of these walls, and that this wonderful time would go on endlessly. I let my mind drift and saw images of all the things I had done with Niles and tried to imagine what new walls would be torn down, what new taboos broken, and how far down the spiral of masochism and submission I would travel to reach new heights and highs.

Niles was starting to look tired. He had been taking antibiotics regularly and I knew that they could tire him as much as his condition. When he said he could use a snack, I was surprised to see that it was nearly eleven p.m. I made two turkey sandwiches on whole grain bread with lettuce and tomato and to give it a personal touch, I mixed ketchup and mayonnaise together to make an ad hoc dressing. Tea and biscuits completed the snack. I cut the sandwiches in points and gave him three of the four pieces. I ate the last one. Eating didn't seem to perk him up and when he suggested that we move into the bedroom, I agreed. Obviously, he hadn't gotten quite enough rest today, still afflicted as he was by swollen bollocks. I had no expectations of playing when we stripped our robes off and climbed into bed. When Niles put out his arm so I could cuddle into his shoulder, I assumed we were just going to go to sleep.

But Niles is and always will be Niles, the horned and ever-ready god of savage love, and he had different plans in mind. Like the night before, as soon as I started to drift off, Niles was on me like a beast. Startled, I cried out in fear, protest, and surprise. I felt his cock, long and hard, throb against my belly. He used one of his legs to hold mine open and pinned me down with his body. He worked a hand between us, then between my legs, and dug two fingers into my dry quim. I screamed at the pain but that and my dryness aroused him more. He redoubled his efforts to hurt me inside, bestial growls resonating from him as he drove his fingers deeper into me. I didn't come and the pain was getting to be too much to bear. I whimpered his name over and over until he clamped his free hand over my mouth and used his thumb to pinch my nostrils shut.

Struggling for breath, I came hard, drenching his fingers. My weak efforts to fight him ceased. I kissed the hand covering my mouth and let all resistance flow out of me. Niles felt this surrender and with hard probing fingers, touched the magic spot, and gave me a racking orgasm. He flung himself onto his back and, before I could catch my breath, he grabbed my breasts. He used them like handles to pull me across his chest, face up. My head hung face up over his shoulder, my breasts flattened out; my derriere, pressed against his belly, was positioned a couple of inches above his cock and left my holes exposed for penetration at will. My knees were bent, my legs were splayed open and my feet were the only part of my body touching the bed.

Niles crudely thrust his thumb into my quim then took it right out. Next I felt him working his thumb, lubricated by my girl jam, into my anus. Then two large fingers entered my quim. His other hand closed on my throat and stifled my moans of passion and groans of pain. I gasped for air as he coarsely fingered me front and back, hurting me, stretching me, and getting rougher with each passing second. His fingers in my quim would touch that spot every so often and I would have a smashing violent orgasm each time. The humiliation I felt at being used like this rocked my world and, loving it, I wanted more of it. Being a sex toy, a blow-up doll, a life-support system for a set of holes to be used by him whenever he wanted. The spiral beckoned and focusing only on his fingers inside me, I let myself go.

Then his hot fudge voice whispered, "Like that, don't you, my little slut? Little bitch slut, look at this slimy cunt." He manipulated his fingers inside me, front and back, emphasizing each word with a stab of pain. I whimpered and moaned in protest and belied my words by squirming seductively on his fingers. Sluttily, I used my muscles to squeeze and caress them, a silent plea for more. Suddenly Niles flipped us both over onto our bellies. Now I was on the bottom and he on top. He repositioned his fingers inside me without bothering to take them out. Pain ripped through me and I put up a struggle. The hand on my throat moved to the back of my head and smashed my face into the pillow. He called me a bitch and a slut and told me that I would learn to accept whatever pain he wished to inflict upon me. Leaving his two fingers in my quim, he "popped" his thumb in and out of my anus, working the muscle cruelly and making me sob into the pillow in ecstatic pain.

His cock dribbled pre-come between my thighs and I craved having him inside of me. Still thumbing me very roughly, Niles continued to grind my face into the pillow until faintness from lack of air and subjugation of my will to his made me stop my feeble struggles. When he felt no resistance against his fingers, he stopped these forms of torture and humiliation and dreamed up a new one. Rolling off me so that he could lie on his back, he forced my head down to his groin. "Lick that pre-come off me, off my dick and stomach! I don't want one drop left behind," he snarled at me. I lapped at his juices greedily, and as I lapped at him, he pulled my legs until my quim faced him. I thought, hoped, prayed that he was going to penetrate me. But instead Niles pulled and pinched my labia and clitoris, and smashed and squashed my clit beneath his thumb.

When his hands steered my head toward his cock, I opened my mouth hungrily to take him. He was so hard, so long and thick, and I ached to have him in me. I put up a slight fight but I was wholeheartedly cooperating with him. Best of all, Niles knew it. Once his cock was jammed in my mouth, he started to taunt me. "How do you like being treated with no respect? Do you like it? Do you? Of course you do. I'm going to degrade you, treat you like a slut, like the whore that you really are! And don't tell me you've never been a prostitute. I won't believe you. You do this too well, you slut. Suck me, bitch, go on, suck me!" His voice, which could be so gentle, so calming, so sexy at other times, was guttural and contained more than a hint of menace. Disdaining the soft caress of my lips and tongue, his cock banged ceaselessly at the back of my throat as he snarled this.

Niles's hands tightened on my head and as he said "Don't lie to me, you little slut," he punctuated each word with a hard well-aimed thrust into my mouth. Then he pulled my head off his cock by the hair and demanded that I tell him the truth. "No, Niles," I mewled, "I'm not a prostitute. Never for money, Niles, never." My mouth was swimming in saliva and I gulped some of it down as I spoke. "You're lying. I don't believe you," he sneered and pulled my cheeks apart. He slapped my anus hard and I yelped in pain. Releasing his cock from my mouth, I whimpered his name. "Lying bitch," he snarled and slapped my anus again, harder this time. "But I would do it for you, Niles, really I would, really," I said in a soft and submissive voice, "Please let me sell myself for you. Please!"

He flung me face up on the bed, using my hair as his handle. My quim, sore and aching from his previous violations, was invaded again by three of his long fingers. When his fingers met with dryness, he shoved them up into me hard and hurt me before he touched the magic spot. After my girl jam had bathed his fingers he began to speak in that crude guttural voice again. "Yes, I'll put your cunt up for sale. Make a few pounds off your arse, I will." With a little more menace in his voice he continued, "Yes, that's right. Anything I want. Sell your asshole as well as your cunt. Make some extra quid off of that tight hole, too." "Please no, Niles! Please don't make me fuck them. Don't make me spread for them!" He slapped me and told me that I would do anything he wanted. "No!" I wailed. He slapped me across my left cheek several times, each slap hard and evenly timed. He slapped me until I pleaded, "I'll do anything you want, Niles. Anything."

The slapping stopped but the revilement went on. Niles's hand was exerting just the slightest pressure against my throat. "'Anything you want, Niles," he said, mimicking my tone of voice. "Oh, you've got that right. Anything I want and I want you to spread for them and fuck them front, back and face, too. Might as well make some money off that hole," he said in the guttural voice. He tightened his grip on my throat and made it a little more difficult for me to breathe. He started to growl at me and a frisson of fear shot through me. "Will you stay with me, Niles? Stay with me while they fuck me? Will you?" I implored him. "Yes, certainly. To make sure you fuck them properly and they get their money's worth. And if you didn't, I would be right there to beat you bloody!"

Then he reviled me again, slapping my face and giving me quick chokes. He spat out, "How do you like it? To have your holes treated as openings for my pleasure? To be face-fucked till you puke? How do you like not being treated like a lady? Do you like being disrespected? Huh? Huh?" Each "huh" was punctuated by a slap, forehand then backhand. He fingered me savagely but my quim had gone dry and he noticed. "Why is your cunt dry, Madelaine? Why is it dry?" he asked sternly, and emphasized each word with a deep thrust. Not knowing what to say except "Because you haven't pushed my button," which would have been a correct but unacceptable answer, instead in a small, pleading voice I said, "I thought you liked it dry, Niles. It hurts me more dry and I know you like to hurt me." I heard him inhale deeply in excitement and continued, "Please hurt me, Niles, please, hurt me, hurt me." I wailed and begged piteously; in an instant I came and loved the feeling of it inside me, drenching Niles's fingers.

"Yes, now you understand, Madelaine. I like hurting you. I want to hurt you. Does *that* hurt?" he said softly. The softness of his voice was belied by what his fingers were doing to me inside. Hurtful fingers dug into me, spread me wide inside and at the opening, and a sharp nail speared me now and again. "Niles, yes, oh yes, you're hurting me. It hurts! Please, hurt me, I love it when you hurt me! Please, more!" Impaled on his fingers, I was almost incoherent with passion, almost out of my body from joyous, riotous pain. After he gave me more of the transcendental pain, I gasped out, "I come so hard when you hurt me." Then he touched that spot, pressing into it cruelly and gave me a shuddering, shattering orgasm.

Followed by a pain that made me scream. Immediately an iron hand was clamped over my mouth and a thumb pinched one nostril closed. The sudden loss of air made me quiet down. With great will, I got control over my breathing and learned to make do with what air I could get. My whole body felt suspended on Niles's fingers; my whole being floated on the pain emanating, radiating, from my quim. Calmer now, I reached one hand down my body to caress his hand. When I put my hand between my legs so I could feel his fingers disappear into my quim, I moaned with pleasure and understood the pain. The only finger that wasn't inside of me was his thumb. He touched me deep inside and pressed repeatedly on that spot just as I fully realized that four of his large fingers up my quim were the closest to being hand-fucked that I had ever been.

I felt every bit the slut he said I was; I felt like the whore he swore I was. The incoherent sounds I made as I continued to stroke and touch my stretched opening and his fingers were mixed mumblings of "moe . . . yah . . . ah." The smell of his manly aroma drove me wild. Grabbing his hand, I tried to shove more of it in me, to move it so it hurt me more, and gave me more shuddering orgasms. I smelled his animal scent more strongly now and knew he was very aroused. Tightening his grip on my throat, he gave me the best, and final, orgasm of the night. He yanked his fingers out of me and wiped the slime on my belly. My body was still shaking and trembling and I was barely on the planet.

Niles lay on his back and gently drew my head into the crook of his shoulder and stroked my hair. I cuddled up to him and I fell asleep thinking how lovely it was to go to bed smeared with dried girl jam and not care.

THIRTY-ONE

After our exhaustive antics the previous night, I woke up around one. I hung out in bed snuggling up to Niles until he woke up around two. When he awoke, Niles told me he was up much later than I was but he didn't say why and I didn't ask. I served him tea in bed, then dressed and ran out to the bakery. I wanted fresh pastries for him and I knew the bakery would be closed the next day. Upon my return I served him fresh tea and some of the pastries. He bit into his apple danish and asked where my breakfast was. Before I could reply, he pulled me closer to the bed by my arm. Then he ripped back the duvet and exposed his erect cock to me. "Here's your breakfast," he said crudely, then he pushed my head down on his cock.

Although my throat was red and sore from the oral services I had performed for him over the last couple of nights, I fell upon him greedily. Holding my head down, he pumped into my face and it hurt. I started to gag and tried to control the depths of his thrusts with my lips and tongue. "Did you forget what I told you about face-fucking? Did you? No lips or tongue, no sucking, no pleasure for you! Now just open your mouth so I can fuck your face," Niles snarled at me. My jaw dropped in immediate compliance. He pumped my face until I started to gag and heave from deep down in my belly. I thought he was going to fuck me until I vomited again, but after one very violent heave, he let me go. Keeping only his engorged knob in my mouth, I gasped for air as long as I dared. I was afraid that he would deprive me of his lovely organ if I let it fall out of my mouth. When I had recovered, I sucked him eagerly.

I didn't care that my throat hurt from the deep poundings it was taking. Niles, the god of cock, had need of me; he needed me to service him, and part of that need was to abuse me and I would not deny him. I had given him my body for his use, abuse, and ultimate pleasure and I had meant it. For the time I was with Niles, Niles owned me; I was his possession, to do with as he wished. I had come to crave the cruel way he handled me; I loved him for his sadism and brutality and because he understood my needs without being told what they were. Not once in all the time we had been together had I given him a "menu," which would have been a list of "no-no's," a list of things I didn't want done to me. The only safe word Niles had given me was "mercy" and I had only said it once. And even then I did not want to say it.

Each time I had been with Niles, I had gotten deeply into sub-space. I got so high on him, so drugged by his pheromones, that I felt like I was orbiting another planet, rocketed out of this world into a palace of sadism created by Niles. Sometimes, I was so overcome that I was unable to speak. All that kept me attached to this world was an invisible umbilical cord of love for the master and passion for Niles. Even after he throttled me until I passed out, even though he used my face and openings cruelly and at will, the first and only word on my mind was "Niles."

My face was still being used as a fuck-hole while I thought this. Niles's cock was delicious to taste, lovely to look at and have inside of any of my openings; I even loved the way he degraded and reviled me because he knew just what to say or do to send me soaring. He thrust harder into my mouth, hitting the sore spot with each thrust. I was gagging and coming simultaneously with each thrust. Holding my head down, he thrust and pounded into my mouth until he himself could no longer take the pain of his exertions. He got up and pulled me off the bed by the hair, which had become his favorite way of moving me around and controlling me. He bent me over the bed, face down, and told me to "stay."

Taking up a cane, he gave me ten hard strokes. Each stroke ripped a scream from me. After I had taken the ten strokes, I was reeling. Then he pulled me by the hair and spun me around to face him. He kissed me roughly and then he let me go so suddenly that I almost fell down. I had barely regained my footing when he commanded me to make him a fresh cup of tea and bring it to him in the reception room. He spun on his heel and strode off. I staggered into the kitchen and made the tea, serving it to him on a tray with some more pastries. As he ate, I sat on my spot on the floor next to the sofa and awaited his pleasure.

His pleasure was to lounge on the sofa and watch TV. I was to remain silent and unobtrusive until he had need of me. Tired from our earlier activities, he didn't require any sexual services from me. His commands were for tea, more snacks, a bath, and other household slave duties. I was happy to do everything he asked of me. When I bathed him, I took a long time massaging him and washing his hair, loving the hairless firmness of his skin. As I performed the towel ritual, he sat there like a prince who expected these services and let me dry him off in a worshipful manner. Then I helped him back into his robe, put his slippers on his feet, and led him back into the reception room. I asked if I could bathe in his dirty water and he granted me permission. Hurriedly I bathed and donning a sexy robe of my own, lace-topped thigh-high stockings and high-heeled shoes, rejoined him in the reception room. His green eyes lit up when I entered the room. Even if he didn't feel like playing, I felt there was no reason I shouldn't be dressed in a way that pleased us.

We smoked several spliffs and relaxed all afternoon. At nine, I made roasted chicken with mashed potatoes and gravy, and sweet petit peas for dinner. He ate with relish and thanked me warmly for making him such a nice meal. I glowed inside at his words of praise; it thrilled me to hear them. Who doesn't enjoy being appreciated? I smiled the whole time I cleaned the kitchen, thinking of his words. When I rejoined him in the reception room, bringing him fresh tea and chocolate-covered biscuits, I was floating on air. Niles gestured that I was to take my usual spot on the floor and await his next command. He told me to make myself "small," meaning that I was to be still and silent until he needed me. I curled up in a tight ball next to the sofa so he couldn't see me and retreated into my mind, thinking of all we had done. I don't know exactly how long I stayed like that but it was long enough to send me off-world.

I was so deeply into my head-space that the first time he called my name, I didn't hear him. He kicked me to get my attention. "Yes, Niles?" I said as I slowly returned to Earth. "I'm tired, let's go to bed," he said. "As you desire, Niles," I replied in a soft submissive voice. I helped him up and we went to bed. But not to sleep, as I had thought. As soon as I had a whiff from his armpit, he demanded service from me. I waited for him to grab me by the hair but instead he ordered me to kneel on the bed. After I had assumed the position, he asked me what I thought I could do that would pleasure him. I offered to suck his cock but he rejected that by slapping me in the face, then demanded that I think I something else. Timidly I said, "Please, Niles, please let me caress and worship your anus. Let me use my tongue to pleasure you there. I want to lick you and taste the sweetness of you."

He slapped me, forehand and backhand. Then he grabbed the back of my neck, squeezed it hard, and shook me. "What did you offer to do?" "I asked to be allowed to worship your anus, Niles." He slapped me. "Language, Madelaine, language. "I want to worship you," he said in a mocking voice. Changing his tone, he said sternly, "You are not to speak like a lady. You are to speak like the slut and whore you are. Now say it again and say what you mean, and this time I want to hear filth coming out of your mouth." I took a deep breath and whispered, "Please, Niles, let me lick your asshole, let me put my tongue up your ass," I pleaded as I struggled to find words filthy enough to make him happy. "Let me lick the shit out of you and clean you with my tongue, please, Niles! Please let me eat out your asshole. I want to lick your shit chute. I want to suck your asshole, I taste to you, to eat you, please let me, please."

"Then do it," he snapped at me, "and you better do a good job of it." With that, he pushed me over backward so that I was face up on the bed. He straddled my face, spread his cheeks, aligned his asshole with my waiting mouth and tongue and sat on my face. "Stick that tongue out, asshole slut," he growled at me. I stuck it out and he started to rub his asshole on my mouth and tongue. "Eat me out! What are you waiting for?" When he said that, I began to lick him and suck on his hole, probing him with my tongue. "Yes, slut, that's better. More licking." I tongued him hungrily, amazed at how good it felt to be degraded this way. When his asshole and surrounding skin were slick with my saliva, he rubbed his asshole all over my face and smeared my face with my own anus-flavored spit.

A new barrier had been broken and I wrapped my arms around him and began to lick and probe him, caring about nothing other than his asshole and my tongue in it, on it, around it. I turned into an asshole licking and sucking beast and lengthening and hardening my tongue, I used it like a cock to fuck him. "Yeah, oh, yeah, now you've got it," he moaned, spurring me on to greater efforts. When I puckered my lips and sucked his asshole he groaned and moaned in pleasure. Excited that I could please him this way, I began to dip my tongue into him as I sucked him; three hard sucks followed by a dip into his hole over and over again. He was going wild, holding his cheeks open for me so it would be easier for me to eat him out. Occasionally he would rub his asshole all over my face saying, "You like that, don't you, you little slut. Don't you?" I moaned agreement and continued to eat him out.

I could have licked him till the sun rose in the west, but instead he climbed off of me, turned around and straddled me again, this time facing me. His legs pinned down my arms and he was very close to my face. His gorgeous hard cock was in his hand and he was stroking it. I begged him to let me suck him off but he denied me that pleasure. "You'll get my spunk, all right. Right in your face." He continued to stroke himself and once in a while he would slap me in the face and revile me. He changed tempo and I knew he was going into one of his come strokes. I moaned and whimpered, "Yes, please, please come in my face. Shoot your hot spunk on my face and let me lick off what I can. Come on me, please, Niles, shoot it on me." He growled and stroked harder and soon he shot his hot pearl jism. He started to come in my face and reaching down with his free hand, he smeared his spunk into my skin as he spurted on me.

He fell off me onto the bed next to me and put out his arm. When I nuzzled my sticky face into his armpit, he trapped my face there. I could breathe but I wasn't getting a lot of fresh air; all I could do was offer no resistance and drown myself in his scent. When he released me, my face was covered in dried come mingled with his fresh wet sweat. He offered me the crook of his shoulder and I snuggled up against him, savoring the warmth and strength of his lean body. Niles fell asleep before I did and as he slept, I gazed upon his sleeping form, eating him up with my eyes. I licked my lips and tasted him on them, and thought of what I had just done with him, of how I had spoken the filthy words he wanted to hear, and the utter abandon that I had shown at his command. I felt uplifted and freed of another taboo and wallowed in the mind-blowing humiliation of his actions and words, and mine. It took me a couple of hours to fall asleep, hours in which I relived "eating him out" over and over. It was near dawn when I finally drifted off to sleep.

THIRTY-TWO

It was late in the afternoon when we arose. We had been partying and playing so often that after such a nice, long sleep, we felt quite perky when we finally rolled out of bed. Niles headed for the sofa and waited for his tea and biscuits, which were not long in coming. I was feeling playful but in a sexy show-off flirty way. Retreating to the bedroom, I dug through my suitcases and re-entered the reception room wearing my black satin and lace corset, a sheer black lace top, lace top thigh highs, a lace g-string, and over it all, I wore my fluffy black crinoline. The "Niles pumps" held my feet in delicate bondage on stiletto heels; I put on makeup because, well, that's part of what a girl does when she plays dress up. As I walked down the long hallway to the reception room, I made sure my stilettos clickity-clicked on the hard floor. I knew the sound of them would make Niles's radar go off and he would be watching the door for my "entrance."

I did the "model's runway walk" when I entered, placing one foot directly in front of the other to give my hips, and crinoline, that sexy sway. But as I did it, I held Niles's green eyes with mine and flirted with him, lifting my crinoline and doing a tame version of the can-can, flouncing down to the floor so the crinoline spread out around me like the petals of a big black flower, and finally crawling to my spot on the floor next to the sofa in the cat-like way I perfected as a dancer. All this time his green eyes were twinkling and when I got to the sofa, Niles took my head in his hands and gave a hard smooch on the lips, even making the "muwah" sound. Then he handed me a hit of E, saying that these were the last two we had. He left a message for Leon and two hours later the answer was "come by, but later on."

We passed the two hours by watching television. After channel surfing for a minute, we came upon a very popular nationally televised dog show, *Cruff's*. It was one of the most amusing dog shows I have seen. None of the dogs were pedigreed animals, they were just a bunch of the cutest mixed breed, family owned and trained, dogs that were really smart. Their tricks included doggie obstacle courses, returning a dropped hanky to their owner, jumping through hoops, and some other tricks as well as the usual "heel-sit-stay-rollover-play dead, etc." routines. We laughed as we watched their antics, little knowing that each of us had taken on a role in the show. Niles was my owner/trainer/handler and I was his smart, cute, mixed breed doggie.

After the dog show, Niles decided that we would leave for Leon's place in another two hours, which would give him plenty of time to rest a little longer and do his man thing without rushing. I decided to leave on my little outfit because it was fun and pretty and sexy, like a high school prom queen gone bad, or gothic. I helped Niles dress and off we went, forgetting to bring his new toys, the cane and flogger, along to show Leon. What a ride it was to Leon's place! He lives way out in the east near a place called Gravesend. There is some contention over the name Gravesend; the "romantic" version states the place got its name because during times of plague it was the outermost reaches so that was were the bodies were buried and the graves ended. Hence, "Gravesend." The more pragmatic version states that a long time ago there was a very wealthy man named "Graves" who owned much land but the current town was the outermost boundary of his property. Being the last bit of Mr. Grave's land, it was named Gravesend.

Well, however the place got its name, it was a good seventy-five-minute ride to it. We passed Primrose Hill where Niles and I had seen the comet, Hale-Bopp, drove by the London Dungeon and the Tower Bridge, through the adorable town of Greenwich with its historical sights and where the "Cutty Sark" was in port. And we still weren't there yet. Fortunately soon after that we hit the highway and driving became much easier for Niles; a straight run to Leon's in fifth gear was less strenuous than driving through central London. I was uncomfortable in my corset during the long ride, but if Niles with his swollen bollocks could stand the strain of the hard drive, I certainly wasn't going to whine about my corset. Relief was evident on Niles's face when we arrived. A good sit down would refresh him as well as a nice visit with his friends.

Leon's place was a charming two-floor house with an unassuming front yard and a spacious garden in the back. Downstairs comprised the reception room and dining area, eat-in kitchen, and the bathroom; the second floor consisted of three rooms: the master's bedroom, the guest bedroom, and another room where Leon ran a piercing business. Best of all, the dungeon was a chamber underneath the reception room, its recessed O-rings were almost completely concealed by the carpet and one had to look hard to find them. A perilous wooden rung ladder led straight down into the chamber which was well equipped with a stockade, bondage table/torture rack, jail cell, acrylic potty chair, and X-frame, all made by Leon. A plethora of whips, canes, paddles, tawsers, and other instruments of discipline, miles of rope for bondage, cock-and-ball torture devices, electro-simulators, dildos, butt plugs, gags, blindfolds, hood, shackles, nipple torture toys, leather wrist and ankle restraints, locks, speculum, and medical toys on shelves lined the walls, making quite an impressive and intimidating display when first beheld.

Once again I was introduced to Leon's live-in slave girl, Barbie, the woman Leon had taken to the Sex Fetishists' Ball and had been the star in many of the videos Leon made, both as his submissive and as the mistress to submissive males. I had watched some of these videos at a friend's house in Florida. She loved them because they taught her how to be a better dom and she had a masochistic side as well. Leon had taught Barbie everything she knew as a domina and she had a creative teacher. Leon had been into tying women up as early in life as his teenage years. BDSM was an integral, up front and in-your-face part of Leon's life and he was a celebrity on the local scene as well as at selected venues overseas. After my tour of the dungeon, Barbie and I stayed next to our masters, me on the floor and she on her special slave's cushion, while the men chatted. When Barbie offered to make coffee, I followed her into the kitchen to lend a hand. She carried the two masters' coffees while I brought up the rear, carrying hers and mine.

The men talked and sipped their coffees for a bit, then Leon ordered Barbie to lie across his lap for a spanking. While he slapped her bottom, I was ordered to walk back and forth across the room to show off my outfit. I did so with pleasure, keeping my head down like a good slave so no one could see how broadly I was smiling, happy to be a credit to Niles in Leon's eyes. When my first promenade was too fast, I was made to do it again, slower this time. Leon, who was a corset fetishist, remarked that my corset wasn't completely closed in back. Niles berated me for that, demanding to know why it wasn't closed properly. I whispered an apology in one of my slave's tones that I had done it up myself so I wouldn't disturb his rest and begged him to forgive me my ineptitude.

Niles turned me around roughly, untied my inadequate lacings, evened them out, then properly tight-laced me, making sure the back was fully closed. I felt the difference immediately and began to draw shallower breaths to accommodate my luxurious satin and lace body prison. Happier with my appearance, I was made to walk slowly across the reception room and dining area up to the kitchen door. The door was mirrored, so I paused and flounced and ruffled my crinoline then did a double pirouette to flare my skirt out. Niles and Leon chuckled appreciatively and after the two men's combined sighs of "ahh!" I dropped down on all fours to return to the floor at Niles's feet. Giggling I walked doggie-style, wagging my imaginary tail, my pink tongue lolling out like a dog's. When I sat down doggie-style, I rested my chin on his thigh, like I had seen many a dog do then sat there with the amiable aimlessness common to dogs until they are called upon by their masters. To my delight, Niles caught on immediately: I wanted to play *"Cruff's."*

Niles gathered up my hair in his large hand and rising, he used it as a leash to pull me across the floor. As we crossed the room, I knew from his hand's hold on my hair that we were in the same space. I scuttled next to him on all fours, making sure to keep my shoulder in constant contact with his leg, which would assist me in knowing what direction to go or action to perform. It reminded me of how I controlled a horse I used to ride, only this was "dressage for dogs." And happy, high me was the dog. When we crossed the room the second time, Niles turned me around in a tight circle, my shoulder still pressed up against his leg. In a dog trainer's voice, he commanded me to sit then let go of my hair. Casually, he walked to the far side of the room, offhandedly telling Leon that we had watched a dog show that afternoon. Then, Niles turned and faced me, one leg straight and the other bent at the knee, one hand on his hip and the other against the opposite thigh. Niles looked me straight in the eyes; his were all a-twinkle with mischief and amusement, and he was smiling.

The child/woman in me, the bitch/dog in me, and me, myself, and Madelaine melted at that look. Bless the goddess! Niles's charm, his brutally handsome wide face offset by dimples and cleft chin, those green eyes, the long hair, his scent, physique, and beautiful genitalia could only have been Her gifts. From the Horned God, Niles had inherited his dark sexuality, his love of savage sex and sadistic tendencies, and his high sex drive. A highly lethal combination.

I hadn't taken my eyes off him for one second while this went through my mind. When Niles patted his thigh in the "come here" action and concurrently made the smooching noises one makes to call a

dog, I was ready for him. I sprung off the mark, and wagging my imaginary tail, trotted to him in my best doggie manner. When I reached
him, I planted my outside shoulder firmly against his leg, swung my
derriere around, and laid down with my head next to his feet. Just like
the *Cruff's* dogs had done. Niles's "aw . . ." was in a tone of voice that
said "how cute!" This prompted Leon to ask if that was what the dogs
from the show did. Niles's reply was to say, "yes," and pat me on the
head. I wagged the tail I didn't have and when he made a "sit" sound
accompanied by a gesture, I sat obediently. Then Niles used my hair
as a leash and, after seating himself comfortably, pulled me to the sofa
at his feet. He let go of my hair and laid his warm strong hand on my
head. He rested my head against his thigh and stroked my hair affec-
tionately.

Quite suddenly, Leon and Barbie went off on separate missions of
their own. Leon went into the kitchen and Barbie, up the black wrought
iron staircase to the second floor. After they had left, Niles commanded me to lie across his lap in what he hoped was an uncomfortable position. But merrily rolling along on E as I was, very little
bothered me and being laid out across his lap wasn't bothersome at
all. When Niles asked me in a rude tone if I was uncomfortable, I
sweetly replied, "No, Niles!" So he made me uncomfortable by cross-
ing his legs so my derriere protruded more and by holding my fore-
arms together at the small of my back. His first spanks were the "soft"
ones that many women, myself included, think are just a little too hard
to be "soft." But I was very aroused and didn't need a warm up so I absorbed each smack as if it were a drug I was addicted to. When Niles
started to spank me harder, I came.

Leon and Barbie rejoined Niles and me within seconds of each
other. Leon had gone to the bathroom while upstairs Barbie had properly cuffed herself. Niles continued to spank me and occasionally
dipped his fingers between my legs, making lusty animal groans of
pleasure at the wetness he found there. Then Leon ordered Barbie
over his lap. Unlike the hard, learn-to-love-the-pain Niles was giving
me, Leon spanked Barbie in a style that seemed to be long-established
between them. As Leon landed blows on Barbie's bottom, they carried
on an almost desultory conversation about the previous night's fun

and games. Barbie had taken quite a hard beating from him but her butt wasn't sore because she had taken most of the blows on her back.

After a time, Niles pushed me off him onto the floor and a minute later, Leon rid himself of Barbie the same way. Leon strode over to the dungeon door embedded in the floor, opened it and, with a hand gesture, ordered Barbie down the precipitous ladder. As soon as Leon and Barbie had cleared the ladder, Niles kicked me toward the gaping hole in the floor. I was so grateful when he went down the ladder first! High and wearing high heels, if I fell, Niles would catch me or at least cushion my fall. Fortunately no such thing happened and I breathed a sigh of relief when both feet were firmly on the floor. And there I was in the well-equipped underground chamber of a famous male dominant with the handsome, sadistic man and master of my dreams!

As far as small underground chambers go, this one was the best equipped I had seen. And cute, too. The walls and ceiling were white plaster with dark wood beams; the ceiling was very low. Not low enough that a six footer would have to stoop but low enough to interfere with an overhead flogger stroke. In one corner was a very small cell containing a child-size wooden stool and a bucket; imprisonment was behind cast iron bars. A red leather bondage table took up the whole right wall. On one wall shared by the cell was a securely mounted X-frame. An acrylic potty chair was stowed under the bondage table. Hanging from the ceiling by chains, parallel to the bondage table and just a couple of steps in front of it, was the stockade. The wrist and head holes were lined in red leather and there was a big old key hanging in its big old lock; all the better to secure you with, my dear.

A variety of hooks and eyes, clips, and chains hung from the beams and ceiling. Part of one wall was covered by whips, canes, crops, paddles, single tails, and the like, hanging from cup hooks. In the wall near the end of the bondage table was a small alcove that had shelves from end to end. The shelves were packed tight with nipple clamps and other nipple torture devices, many interesting cock-and-ball torture devices made by Leon, dildos, butt plugs, vibrators, and electro-stimulation toys. There were latex and leather hoods, wrist and ankle cuffs in leather, and standard police-issue handcuffs. The shelves were so crowded with toys that I couldn't identify some of them because they were so concealed by their neighbors. Every time I looked, I saw something new.

Niles was sitting on the bondage table and I was kneeling at his feet when Leon commanded Barbie to bend at the waist. He clipped her wrist restraints together behind her back then attached the clip to one of the chains in the ceiling. Her boobs hung down and Leon began to play with them.

Well, that was all I saw of them for quite some time. Niles searched around and found a toy he wanted to play with, namely a cane. First he sat on the bondage bench and stood me in front of him but couldn't get a good swing no matter how he sat. The wall was too close. He dragged me towards the stockade. I moaned with fake distress but I was getting excited at the thought of being caned so cruelly while restrained in a humiliating position like this one. Niles opened its maw and roughly manhandled me into it. My hair fell forward and I couldn't see much except the floor for a few feet around me. Leon left Barbie and came over to lend Niles a land with the lock. Once enclosed, both men yanked my crinoline off; no easy thing to do since it was under my tightly laced corset. But determination wins out over mere inconvenience. Soon the crinoline was at my feet and Niles ordered me to kick it aside. I stepped out of it and in one clean kick, launched it across the room. Leon returned his attention to Barbie and Niles's returned to me.

Niles began by beating me with the thin whippy cane he had in his hand. It was good, the beating was technically near-perfect but the canes I had given Niles felt better. I ate it up anyway and rocked into each stroke until he beat me so hard that I started to wiggle my sore derriere out of the line of fire. Imprisoned in the stockade, true evasive actions could not be taken. Suddenly the cane strokes stopped. After a few seconds, a dog whip landed on my derriere. I didn't like that at all. Much to the amusement of Leon and Barbie, I complained loudly about it but at least Niles stopped using it. He took up a crop and used that on me but I didn't like that much either. "Niles, please, I beg a favor. Don't use that thing on me anymore. It doesn't hurt good. Use the canes, Niles, please use the canes!" I pleaded. And Niles, the dark knight, used the cane on me right up to the moment when Leon came over. Leon had unstrung Barbie and she had gone upstairs, leaving me alone in the dungeon with the two sexy masters.

Both men stepped behind me and Niles pulled my g-string aside. His two fingers plunged into me. I was dripping and my g-string was soaked. Niles withdrew from me and Leon stepped up. Leon's fingers were much smaller than Niles's, three of Leon's fingers felt like two of Niles's. Smaller fingers or not, Leon went right for the magic spot and gave me a series of body-shaking orgasms. They removed my g-string with only slightly less trouble than the crinoline and I was ordered to kick that aside, too. I tried to aim it near the crinoline but the kick went wild.

Niles picked up the cane and continued to beat me with it, more moderately this time, while Leon fiddled with something in the corner. At a signal obviously unseen by me, since all I could see were feet through the curtain of my hair, Niles moved in front of me and Leon stepped up behind me. I heard Niles unzip his leather pants and soon saw his lovely cock enter my limited range of vision. As the hot, silky skin of his cock parted my lips, something cold and hard penetrated my labia. In tandem, Niles worked his cock down my throat as Leon worked a dildo every bit as large as Niles's cock into my quim. Fleetingly, I wished there was a dildo up my ass, filling up my last hole, which would have fulfilled yet another one of my fantasies.

Having Niles in my mouth usually consumed all of my attention but Leon was doing a good job of claiming his fair share of it. Leon was very skilled at using the dildo exactly like it was his own cock. Holding onto my hips, his own hips punished my cheeks as he pounded into me. His black jeans chaffed against me as he thrust and this aroused me more; I wanted to rock into him, to thrust back and let him ride me hard. But the stockade and Niles's cock in my mouth made my motion very limited. Sensing that Leon now held more of my attention than Niles did, Niles backed off and began to beat me in the face with his cock. I trailed my mouth after it, trying to recapture it and fill my hungry face hole with it.

"You know, Leon, I've had this slut for a while now and I know she's a greedy little bitch, but I don't know just how greedy she is." On the "yeah?" of Leon's "Oh, yeah?" each man slammed into their respective hole harder and deeper than before. Impaled front and back by their cocks, I resigned myself to their pleasure and mine. Every couple of minutes a hand would probe me for wetness. I could tell Niles's touch from Leon's; both touched me roughly but Niles's fingers were so much bigger than Leon's that it was easy to tell them apart. Neither owner of the fingers was disappointed that when withdrawn, the fingers came out slick with my juices. The slimy fingers were wiped off on my back, cheeks, thighs, whatever was in easy reach. They laughed at how much I came.

Niles stepped away from Leon and I while Leon worked the dildo deeper and deeper into me. Leon was so skilled with the dildo that he found the magic spot with it, and once having found it, took great pleasure in hitting it often. Each time I came, I took a little more of the dildo into me, so abandoning myself to it that I began to use my muscles to help him get more in. Weak from coming, I was glad of the stockade holding me up. Especially when Niles rammed his cock back down my throat. Immediately Niles began to search out the soft spot in the back of my throat, not caring how much or how often I gagged or gasped for air between savage thrusts. His sadism inflamed each time he hit the spot and I would heave from deep down in my belly. The heave would force Leon's dildo out of me and Leon would have to work it back into poor little me.

The two of them fucked me for a long lovely time and I gloried in their attentions. I wanted to show one of them my love of what they were doing to me and for me but all I could move was my feet. Balancing on one foot, I extended the other one back and rubbed it tenderly on Leon's leg. "What's this? She's rubbing her foot on me leg!" Leon said to Niles. "Oh, that means she likes it," responded Niles, a chuckle in his voice. "Does she? Good!" came the reply from behind me, accompanied by a few special pumps. Suddenly Niles began to fuck my face very hard, the kind of "hard" that ultimately led to vomiting. When Niles start to pump me like that, Leon sat down on the bondage table and deprived me of the warmth and excitement of his body but, thank the goddess, not of the dildo. Leon manipulated it in a most creative way and I loved having it inside of me.

All this time, Niles was still fucking my face like it was just another hole and my heaving turned to near-vomiting. Snot was running down my face and onto Niles's cock, my arms were tingling from their imprisonment but still I didn't pull away. It never crossed my mind to say my word. My mouth filled with vomit and I kept swallowing back down every horrible mouthful that came up, some so far up as to explode around Niles's cock. He knew I was puking up and swallowing it down and it brought out the beast in him. After one particularly brutal and well placed thrust which I almost wasn't able to swallow back down, I wrenched my head free and said, "Niles, I'm drowning. May I please have a tissue?" They laughed but Niles got the tissue and wiped my face with it, even holding it to my nose so I could "blow" on command. Sighing with relief and gasping with lust, I took many deep and much needed breaths. I had, with my silly request, bought myself the small respite I needed to take more of this deliciously dirty desirable misuse. Niles was right; I was a very greedy little bitch.

Then Niles said, "No pleasure for you! Just open your mouth so I can continue where I left off!" Immediately my jaw dropped open and I positioned my tongue over my bottom teeth to protect his shaft from them. With a lust-filled growl, he said. "Oh fuck! Oh hell! Look at her, just look at her!" He grabbed my head in his massive hands and positioned it so that my mouth was aligned with his cock like a cunt. Then he drove his cock into my mouth and down my throat. Leon was seated on the bondage table, still manipulating the dildo with such expertise that his hand was wet from my come. Almost roaring, Niles tightened his grip on my head and brutally forced his cock so far down my throat that he cut off my breathing. I could get no air through my nostrils and none through my mouth. I held still for as long as I could. Leon worked the dildo in deeper. Although I was lightheaded from lack of air, I began to struggle against the double invasion.

Resistance, of course, was futile. More snot exploded from my nose and bile filled my mouth. But most humiliatingly of all, the heave caused two small farts to be forced out of my butt, which was only a few inches from Leon's face. I was happy that my hair covered the red stain of shame creeping up my neck to my face when both men laughed. My farts must have been a clarion call because they both withdrew from me at the same time. With some help with the lock from Leon, Niles freed me from the stockade. Taking advantage that my hair was already flung forward and easy to grab, he gathered it tight in his hand and forced me to my knees. He tried to walk me across the floor like a dog but my upper arms were numb and I fell forward. Undaunted, Niles simply dragged me across the floor to the bondage table caveman style until I was at Leon's feet. He used my hair to wrangle me into place between Leon's open knees. Leon unzipped his pants and took out his cock.

I hardly needed Niles's rough hand "forcing" my head down on Leon. Leon had a long limber one with a Prince Albert. I fell on it, remembering all the pleasure Leon had given me. Niles started to rough things up but thankfully, I felt Leon motion Niles away. I loved all the face fucking but it was nice to give head my way for a change. I was ready to try a little tenderness. And, I was sure that if I did something Leon didn't like, Leon himself would let me know. I sucked Leon, made love to his cock, gave him a blow job (we girls understand the differences among these actions), played with his ring, licked and worked his clean shaven balls to my heart's content. Leon's gentle hands lifted my head and he thanked me. Then he climbed over me, handed me back over to Niles, and went up the ladder.

From behind me, Niles swung into Leon's place and forced my head down on his cock. He was enormous and rock hard from watching me suck Leon. It didn't take him long. Several hard thrusts and soon I felt his hand on the back of my head. I turned into a growling bitch, gnawing on his cock, making myself gag on it. Niles groaned as my mouth worked him hard. After a couple of more hard thrusts, Niles came in my mouth. Making animal noises, like a dog with a bone, I swallowed it down, sated. After a few minutes had passed, Niles announced to me that we would be spending the night at Leon's, in the middle room upstairs. I went up the ladder first and Niles sprinted up behind me. A few short steps across the reception room and we were tiptoeing up the spiral staircase to the guest room with its dark blue moon and stars motif duvet, pillow cases, and curtains. An otherworldly setting for a night that had been spent off-world. I fell asleep as I usually did, inhaling Niles's pheromones as I drifted off.

THIRTY-THREE

Everyone slept late the next day although Leon and Barbie were up long before Niles and me. About midafternoon the delicious smell of coffee woke us up and we followed its enticing aroma downstairs to the kitchen like we were being led by the nose. Leon and Barbie were in the reception room sipping their fresh brew when Niles and I staggered down the spiral staircase. They took one look at us and started laughing. All I was wearing was my coat because I had no clothes other than the outfit I had on last night and Niles was in his sexy underwear and his black turtleneck and his socks. We borrowed toiletries then Niles went into the reception room while I brought coffee for two, twice. Niles said he was hungry and Leon and Barbie shook their heads ruefully; there wasn't even that old standby, eggs, in the house. Besides bread, there was nothing to eat except peanut butter and jelly.

If that was all there was, then that was what I would make. As I rooted through the cabinets looking for the peanut butter, I came across some candy, called "Maltpleasers" (malt powder covered by chocolate; we have them here too but call them "Malt Balls"), and a tin of "crisps," the British word for potato chips. I had all I needed to present Niles with a cute, if not healthy, meal. I made him two sandwiches, cut in points, and arranged the candies and crisps between the four pieces of PB&J. I presented it to him like it was rack of lamb or Duck l'Orange and he accepted it with the same grace. Leon said to Barbie, "when I want a snack, why doesn't mine look like that?" I was a little embarrassed. It hadn't been my intention to show Barbie up but she seemed to take it that way.

I cleared away Niles's plate and when I returned to the reception room, Leon told Barbie to lend me something to wear, pointing out that I couldn't sit around in my coat all day. She returned with a drop-over-the-head mini-dress, that although too big, was a big improvement over the coat. It was cute and sexy and I went upstairs to get my shoes. Of course, I combed my hair and put on makeup; there was no reason not to look sexy and looking sexy is fun. Niles told me to bring him his leather pants and his boots so I brought them down to him. As he zipped them up, he turned to me smiling and showed me he had a hard on. There was that twinkle in his eyes that I knew was the promise of more fun, games, rough sex, and submissive/masochistic limits to test and push and finally, break down. I was tingling with anticipation but the men seemed to be in no hurry. They sat and chatted together as if Barbie and I weren't there, until they needed something: tea, coffee, cigarettes, the hash tray. After the mission had been completed, we returned to our respective spots on the floor at the feet of our masters.

I don't know how long the men sat and talked. I do know that Barbie and I dozed off occasionally and were awoken by laughter or by a gentle shake when a service was required, usually fresh tea or coffee. Then we'd doze off again. Living in a timeless environment with dark heavy curtains, no clocks to be seen, no one wearing a watch, not even a church bell in the distance by which to gauge the time, life became a dream. Time was nonlinear, a loop, and if I had to be in a loop, I liked the one I was in. Just the two masters, and their slave girls, the music, the dim lights, the promise and threat of what lay beneath the dungeon door concealed by the carpet and mind-altering drugs to enhance the experience for one and all. But now the men were hungry for dinner so instead of sex and drugs, or peanut butter and jelly sandwiches, we had Indian food delivered. It was delicious; London has the best Indian cuisine I have tasted. And no one had to be bothered cooking.

We lounged around in the reception room, smoking joints and cigarettes, burping (which they considered hilarious), and after a lovely but indeterminable amount of time, the E was passed around. Barbie and I were sent to change our clothes. I didn't have much of a selection but I had worn so many things the night before that I was able to make an outfit using just the lace top, lace topped thigh highs, and my pumps. Barbie was downstairs already, wearing only a corset, stockings, and of course, pumps. Authoritatively, Leon strode across the room and opened the trap door to the oubliette. Barbie, Niles, and I went down the steep ladder and lastly, Leon. He gave the trap door a deliberately hard slam, as if sealing our fate. At its tone of finality, I felt a lightness of being and a white hot surge of anticipation, accompanied by a spurt of wetness.

It was a little awkward at first. Barbie sat on one end of the bondage table, Leon was in the middle, and Niles sat on the other end. There was no room there for me to sit so I knelt on the floor at Niles's feet. He gestured that I was to kneel between him and Leon so I moved as instructed. Once I was settled back on my heels, Niles pulled me forward into an upright kneeling position with my torso on the table and kicked my legs open. Roughly, he crushed me against his thigh and held my head behind his back with a strong arm. To my left was Leon and I was pressed up against him too, seated were he was. I found his nearness to be comforting and exciting as well as humiliating, delightfully so. Niles spanked me on my sore buttocks and on my quim. Each time he slapped me there, I came. When he slapped my anus, I tried not to cry out in pain but I couldn't help myself.

There was more than just turning the physical pain into pleasure in play in this little scene. There was the fulfillment of a longtime fantasy: to be on exhibit as a pleasure slave to a cruel handsome master, the humiliation of coming so frequently and violently in front a man I hardly knew and finally, the emotional impact that this man knew something so intimate about me, namely that anal pain made me come. Involuntarily, I wrapped my arm around Leon's calf and stroked it. When Niles next slapped me there, I clung to Leon's leg passionately and whimpered in agony at the ecstasy of it all. Niles stopped beating me and I went delirious with desire for more but before I could express this in any way, I felt Leon's fingers between my legs. In contrast to the hard anal slapping I had taken, Leon's fingers were almost gentle as he explored my folds and furrows. I had been coming so furiously that my thighs were smeared and sticky. When Leon's fingers met with this ooze, he said "Oh, fuck, yeah! I can see why you like this one." Niles laughed.

Barbie left; maybe of her own volition or maybe at some signal from Leon. For the second night in a row, I was left alone with the two men. Even I find it hard to describe the head space I was in. I was elated that Niles could get me into such a deep space by his smell, a look, a growl, even a sniff. I was tingling with anticipation and expectations but content to leave myself in Niles's hands and not really care. He would do what he would do; I would do as he wanted. I was fearful yet thrilled by the fear. I was overjoyed to be living out these fantasies, and more importantly, being with someone so skillful that the enactment was better than the fantasy itself. Niles brought out the masochistic side of me I had journeyed here to discover and embrace and my new love of pain, when incorporated with my submissive desires, imparted a new darkness, a new aspect, a new burning fire to decades-old fantasies.

Niles stood me in the middle of the floor, my derriere facing Leon. Niles ordered me to spread my legs about three feet apart, then kicked them open a little wider. He commanded me to brace my hands on my knees but to keep my back at a forty-five-degree angle. Then he told me to bend my elbows and see how close I could get my body to my thighs. I could almost rest my torso on them. A pleased "uh-huh" came from him. Then I waited for him in that position as he tested several of Leon's canes while Leon remarked about this cane or that. As each cane whipped through the air, making that whooshing sound I had come to love and fear, I whimpered in lust and fear. I begged Niles "No, please" in a hoarse voice that really said, "hurry up!" Smiling, Niles showed me the cane he had selected; impulsively, I kissed it. He stepped around me, told me to lock my elbows, then he let fly at my cheeks, still red, striped and sore from the previous nights.

The first stroke was hard enough to make me fling my head back to help absorb the pain. When I flung my head, my long silky hair fanned out and landed like a gentle flogger on my back. Niles muttered, "Oh, fuck, bloody hell," but in spite of the crass words themselves, his tone was like a caress filled with lust and appreciation. He thought I was beautiful then and I knew it. He hit me again, harder this time. My knees buckled slightly but I held position. If my knees buckled on just the second stroke, I knew this caning was going to push me to the brink. He waited for me to recover before cracking the cane across my ass again. I was more prepared for the third stroke, although it was harder than the second. The more I took, the harder Niles caned me,

giving my ass several more increasingly harder strokes with less re-
covery time in between.

A very savage blow caused me to fall forward. I had to brace my
palms on the floor to support myself but I hadn't closed my legs.
"Stay!" came Niles's voice from above and I froze in that awkward and
exposed position. I hadn't forgotten about Leon watching us and I
doubt Niles had either; I was sure some of this was for Leon's benefit.
Niles stood directly behind me. In the new position it was very easy
and enticing to cane my quim and I felt myself blush with shame at
how much I wanted him to. Niles, my pagan angel, began to do just
that. I screamed in pain and humiliation each time the cane hit my clit
and made me come. After one stroke, the final one, which landed directly on the bone and bit into my lips cruelly, I curled up in a little
ball on the floor, protecting myself. In a flash, Niles was in front of me
and helped me up. Sobbing softly, I clung to his strong neck; my arms
looked delicate and bird-boned compared to his large head and broad
shoulders. His strong arms encircled me and supported me.

Putting my lips to his ear, I begged him to stop. Very quietly, so quietly that maybe Leon didn't even hear, Niles whispered back in a gentle voice, "What do you say?" I held him closer for a few more seconds
and took a deep breath. I stepped back from him and looked into his
eyes. Making my expression seductively submissive. I resumed my
original position in the center of the floor. I held his eyes in mine as I
did this, an invitation for him to pick up where he left off. He muttered
"bloody hell" as he stepped behind me then flailed the cane against
my quim. I took the first stroke, and the second, but we both knew
that the third stroke would be the last. I didn't flinch when he drew his
arm back and he didn't pull the stroke. Burning pain; I almost collapsed. Before I could fall, Niles put his arm around me and held me
up, held me to him. His other hand pushed the hair back from my face
and stroked it. All the while Niles was murmuring "good girl" and
other endearments and planting little kisses on me. Finally, I regained
my balance.

His tenderness lasted just long enough for me to recover then Niles
stripped me of my lace top. He commanded me to stretch my arms

over my head and grab the low beam in the ceiling. Because he wanted my feet apart, even in my heels, I had to stand on tip-toe to do this. Next, he ordered me to lean my head back as far as it would go. Saying "uh-huh" as he walked around me, he made sure all my hair flowed down my back, had me arch my back more, and made little adjustments in my stance until he was satisfied. I hadn't forgotten Leon, not at all. I could feel his eyes on me and the heat of his gaze incited me further.

When the cane landed squarely across my breasts, it took a lot of willpower to remain in position. Niles stepped to my right, the best spot for freedom of movement and a good swing. He hit me slowly and gave me enough time between each stroke to allow me to scream and take a deep breath before landing the next blow. My left breast, being a little larger than the right one, took most of the beating but I knew both my breasts would be bruised and welted from it. In my mind, the marks and welts became badges of honor, badges of submission, markers of another spin down the spiral. In love with this thought, I took several more blows, many more than I thought I could take; determined to fulfill the sadistic desires of my brutal, sexy, handsome master. One extremely hard stroke landed on my nipple and I screamed "Niles!' in genuine agony. I covered my breasts with my hands for a minute, my head down, my hair covering my face, and made sexy sobbing sounds but I would not say "that" word.

I got back into position, arching my back and standing on tip-toe to grab a hold of the beam. Once I was in position, I looked deeply into his glinting green eyes and when I said his name, my voice was a caress. Quickly he stepped in front of me. But instead of him bringing the cane down on my breasts, he placed it carefully between my legs and brought it up in a hard, fast stroke. It landed squarely on my clit and bone, biting into my long pink labia on its way. I broke position and flung my arms around his neck and clung to him, my savage master. I whispered in his ear and pleaded with him to stop, please stop. This time when he whispered back "What do you say, Madelaine?" I hung my head and in a very small voice said, "Mercy, Niles, mercy."

And it was over. He hugged me and kissed me then led me over to the bondage table, where the smiling Leon was still seated. Leon moved to the far end and Niles sat down on the near. Before I could assume the kneeling position at Niles's feet, he patted the table next to him. As I went to sit, he said in a matter-of-fact tone, "no, Madelaine, lie face up, your head against my thigh." I felt the now familiar knot in my stomach when he said this. Looking at the amount of space left on the table, only my head and back would fit. And I doubted that Niles's intent was for me to drape my legs over Leon's lap. The only place for my legs was close to my body, which exposed everything to Leon. Closing my mind to every inhibition that may have stopped me from obeying in the past, I did as Niles commanded. And found myself in yet another new place.

Although this was a favorite fantasy of mine, it almost bordered on being a bathtub fantasy, the kind you think about when you are masturbating and need heavier or more severe fantasies than when you are not flying solo. However, they may not be fantasies that you want to live out. Suddenly, this one was livable.

Leon and Niles talked over my head as I settled myself into position. I had to bend my neck to fit my body in the remaining space. Next I bent my knees and drew them toward my chest but after just a few seconds like that I found I was more comfortable holding my ankles in my hands. I closed my eyes and reduced the men's voices to white noise while I floated on E and sex and smells. A voice said, "Go ahead;" I recognized it as Niles's. "My pleasure," came Leon's response. I felt firm yet gentle fingers slide into me and had a strong orgasm. Leon's fingers didn't seem as interested in hurting me as they did in wanting to figure out what made me come. It had to hurt *and* make me come. Leon believed that giving his slave frequent orgasms, either hurtfully or pleasurably, helped to enforce his control over her. He enslaved her with sex and how good it felt to be so free and come so much.

Leon's favorite method of enslavement was to get his hand inside the slave's quim. He didn't care if it took him two years to stretch her enough to take him; he worked her daily. She began to crave those smashing, shattering orgasms; so much so that when he didn't give them to her, she begged him to do it. Little by little, his control over her was strengthened and new levels of control could be implemented.

He ran his fingers in my folds and furrows and found them dripping and come smeared my thighs. Leon dipped three fingers into me and said to Niles, "Slimy little thing, isn't she?" Niles chuckled affirmatively. I came when Leon said those words. "Madelaine, open your eyes!" Niles ordered, "And look at the ceiling." With great effort I opened my eyes and looked at the ceiling. But the two men were in my sight line and I could see their faces. The look on Leon's didn't change at all when he pushed three fingers back in me and began to touch me inside. It only changed when he found a high pain or high pleasure spot. When he found one he would say "ah-huh" and memorize its location. I was moaning his name and breathlessly saying words of encouragement and pleasure when Leon told me that the only word/sound I was allowed to make was my "word." Otherwise, I was only to moan and groan like a bitch in heat.

I wallowed in the feel of Leon's fingers inside of me and found myself peeking at him whenever I thought he wouldn't notice. Abruptly he pulled his fingers out and I thought I was "caught" but all Leon said to Niles was, "Good cunt, gushes a lot. Small hole, though. Good for fucking but it'd probably take me three years to get me hand in there without rippin' her." Both of them laughed crudely at that and I tried to concentrate on the ceiling and become the willing vessel they wanted me to be. Leon felt me relax against him and correctly interpreted this as a signal for more. He entered me with his thumb and explored it briefly, wiping some of my girl-jam onto my anus. He took his thumb out but before I could protest its loss, I felt the simultaneous entry of two fingers up my quim and a thumb up my anus. The sensation was, as usual, exquisite and I growled with mindless desire as I squirmed on Leon's fingers.

When Niles said "she likes that," I came. When Leon responded, "I know," I came. "Did she come?" asked Niles. "Yeah, twice," Leon said, "once for you and once for me. Now she just came again. Wonder who that one was for?" I moaned in delighted humiliation as the knot of wantonness unwound in my belly. I caught Niles gaze and held it, then I let go of my ankles, reached down, and spread my cheeks. Niles's eyes burned as he watched me spread myself for Leon. Suddenly, the thumb inside my anus was no longer a gentle wand but had turned into something hard, like flexible steel. It drove deeper into me and still I held my cheeks open. It did things to hurt me, this thumb, things I can't describe to you because I don't know how he moved it to hurt me so. But hurt me he did, and each time after I had accepted an especially cruel pain, Leon rewarded me with a great shuddering orgasm. After the first orgasm, my hands flopped loosely at my sides and I curved my back so that I didn't need to hold my ankles to be in the maximum exposure position.

After Leon gave me one last orgasm, he withdrew his fingers, bade Niles and me good night and headed up the ladder. Niles hugged me and cuddled me and asked me solicitously if I was all right. I assured him I was fine, just fine, and his eyes were warm when he smiled at me. We sat there for several minutes in sated silence, my head in his lap, my legs open on the table. Then Niles suggested we go upstairs. He went up first, climbing the perilous ladder with great ease. I followed him, teetering on my high heels and clutching my lace top in one hand. As soon as I could, I tossed it up into the reception room to free both hands for the ascent. Unable to climb straight up that horrible excuse of a ladder gracefully and "appear" in the reception room like the queen of the damned rising from the grave, I scrambled into the reception room on my hands and knees.

Upon my ungainly arrival in the reception room I found Niles already comfortably seated on the love seat and Leon and Barbie on the other sofa. Instead of walking upright to Niles, I walked on all fours, doggie-style, giggling at my silliness and glowing under his smile. Barbie left the room briefly and I took the opportunity to tell Leon that I had enjoyed playing with him. Leon responded by saying that I was very sweet and that he liked my personality. Thrilled by Leon's praise, I rubbed my head on Niles's leg. I was so happy; happy for myself, happy to have been a credit to Niles, and happy to have pleased Leon. Not to be left out, Niles, with a little prompting from me (was I a good girl? did I please you?) said that I had been a pleasure, very nice to be around, excellent in fact and that I was one good little nurse, too.

Then Niles related in some detail to Leon and Barbie what good care I had been taking of him. He told them about the cooking, cleaning, shopping, laundry and how I conspired to keep him lounging around all the time. He said he was getting spoiled by my service; all he had to do was call out what he wanted and it would appear. Then Niles made a joke about a newspaper headline: MAN FOUND STARVED ON SOFA IN MAIDA VALE, which, he said, would be him after I left. Leon and Barbie laughed, Leon looked at me with a new appreciation. I thought I would burst with happiness. I had never left like this before in my life.

We sat for a few minutes then Barbie came in and told us what time it was. We were very surprised at the lateness of the hour; even if we left right away, it would be after dawn before we reached Niles's place in Maida Vale. Although Niles was on the mend, he looked very drained and the long hard ride, especially after our sexual acrobatics, would have been tough on him. Seeing this, Leon invited us to spend another night under the moon and stars in the guest room. Niles accepted immediately and I was glad. Up the spiral staircase we went, and once in the out-in-space room, I took my position in the crook of Niles's shoulder.

But sleep eluded me. I snuggled closer to Niles and in my mind, I relived the night. Do I need to tell you that I came violently with each stroke of the master's cane? Do I need to write that my come smeared my thighs and dribbled down my leg? That every time Niles or Leon's hand touched my quim, the hand came away slick with girl-jam? That I had no sense of time? That I didn't care where I was as long as I was with Niles? Or that the enactment of my fantasies was more magical than the original fantasies? I thanked the goddess for guiding me to London where I met Niles, the sadist and satyr, and the fulfiller of dreams. I watched dawn break on the moon and stars then fell asleep.

THIRTY-FOUR

Awaking under the moon and stars the next morning, I decided that at some time I would like Niles to deliver me to Leon as a "gift" for a day. I knew Niles would do it; after all, he had set up that rape for Charmaine! I laughed at this thought—so unlike the old me—and woke up Niles. He asked what I was laughing at and I told him.

Niles expressed great interest in this idea; saying that he had been wanting to get Barbie alone for quite a while now. Since Leon had expressed interest in me, there was a very good possibility that a "swap" could be arranged on my next visit. I laughed and smiled but I knew that if the opportunity to "get Barbie alone" arose before my next visit, he would jump on it and her. The thought made me sad but I brushed it away and tried to think no more about it.

Leon and Barbie were already up and dressed when Niles and I went downstairs. It was about one in the afternoon, a bright sun-shiny day. We had coffee and Barbie made Niles and Leon an eggs on toast breakfast, the eggs done British-style, which means fried in lard. Although I was hungry too, I declined the offer of eggs fried in pig fat; my stomach just wasn't ready for something so greasy that tasted so yuck. After breakfast, we smoked a couple of spliffs and lounged around for a bit. We had been high on E for what seemed to be days and the relaxing effect of the hash was fabulous. Niles suggested that it was time to go and we went upstairs and dressed.

Niles looked relatively normal but I looked very silly in the corset outfit, especially since when I put my coat on, the wide skirt of the crinoline made the coat stick out ridiculously. And, because I had lost my g-string, my private parts were quite cold. We said our good-byes, the long, polite British kind. Which meant we were there another hour. As we made our final good-byes, I whispered heartfelt thanks into Leon's ear as we hugged and I expressed the hope that we could do it again sometime. We kissed all around then headed out to the car for the ride back to Niles's. My corset was killing me—for some silly reason I had laced it too tightly—and I had to put the seat in the laying down position to relieve the pressure. Thankfully the ride home took less time than it did to get there.

As soon as we had our coats off, Niles released me from the confines of the corset and I was able to draw deep breaths at last. We changed into more appropriate clothes for lounging around the house then I went off to the kitchen to see what I could rustle up for dinner later on. There was plenty of food and all I had to do was decide what to cook. Satisfied, I joined Niles in the reception room and brought tea. My prince was reclining comfortably on the sofa and I took up my position on the floor at his feet. We dozed on and off for the rest of the afternoon and into the early evening. Niles was asleep and I was gazing upon his strong handsome face when I finally faced the fact that I would be leaving in a day or two. Facing up to that made me feel like I had just been punched in the stomach, hard. I pushed the feeling away and adamantly told myself not to think about it and to enjoy whatever time was left to us.

When Niles woke up, he said he was hungry. I proceeded to go through a "menu of dinner possibilities" but Niles said not to cook and that he'd like a couple of sandwiches instead. I hurried off to the kitchen to do his bidding, pleased to serve him and to act like the "good little nurse" he had said I was. Although they were only sandwiches, I arranged them on the plate with some grapes and chocolate-covered cookies and made them look appetizing. As always, Niles was appreciative of my efforts and ate every last bite. I left him to roll us a spliff or two while I cleaned up. When I returned, he was already smoking one and gestured me to light up the other one. I was delighted when he moved his legs just enough for me to sit on the sofa and invited me to join him.

All of this took longer than it seemed and at two a.m., when Niles suggested that we go lie in bed, I readily agreed. As if I needed coaxing to lie in bed with Niles! Although with my care and devoted service, he felt much better, I could see the fatigue in his face and his slow, bow-legged walk told me he needed rest. After we were tucked in and I was nestled in the crook of his shoulder, his long, strong arm encircled me. I sighed and melted at his touch and thought about how much I would miss laying with him like this each night. I kissed him and snuggled in closer. I didn't care that we weren't going to play that night. Niles had been wonderful: wonderful to me, wonderful at reading my mind, and brilliant at fulfilling my fantasies. He put out the light and fell asleep right away. I fell asleep much later; spending the time gazing upon his sleeping face and form, gently running my hands over his lean hairless body, and reliving and reveling in the experiences I had had with him.

I thanked the goddess for sending me a man whose proclivities ran the gamut from romantic to bestial. I thanked her for sending me a pagan god of sex whose brute passion brought out the most primal sexual side of me. If it wouldn't have woken him up, I would have sucked his cock.

THIRTY-FIVE

The first thought that crossed my mind when I woke up today was that I would be leaving tomorrow at about this time. This was to be my last twenty four hours with Niles for about three months. I wanted to savor every last moment with him and soak up his essence; I wanted to hoard it for the long days and nights ahead without him, my horned god of the wood, Kernonous; my wild man of the forest, Enkidu; my first and only master, Monsieur le Marquis. He brought out the sexual goddess, the bitch-slut in heat, and the masochist in me and I would miss them as much as I would miss him. I looked at his face, still strong and manly in sleep, and sighed at having to leave him. I was very concerned about how he would fend for himself after I was gone. Another week of my ministrations would do him good. One word from him and I would have stayed but he didn't offer and I was too shy to ask.

I curled up next to him and in seconds the warmth of his arm enveloped me. I sighed deeply and whispered, "Oh, Niles!" in a voice heavy with emotion. Suddenly I was overwhelmed by my feelings. A stray tear ran down my cheek onto his chest, my nose got stuffy in sympathy, and I sniffled. I was choking with emotion and I had to get a grip on myself. "No, you will not cry!" I silently commanded myself. "No tears! Only happy faces! You will *not* let him see you cry!" Miraculously, thankfully, these silent commands worked. I vowed to do everything in my power to make the most of these final hours with Niles, to make them memorable ones for both of us. I wanted to live on in his memories, as he would live on in mine, until the next time we were together. When Niles awoke, it was to a bright smile and a warm hug, followed by a lovely cock-sucking, then breakfast in bed.

As I prepared Niles's French toast with a dash of vanilla, I noticed that the food supply was running low. I decided to fill the fridge before I left. When Niles took his nap, I would go on an expedition to the supermarket and stock the kitchen. Doing that would serve multiple purposes: obviously, he wouldn't starve or have to shop after I left. And, every time he opened the fridge, he would think of me. Pleased with this plan, I served him his breakfast and sat with him making small talk while he ate. After I removed the tray I set up the reception room for him and helped him into his robe and slippers. I don't know why I loved those worn old slippers of his but I did. Somehow Niles had managed to impart his personal style to them and they were as sexy on him as the most elaborately ruffled shirt. I gave them a sniff before I put them on him and was not disappointed or surprised to find them odorless. The goddess had reserved his scent for his sexualtiy, not his feet.

We moved into the reception room. I settled Niles into his spot on the sofa then got into my spot on the floor. Although the silence was comfortable, I wanted to fill it with words of gratitude for this fairy tale interlude, with fantasies for the future, and a million other things. There was so much I wanted to say to him but I couldn't find the words to express myself. My head was so full of thoughts I wanted to share with him about what I had discovered about myself, and ideas and dreams that I wanted to confide in him, that I ended up saying almost nothing at all. I quietly asked him if, after I had gone, we could still talk on the phone and, you know, "play our games together." He smiled at me, all green eyes and dimples surrounding his strong nose, and said, "of course." I grabbed his hand and kissed it, loving its delicate yet strong shape then laid my cheek in his palm. My heart was in my eyes when I thanked him.

After a couple of hours had passed, Niles said he was going to rest in bed. I helped him into bed and did quiet chores; when I looked in on him half an hour later, he was sleeping. This was my chance to stock the fridge so I wasn't deprived of even one minute of his company. I called the car service and shot off to the supermarket. Disdaining anything he could get locally or was lightweight, I loaded the cart with steaks, chicken, ham steaks, pork chops, veal chops, and cold cuts, yogurt and creme caramel, cartons of juice, bags of sugar, bottles of soda, potatoes, and staples like tea, eggs, milk, and bread. Although I raced through the supermarket like I was in one of those old game shows then took a car service home, Niles was in his robe and slippers and up and about when I got back. At first he wondered where I had gone but he rightly suspected what I was up to. When he heard the car pull up, he looked out the window and saw me arrive with a couple of dozen bags packed with groceries. His surprise and delight showed in his face and his thanks was heartfelt. He sat on the stool in the kitchen and smiled as I unpacked the bags. He made me feel like I had given him the greatest gift in the world.

Seeing all that food made him hungry. First, I accompanied him into the reception room, put on the music, and gave him the hash tray. I wanted to share a spliff with him while I thought about what to serve for dinner. His rolling technique never ceased to fascinate me and I watched avidly as his beautiful fingers twisted up a perfect, cigarette-shaped joint. We talked about cooking as we smoked and soon visions of baked breaded veal chops, mashed potatoes and gravy, and petit peas and diced carrots danced in my head. The creme caramel would be a sweet and exotic finale for a hearty, home-style meal. Inspired, I headed off to the kitchen and emerged an hour later with a laden tray. Niles's "mmm, looks good . . ." was confirmed when upon tasting it, mouth filled, he nodded his head up and down and "mmm"ed again. I went back to the kitchen for my own plate. He was right, it was good. I realized how much I was going to miss him and miss doing all of this and I crushed the thought.

Niles thanked me again when I cleared the plates away. With my eyes downcast like a good slave, my coy reply was "I am so happy to be of service to you, my lord." His eyes started to twinkle and when he smiled, there were those devastating dimples again. I dropped off the dishes and I went to find something sexy to wear. We were going to have a party! Niles was well rested, fed, and perky; I knew from the twinkle in his eyes. I rooted through my suitcase but couldn't find anything I really wanted to wear so I put on black thigh high stockings, black satin opera gloves, a PVC waist cincher and the "Niles pumps." Lots of black eye make-up and several coats of red lipstick completed my "outfit." I liked it; it covered sexy parts but left my genitalia and breasts exposed. I was decorated, not dressed. And the make-up and lipstick would look so lovely when smeared or running down my face. I walked into the reception room with a coy wantonness and knelt before the master with my knees open and eyes cast down.

I could feel his eyes on me, burning into me as they raked me up and down. With an intake of breath, his hand shot out and grabbed my breast. From the depths of the delightful shadowland in my mind, I was aroused before I entered the room. My whole body trembled at just this one touch and I gasped aloud in pleasure. When he told me to prepare the room as he had done on previous nights, I hurried to do his bidding. I gathered up duvets and pillows, broke out the E we had gotten from Leon, turned up the heater and turned down the lights, brought in snacks, whiskey, soda, extra ashtrays, the toys just in case he wanted to play with them, everything I could think of. I performed these errands as sexily and submissively as I could, yet with pride in what I was doing under his glittering green eyes. Once the door was closed and our pleasure planet came into orbit, I didn't want to leave it unless I absolutely had to. If I could have brought the toilet bowl in there, I would have.

When the floor was a white cloud of pillows and duvets, the heater was glowing and radiating its warmth, and everything was to Niles's satisfaction, he rose majestically and looked down at me as I knelt near his feet. As he stood his robe fell open. His beautiful genitals were inches from my face and I moaned with pleasure at seeing them. He let me eat them up with my eyes for a few seconds then he deliberately closed and tied his robe. I whimpered at being deprived of even the mere sight of them but he ignored my wordless pleas. He laid down next to my kneeling figure. "Obey me, Madelaine. Open your mouth." I opened my mouth the way he had taught me to receive a face fucking. To my surprise, he reached for the hash tray and from it, took two hits of E from the little plastic bag. Then he leisurely uncapped the soda bottle. As he did these things, a knot of lust formed in my stomach. A new thought crossed my mind, one that was a new road to heightened pleasure.

In an instant, he became the Marquis and I was one of his prostitutes. I knew the Marquis's taste in pleasure and shared it. I wanted him to drug me, I enjoyed our passions more when drugged. And for him it was double pleasure: it pleased him to give me the drugs because he wanted complete control of me and because he got better use of me when I was high. The drug would remove all ego. Only raw and primal sexual desires, desires that were masochistic, submissive, humiliating, degrading, would remain. The god of pain and desire placed two hits of E on his tongue. I licked one of them off then he handed me the soda bottle. He picked up his whiskey. We locked eyes and made a small wordless toast to each other. Then we swallowed our drugs.

Our eyes still locked, Niles opened his robe and his lovely cock sprang free. I held his eyes in mine as I lowered my head and opened my mouth. He tasted and smelled so good, so seductively feral, that soon I was moaning as I sucked him. I eased my head down on his shaft, caressing him with my tongue and lips, taking more of him into my mouth with each pump of my head. He enjoyed this and allowed me to continue, knowing I loved it. Suddenly, his hands were in my hair and holding my head, forcing it down onto his ever-growing spear. I swallowed as much as I could, still thinking I was giving him "head." But as he got rougher and rougher, I realized that my blow job had turned into a face-fucking. I struggled for air when his knob cut off my breathing and felt him grow even harder when I fought against him.

Savagely, he used my hair to pull my head up. Saliva was dripping from my open mouth, my lipstick was smeared, and the black eye makeup had started to run. I saw the fire dance in his eyes when he beheld the mess on my face and, using my hair, he shook my head hard. Then he said to me in that cold, sneering tone, the tone that the brute within him spoke in, "So, do you still think you're giving me head? Do you? Huh? Huh?" Each "huh" was punctuated by one deep hard thrust down my throat, and a second later, followed by a gag and heave from me. "Open your mouth," Niles sneered crudely, "so I can put that hole to its one pleasurable use!" He said the last three words with a pause between each one, a pause filled in by a deep thrust. The third and final thrust was the deepest, most searching, and Niles held my head down cruelly as I struggled for air.

A second before I vomited, Niles let my head go. I fell against his body gasping for air, my face still very close to his cock and balls. The air was heavily with the smell of sex and I filled my starved lungs with it. With a guttural groan, his hands were back on my head and positioning it over his cock. He smacked my face with his cock a few times before letting it enter my saliva dripping mouth. I was always so hungry for him. I opened my mouth as wide as I could, relaxed my jaw, and placed my tongue over my teeth to protect his cock from their sharp edges. To show him I loved the way he rough-handled me, I gave his cock just the barest caress but it shot through him like electricity. Growling, "Oh, hell, oh, fuck yes . . ." Niles slammed into my mouth and down my throat with renewed lust. Just the sound of his desire for me made me come and I relaxed my head and neck to give him better use of me. The more he used me, the more I came and I loved to come for Niles.

His determined hands held my head in place as easily as if I were a rag doll and I offered just about the same amount of resistance. He pounded into the back of my throat, occasionally hitting the high wisdom tooth on the bottom left side with his hard knob. Each time he connected with the tooth, he growled and groaned; each time I gagged and heaved and felt the bile rise in my throat. But each time, just as I was about to lose it, Niles let go of my head. I was allowed to take him out of my mouth to catch my breath but I voluntarily, no greedily, held his knob between my lips while I regained my breath. When I was ready for more, I took his hands in mine and replaced them on my head. Then I opened my mouth, jaw dropped, tongue out and at the ready, and waited for him to force me down on him.

Our world was a timeless place and I had no idea how long this went on; it could have been ten minutes, it could have been an hour or more. I do know that he moved me into many different positions to use my face, experimenting to see which ones gave him the best access and to see the ones that humiliated me, excited me, exposed me. I do know that I ate him greedily in each position whether it was awkward, humiliating, uncomfortable, or hard to breathe. After a final brutal pounding, I collapsed on his belly and lay there gasping and moaning. The black make-up stung my eyes and ran down my face, my lipstick was long gone, my hair was a rat's nest, and the taste of snot was in my mouth. I never felt more beautiful, more desirable than at that moment. Niles put his hands on my head and gently began to stroke my hair and smooth it down.

I sighed in contentment and draped my arm across him. His touch was affectionate and soothing and this aroused me as much as his earlier rough treatment of me. My mind was screaming for him to penetrate me and my quim creaming anew. My thighs were almost stuck together from my own dried girl-jam. I sobbed his name as I curled up next to his body, my face still pressed against his flat, hairless stomach. Shaking with passion, I kissed his warm, Niles-scented flesh. From the semidarkness above came his voice, filled with tenderness, "You've been a very good girl, Madelaine, quite excellent. I'm very pleased with you. If you could have any wish you wanted that I could grant, what would you wish for?"

Overcome, I rested my head on his belly and looked up at him. It took me a minute to stammer out, "Oh, Niles, I couldn't name only *one* thing! You know what I like better than I do. Please pick something for me." And I meant it. "No, Madelaine, tell me the lot of them," he said encouragingly. Carefully considering my choices, I said in a voice husky with passion, "I would like you to fuck me in my cunt even if it's only for a little while. I want to feel you there, stretching me, filling me up. I would like you to choke me, Niles, choke me until I pass out and when I wake up I want to be in your arms, your face close to mine, your fingers inside of me. I want you to cane me, master, and cane me hard. I want to go home with marks that will last for days." A small sob escaped me when I said that: mementos of my trip.

"Go on, Madelaine. Is there more?" he asked softly. I took a deep breath and went on in a voice just as soft. "I want to worship you, Niles, my master, my beast-god, the one who made me. I want to eat out your asshole and put my tongue in you. Taste you, smear your cream on my face, adore you and abase myself." Even more softly, and perhaps with a tinge of embarrassment or humiliation in my voice at asking for this, I added, " And I would like to you sodomize me, Niles."

It thrilled me and humiliated me to speak those words to him, to hear myself ask aloud to be anally penetrated. After speaking those words, a frisson shot through me and I came.

Gently but firmly, knowing my shaky state, Niles helped me up to rest my head on his shoulder. I nestled into the familiar, soon-to-be-missed, crook and deeply inhaled his scent. It nearly knocked me out. He caressed my face, making me melt, and planted kisses on the top of my head. I stretched out next to him and pressed my body close, wanting to soak up as much of him as I could. After planting one firm kiss on the top of my head, he said in a lover's voice, "I think those things can be arranged, Madelaine." A passionate groan escaped me and I buried my face in his chest. He pulled the duvet up to cover us both and we fell into an easy synchronized breathing. Soon we were asleep.

THIRTY-SIX

We only slept for about an hour, just a little nap, really. Niles awoke before me and kissed me awake. I was on my back and his arm was under my shoulders. He held me tightly and I luxuriated in his warmth, his strength, and his scent. His hand was between my legs and I was creaming from his gentle, expert touch even as I slept. He nuzzled his lips into my ear and with his fingers stroking me inside, he whispered, "What were we talking about before our little nap? Oh, yes," he breathed teasingly, touching me and making me come again, "your five wishes." "Yes, master," I breathed. He looked into my eyes and said, "What was my answer? Oh, I recall, I said those things could be arranged."

He was on me like a wild thing before I could reply or draw breath. He pushed me to my side then from behind wrapped his arms and legs around me. When he rolled over, he took me with him. Now both of us were face down on the duvet. He smashed my face into a pillow and used his legs to spread mine wide, frog-like. His hard cock deliberately poked and probed my quim, seeking my hole. In spite of the flood between my legs, Niles was making his entry as painful as he could. After all the slapping, punching, biting, and caning my quim had taken, it was sore and sensitive and he could make penetration as painful as he wished. I clung to the arm encircling my neck and tilted my hips up to give him better access. I whispered his name until finally, thankfully he drove his cock into me in one long stroke.

His deep entry transported me into momentary silence and utter stillness while I absorbed the length and breadth of him. I dug my fingers into his arm and panted through my mouth as I felt myself stretch to accommodate him. When Niles felt me come, he began to pound into me without pity. Pinned down by his body, my legs immobilized by his, my arms enclosed by his, I abandoned myself to his cruel attentions and wallowed in them, oh-so-guiltlessly enjoying the many orgasms he gave me.

After one smashing orgasm, something changed in me and I began to fight him. I tried to get away from him, futilely pulling at his strong arms with my small hands, and jerking my legs in a doomed effort to free them. My struggles only incited him further and he humped me faster and deeper, growling like a beast. Silent no more, I kept mewling, "Please, please . . ." over and over, not even knowing what I was pleading for. His cock still buried in me, he knelt up behind me and dragged me to my knees. My hips were high but my upper body was still face down on the bed. My arms free but useless, he violated me this new way. I wailed as he rammed into me and to silence me, Niles took a pillow in one hand and held it over my head. I thrashed against it but I was no match for him and soon the lack of air made me weak. I ceased my struggle and started to go limp.

Niles felt this and used his cock like a weapon, spearing me over and over. Right before I was about to pass out, he pulled the pillow up from my head. Air, delicious air, smelling of his pheromones and our sex flooded my nose. As air filled my starved lungs, he held me by the hips and used his cock like a battering ram. Soon he was so deep inside me that his knob pounded into my cervix. I moaned in pain and writhed under his onslaught. After a particularly hard stroke, I screamed and began to pull my own hair, calling his name repeatedly, mindlessly. He wrapped his arms around me and toppled us face down on the bed. I put up a small struggle against the weight of his body while he again pinned me down spread-eagle. I came so hard that my whole body spasmed and shook and my cunt muscles went crazy squeezing his cock.

"Five wishes?" he sneered. "Here's your first one, then! Do you like it? Huh? Huh?" He emphasized each word with a brutal thrust. "What were your other wishes? Let me think." His teasing worked. "Oh, master, thank you for fucking me. Please more . . ." I groveled. "More what?" he said. "More of this?" he grunted as he pummeled into me. "Just more, more of anything, master, more of anything you wish . . . use me, hurt me, I don't care . . ." I trailed off. "Oh, yes," he said in a deceptively sweet voice, "you asked to be caned, to be choked, to worship me, and to be sodomized. I remember now." I groaned in pleasure at his words as much as the feel of him inside me. I had come so much there was a huge wet spot on the duvet.

As Niles pulled his cock out of me in one swift motion, he said, "I think I'd like to cane you before I sodomize you. I want to rape your ass after it's red and welted from beating you." He was out of me completely now although kneeling between my open legs. I was still panting, limp from his penetration, when he grabbed me by the arm. Niles pulled me to my feet and steered me to the arm of the sofa. He pushed me down over it and left me there while he found the cane. I clutched the sofa and made involuntary "mmmm hhhhmmm" sounds interspersed with little dry sobs until he returned.

Niles smacked the cane against his hand a couple of times so I could hear the whistling sound it made as it sped through the air and the *crack!* it made against his palm. My incoherent babbling increased but he waited until I begged him to hit me. I pleaded with him to cane me, to please do it and make it hard, to hurt me, to cane me until I couldn't stand, or stand it, any longer. Niles, my savage lover, didn't disappoint me. The first stroke was as hard as I hoped it would be and I relished the pain and simultaneous orgasm it gave me. He waited for me to absorb it all but I was out-of-my-mind greedy for it. I begged him to keep hitting me and stuck my derriere out to entice and incite him. The second stroke landed, followed quickly by a third, fourth, and fifth stroke. He kept up the pace and after about twenty-five strokes, I felt his large warm hand massaging my cheeks to keep the skin loose for more punishment. I loved the feel of his hand on my red and swollen flesh and when his finger dipped into me, just slightly grazing my clitoris on the way in, I had an orgasm so intense that my knees almost gave out.

When he felt the ooze between my legs, I heard him gasp with delight. His touch drove me insane and I began to beg for more strokes. He stepped back and let fly. The cane landed squarely across my buttocks and my scream was one of pleasure, followed by "please, more, please . . ." over and over. After another twenty-five strokes, again I felt his huge hand massaging and squeezing my buttocks, getting them ready for "more," then his finger entered me anew. I had come so much my thighs were smeared and sticky but still I wanted more: more pain, more pleasure, more of him and his sadistic desires. I was inflamed by them and thrilled that he shared his sadism with me. I begged him to go on, not caring when he said that more strokes would probably break the skin and I would bleed. The word "bleed" rocketed me into another dimension; I hadn't bled for anyone before and I wanted to bleed, to bleed for him and for me. "Please, master, please, Niles, make me bleed, I want to! I want my blood to flow, please, please, beat me, beat me!" I babbled urgently.

The next stroke was so hard my knees buckled. I gripped the sofa so I wouldn't collapse. The succeeding strokes were equally severe but I embraced each one as much as my mind and heart embraced the sadist who was beating me. I didn't need to look at my derriere to know it was red, swollen, and welted. I loved the thought of it and conjured up a mental image to match the reality. I was still moaning in pleasure from this image when the next stroke landed. Searing pain and a violent orgasm ripped through me. I felt the skin break and imagined I could feel the drops of blood rising to the surface but by then I was so crazed for him, for it, that maybe I wasn't imagining it at all.

"You're bleeding, Madelaine," came his gentle voice from behind me. "Bleeding and welted." "Yes, master, thank you, master, more please! Please more!" I implored him. But instead of the cane, the next thing I felt on my inflamed buttocks was his hand. His sex smell domi-

nated the room, invaded me, and conquered me. Again I begged him
to continue, wiggling my derriere at him, but he denied me. Instead he
ordered me to stay there and went into the bathroom. Niles returned
with a wet cloth, dry towel, and a tube of something. His touch was a
caress when he blotted the blood away. A second later the wet cloth
was on me blotting up more blood. I was moaning and babbling, not
knowing what words or sounds were coming from me and not caring.
All I wanted was his touch and more of what he was giving me. But
soon the wet cloth was gone and I heard strange little sounds from behind me. I realized that he was taking out whatever was in the little
tube he had brought from the bathroom.

It was a styptic pencil. As soon as Niles rolled it on my bleeding
welt, I shrieked in surprise at the burning sting. He pushed my head
into the sofa to muffle the sound and continued to apply the pencil
until he was satisfied. Still pushing my head into the sofa, I felt his
thumb enter my quim. "Slimy girl, dirty slimy girl," he said in a teasingly cruel voice that drove me to further insanity for him. Abruptly
the thumb was withdrawn. Just as abruptly, I felt two fingers enter my
quim at the same time the thumb invaded my anus. I growled at the
invasion but I began to work my muscles to caress the fingers and
thumb inside of me. I couldn't stop coming; I didn't want to stop coming. All I wanted was more and I danced on the fingers and thumb inside of me to get it.

"Oh, bloody hell, fuck, yeah . . ." Niles growled. The hand pushing
my head into the sofa moved to my hair and grabbed it at the roots.
His fingers and thumb were still implanted in me when he used my
hair to pull me into a back-arched standing position. Using my hair
and holes to control me, he roughly maneuvered me into the bedroom. Once there, the hand grabbing my hair released it but I was not
to be freed. His fingers and thumb still embedded in me, his free arm
encircled me. Then Niles picked me up by the holes and tossed me on
the bed. The fingers and thumb gone from me, I landed face down and
in an instant he was on top of me. He wrapped his strong arms around
me and crushed me to him, pinning me to the bed. His legs kicked
mine apart and spread them wide. I was grunting and moaning mindlessly and twisting my head unconsciously from side to side when I

felt his hard cock probe between my cheeks and roughly, cruelly seek out my anus.

"Oh, yes, I remember another of your wishes," Niles said nastily as he held me down and sought out my hole. "You wanted me to sodomize you, didn't you? 'Sodomize me,' you asked me. I'll sodomize you all right, Madelaine! You'll feel my dick in the back of your throat before I'm through with you!" he snarled. With that he tried to ram his engorged cock straight up my ass. Although his earlier fingering of that opening had stretched it some, I was still very tight and he was still very well-endowed. "No, Niles, please, not like this, please not like this!" I implored him. "How then?" he sneered at me as he attempted to spear me a couple of more times. But I was too tense and too tight to let him in. I pleaded with him to go slowly, saying that it would still hurt me, but please just go in slowly I beseeched him. Once he was inside me and I became adjusted to his size he could pound me to death. He tried once more but very roughly and I screamed.

Niles tightened his grip on me and spread my legs farther, wrapping his own around them to keep them open. His cock was poised just outside my anus, I could feel it there between my red, swollen cheeks, ready to impale me. "Please, Niles . . ." I entreated, "please!" "Please what, little slut? Please what?" he snarled. "I know, I know how to get you inside of me," I stammered. "How, then? Tell me!" he demanded. "Let yourself get a little soft, Niles," I implored him. "Soft? Why would I want to sodomize you 'soft'? Where would the enjoyment be in that?" he asked cruelly. "Niles, please listen. If you get a little soft then you can pack as much of your cock into me as you can. After you're packed into me, you can grow, Niles, grow as big as you want and I'll have no choice but to take you," I whispered, overcome by what I was saying, what I was offering him.

I felt him soften up a little and I relaxed into his arms and took deep breaths. He entered me slowly but it was still painful. Deliciously, exquisitely painful but I wanted it so very much. One long moan came out of me as he did what I urged. When he had as much of his cock in me as he could, I felt him begin to harden. The sensation was incredible. I felt my muscles and my rectum stretching to accommodate him as his cock grew into a pole on which to impale me. My body shook and guttural "hhmm, hhmm" sounds emitted from my mouth as he grew to full size. "Bloody fucking hell, that feels good! Does that feel good to you, Madelaine?" he asked me as he began to thrust and pump into me. "Yes! it feels incredible. Yes, do it to me, Niles, sodomize me, your cock is so big, so hard, it's stretching me so much, please, please! Hurt me, pound me, ram me! I want it, I want it . . ." I trailed off. My words turned into delirious mutterings when he did exactly what I asked.

I grunted and groaned and growled like an animal under the onslaught of his cock and his overwhelming smell. My pleasure was increased tenfold when his body smacked into my welted, swollen cheeks with each thrust and stroke. I begged him to go on, to keep sodomizing me and not to stop. But he did stop, his cock buried deep in my anus. "What did you say, Madelaine? Remember your language!" "Yes, master, yes, Niles. Please ream out my asshole, Niles, please! Fuck my ass, fuck it deep and hard, stretch me, hurt me! I want my hole to be gaping open when you are finished," I pleaded, almost frantically. "That's better, Madelaine. That's what I like to hear!" Although I didn't think it was possible, Niles managed to grow even bigger and harder until he was deep into my entrails. My hole was screaming in agonized protest but I ate it up, this wonderful amazing pleasure-pain he was giving me.

Limp and unresisting in his arms, I took all he had to give. Niles thrust, pounded, and rammed me like a wild man until I felt him go into one of his come-strokes. Grunting and snarling like a beast, he used me almost brutally, unheeding of my own screams and exhortations for him to come, please come. I begged him to give me a come enema, I promised him I would hold it in me if only he would give it to me. I felt his excitement mount when I said that. His arms squeezed me like a boa constrictor and I felt him pull an inch or two of his cock out of me but he continued with his come-stroke. With a final growl, he spurted his hot jism into my ass. "Yes, yes, yes . . ." was all I could say.

Niles let me go and rolled off of me. I was too sated, too exhausted, to move. Our sex had drugged me as effectively as any narcotic. When he got on his knees between my open legs and spread my welted cheeks, I offered no resistance. When I felt his breath on my hot, stretched hole, I moaned in mixed pleasure and humiliation. Then I heard him say, "Madelaine, your hole is hanging open and I can see my come inside you. You promised me you would hold it in. How can you hold it in when your hole is so big?" Each word deepened my joy and my humiliation and submission. "I'm sorry, master," I said in a small voice. "Sorry? What good does 'sorry' do me?" he sneered. "I want that hole closed! Hold your cheeks open."

I reached back and spread my beaten cheeks. They were hot under my hands and I could feel the welts on them and where he had broken the skin. I don't have the words to describe how I felt: sexy, humiliated, beautiful, dirty, desired, used. I buried my face in a pillow and awaited what was to come. His fist smashed into my sore hole. The pillow muffled my screams as he punched my hole over and over until it closed and trapped his come inside me. "Good girl, Madelaine," he said almost sweetly as he stretched out next to me. I rolled onto my side to face him and began to nuzzle and kiss him. He extended his arm and offered me the crook of his shoulder. I snuggled into it and got my nose as close to his armpit as I could. Our lust slaked for the time being, we both took a little nap.

THIRTY-SEVEN

I awoke before Niles and looked at the clock; again we had been asleep for less than an hour. Sliding quietly out of the bed so I wouldn't disturb him, I padded on bare feet to the bathroom to clean myself up. As I was sitting on the toilet, Niles appeared in the doorway wearing his robe and slippers and smiled wickedly at me. I knew what he wanted, or wanted to hear: me ridding myself of the come enema he had given me before our nap. Sitting there naked on the toilet and knowing what was expected of me, I felt the glow of submission warm me. His glittering green eyes watched me keenly as I pushed and strained to obey his unspoken command. Suddenly his come exploded out of my bottom, making embarrassing "raspberry" noises. These noises were humiliating, deliciously so especially under his keen eyes. Again, I blushed.

When his precious cargo was out of me, Niles continued to stand in the doorway and watch me as I gave myself a bird bath in the tub. As I dried myself, he turned on his heel and strode off to the bedroom. I knew that when I was finished, I was to join him there. I dried myself quickly and hurried down the hall to the bedroom. I found him ensconced on the bed, his robe and slippers off and covered to the waist by the duvet. His eyes were warm now and when he extended his arm in the familiar way, I jumped to take my place next to him. I stretched out beside him and luxuriated in the warmth and strength of his body. His other arm curled around me and hugged me to him. I almost choked on the emotions welling up inside of me. One tear fell and landed on his chest. Then a small sob escaped me and he hugged me tighter.

"Oh, Niles . . ." I whimpered, clutching him to me. "I know, Madelaine," he said gently as he rolled us both over so that he lay on top of me. I wrapped my arms around him, entwined my legs in his and kissed his face and neck and shoulders. He stroked my face and I melted. His lips met mine and he began to kiss me, slowly, deeply, passionately like when we had first met. My lips parted and my tongue caressed his; I felt the wetness between my legs and started to rub my hips against him. His lovely cock was hard and having it inside of me was all I could think of. Niles rubbed his cock on my belly, teasing me, making me wild for him, but he didn't penetrate me. I was mewling like a cat in heat. My tongue sought his, I ran my hands up and down his back, and drawing my legs up, I used my feet to caress his legs. I writhed under him shamelessly and felt another orgasm drench my quim. What lovely torture!

Suddenly he rolled off me, leaving me cold and alone on the bed, depriving me of the warm brutality of his body and kisses. I almost wept in protest. But when he reached across his chest and grabbed me by the arm, he startled me and I cried out in surprise. My cry spurred him on. He dragged me across his chest as if I weighed nothing and plopped me down half-sitting, half-prone, on his left side. Before I could settle down, his hand was on my throat, squeezing, squeezing, squeezing. I clutched at the hand on my throat but I was no match for his strength and determination. My body began to shake and I gasped out "Niles . . . !" Then utter blackness descended and I collapsed in a faint on his chest.

When I came to, dazed and a little scared, I was on my back on the bed with his fingers deep in my quim. While I was unconscious, he had been fingering me and working the magic spot inside. I could feel the puddle of girl-jam under me but I couldn't see him. I called his name and his broad handsome face loomed over me. He pulled his fingers out and grabbed me roughly. I begged him to wait, to please give his slave a minute to collect herself and he granted me a small respite. In answer to my plea, he manipulated me like I was a doll, his arms encircled me and pulled me close. I nuzzled against his chest. I matched my ragged breaths to his even ones and soon I felt sleepy. Although I was on "his" side of the bed, I thought we were going to take another little nap. These last fantasy-filled hours had been the things my dreams were made of—how could I ask for more? Besides, Niles's swollen bollocks must have been really hurting by this time. He was so virile, I kept forgetting he was still a sick man.

But Niles was full of surprises. When he pulled me across his chest, I thought he wanted to change places with me so he could sleep on his side of the bed. I went groggily, only to have him grab my hair and force my head down to his crotch. He rolled onto his side and pushed my face between his buttocks. Then he commanded me to eat out his asshole, crudely adding that I had better do a real good job of it and that he'd better feel my tongue deep inside of him. Thanking him greedily, I spread his cheeks and plunged my face between them. His big hand was still in my hair and guiding my all-too-willing head into place. He bent one leg to give me more room to obey him.

I wanted to start by truly worshiping his sweet asshole, all pink and brown and delicately pleated. I wanted to caress it with my tongue, give it long paintbrush licks; I wanted to pucker my lips and suck on it while I gently teased the hole, and use my tongue in different lengths and firmness to give him as much pleasure as possible before I entered him. Master Niles had a different idea: he wanted it hard and deep and right away. I obeyed him and rammed his ass with my tongue, which I had rolled and stiffened into a little cock. I felt my tongue breach his muscle, felt his muscle close on the tip of my tongue and I came. I tongued him and tongued him until my jaw hurt. The hand holding my head let it go and I took a deep breath.

Lust filled me again and I began to worship him the way I had wanted to from the start: the caresses, the paintbrush licks, and the sucking and kissing I was so fond of. I knew he liked what I was doing because he relaxed and rolled over a little to spread himself more. When he reached back and spread his cheeks for me, I knew he was enjoying my tender devotions. Occasionally he'd moan, "Oh, bloody hell" or "Oh fucking hell," and his manly aroma would almost suffocate me. I knew that I was pleasing him and renewed my efforts, wrapping my arms around his hips so he couldn't get away. Soon his hand was on my head and Niles was pumping his ass up and down on my tongue, much like the way he pumped his cock into my face. I stretched my tongue out as far as I could and moved my head to meet his thrusts. This intensified and deepened my entry into his sweet anus. I reveled in eating him out; the dirtiness of what I was doing turned me on. But he tasted and smelled so good, it all seemed so natural that I should be doing this to him. I never wanted to stop. I lapped at his tender opening until he pulled me away.

Niles rolled onto his back, grabbed me under the arms then pulled me up to rest my head in the crook of his shoulder. I thanked him over and over for allowing me the pleasure of worshipping him. After I thanked him, he gently licked my lips and tongue-kissed me. The same lips and tongue that had just been in his sweet asshole. Although he had done this before, this gesture was a very powerful one to me. "What manner of man is this?" I thought with love. Most men I had known wouldn't even kiss me after I had sucked their cock, never mind ate out their asshole. We laid in each other's embrace for a little while, enjoying the closeness and intimacy we shared. My swollen buttocks still ached from their caning and I relished the sensation, and the arousal it stirred in me. Hungry for him but without opportuning, I trailed my fingertips over his chest then my hand strayed down to his cock. He was starting to get a hard-on and I stroked him until he was rigid. He groaned while I touched him and soon his arousal was as great as mine.

He tossed me off him and onto my stomach then he mounted me from behind. His arms pinned mine to my body and his legs spread mine wide. I felt him probe between my reddened cheeks and I relaxed for him. I laid still as he entered my ass in one long stroke but I couldn't stop myself from making guttural animal sounds as he stretched and filled my hole. My quim gushed and ached for him and I whispered his name over and over. He started to pump me but not as hard or as roughly as he had earlier; this time his use of me was more gentle. As I became looser, he began to pump me a little harder and I rose to meet him. Then he changed the angle of his entry. Instead of stroking straight up into my entrails, he aimed his cock downward, toward my quim.

When his hard knob brushed lightly against the magic spot in my quim, ego departed and left naked lust in its place. Mindlessly I made those "hhmm, hhhmmm" and "uh uh uh" sounds and growled like a beast. Niles knew he had come to a new wall which needed to be breached and with his cock he sought out that spot through my vaginal wall. Skilled lover that he was, it didn't take him long to find it and hit it dead on. When he connected, I had a painful, humiliating, squirting orgasm that was the most complete and satisfying orgasm I had ever had in my life. I laid limp in his arms and let him do as he pleased; the feeling and the orgasm were so intense I don't think I could have done anything else. He hit that spot every fourth stroke with the same effect: a painful, humiliating, spurting orgasm that left me weak and gasping. After several of those mind-shattering orgasms, I began to wail that I couldn't take any more, that I was weak from coming so much but he knew I didn't want him to stop.

Giving me one last shuddering, shaking orgasm, he pulled out of my ass. My quim was drenched and having muscle spasms when he entered it. I cried out in pleasure and egged him on, exhorting him to fuck me, yes, fuck me in my cunt, it's so wet and hungry for you, please do it, do it now. He did fuck me but it wasn't a brutal pounding. It was the fucking of two lovers, not of two bestial growling things. This endeared him to me more than anything else he had done and no one could deny that we had done plenty. When I came with him in my quim, I almost wept from the passion I felt. Niles felt it, too. I was so wet I felt as slickery and slippery as an eel. As he slid in and out of me, my quim made squishing, almost slurping, sounds and this increased our excitement. I urged him to fuck me, fuck me more, please fuck me and don't stop, please don't stop. He groaned "oh, bloody hell . . ." then he held me tightly and went into a hard come stroke. I begged him for his pearl-jam and a few strokes later, he gave me what I wanted.

We laid that way for several minutes, breathing heavily. The room smelled of our sex. The sheet beneath us was soaked with our juices and sweat. Both of us were too exhausted, too sated, to move. When he pulled out of me and rolled onto his back, I hurried to snuggle up against him and absorb as much of him, of his essence, of his sadism, as I could. Although I didn't want to, I looked at the clock. I had to leave in an hour. I fought back the tears.

THIRTY-EIGHT

"Oh, Niles, I have to leave," I whispered, pain in my voice. I clung to him almost desperately; I couldn't rip myself away. I writhed against him, entwined my legs in his, rubbed my feet on his, stroked his chest and kissed his neck and shoulders and faces and hands. His lovely large hands. Feeling my need to be close in these final moments, Niles returned my embraces and stroked my head, saying, "But you'll be back." Then he kissed the top of my head. This small gesture nearly made me break down and cry. Instead, I gave him one last full body hug and got up to pack. I put the kettle on and pulled out the suitcases. I tossed everything into them willy-nilly and made a last run through the house. When the kettle whistled, a fully dressed Niles joined me in the reception room. It was still a mess from our earlier escapades. I started to clean it up but Niles stopped me and sat me down next to him on the sofa. He put his arm around me and we drank our tea.

I wanted to tell him how wonderful these weeks had been, how wonderful *he* had been but words failed me. All I could do was look at him and say, "I'm going to miss you!" He smiled and repeated that I'd be back, and added that "this" had worked out very well, very well indeed. But when he offered to drive me to the airport, I thanked him politely and told him no, I would rather take a cab. He asked why and I gave him a jumble of answers: he looked tired, it was a long round trip, the ride would be hard on him, it was early in the day, blah blah blah. But he knew I was telling only half-truths. Then I came out with it: seeing him at the airport was too final, too real, too much of a departure. I said I would rather take the cab and leave thinking of him here, in the funky flat in Maida Vale, where I enjoyed so much pleasure and learned so much about myself.

We spoke about keeping in contact right up until the second the car service arrived. I asked the cab driver to handle the luggage as I said my last good-byes to Niles. And then I learned another thing about him. He never said "good-bye" unless he meant it; he preferred to say "see ya later" or "see ya soon." Before I closed the cab's door, I turned and waved to him, and between hand-blown kisses, I called out, "See ya soon!" My smile hurt my face.

THIRTY-NINE

What can I say about the ride to the airport? That I was numb? Yes. That I felt like I had left a piece of my heart behind? Yes. That I was in an emotional limbo? Yes. That my body still craved him? Yes. That I cried a little on the plane? Yes, I did that, too. I tried not to think about leaving him, especially under such circumstances, but the plane ride back to Miami was long and boring and I couldn't help myself. Unable to sleep, I used the time to make little notes in the margins of my journal so nothing would be forgotten, and in doing so, re-read every word I had written. Knots formed in my stomach as I visualized what I read and I choked back the occasional dry sob when what I read some of the things we had done together. I explored my feelings, digging deep into my soul and psyche and being honest with myself about them. I liked what I found but the wrench of leaving him hurt. I kept reminding myself of Niles's words: "You'll be back," and I knew I would return to Niles, to the master who made me, and to the new pleasures and humiliations, new joys and degradations, and exhilarating, liberating new experiences that awaited me there.

EPILOGUE

Renee was waiting for me at the gate. When I got off the plane, she said to me, "Madelaine, you're *glowing*."

The glow lasted several weeks. I floated on air. Niles's raw erotic power, his rampant and unchecked sexuality were potent aphrodisiacs that easily stretched the five thousand miles between us. Scheduled and surprise trans-Atlantic phone calls kept us connected. I sent him little gifts, music cassettes mostly. I dedicated *The Art of Sensual Female Dominance* to him, and when it was released, I sent him a copy, signed of course, and embellished with a slut-red lipstick kiss. I wrote him letters. Even though I knew Niles wouldn't write in response, I knew he kept the letters. And the "self-portraits" I sent him. One night during a wee-hours, super-hot phone call, he ordered me to shave my quim. Razor in one hand and phone in the other, I did as the master bade me. Then I took "self-portraits" of the exposed newly shaven area and mailed them to him. After another call, I wrote up a slave contract/wish list and sent it to him. The receipt of the slave contract/wish list prompted more hot, steamy late-night phone calls.

We got out our calendars and planned the date for my return. The adventures of Madelaine would continue.

GLOSSARY:
A BIT O' BRITISH SLANG

bobbies: cops

bollocks: the balls and groin area

bouncy: wanting to dance; restless

bum: buttocks

chips: french fries

crisps: potato chips

dust bin: garbage can

fanny: vagina

muwah: the sound your lips make when you blow a kiss

"p": pence

post: the mail

quid: one British Pound Sterling

quim: vagina

shag: intercourse

spiff: joint

spunk: semen

About the Author

Claudia Varrin, is a longtime member of the BDSM scene, both publically and privately, and through her writings, public appearances, magazine interviews, and television and movie appearances has become a well-known advocate of the BDSM love style. She gives generously of her time and donates books and other items of interest as often as possible to worthy causes. Varrin is travel-crazy and can be seen at Fetish events in London, Paris, Amsterdam, Prague, Houston, Boston, Fort Lauderdale, and many other cities near and far, all the while promoting tolerance and understanding of the BDSM community.

Varrin lives life among the incurably curious, which often confuses some people as to whether she is "truly dominant" or not. Varrin thinks of herself as an author and artist first, whose understanding of dominance and submission has led her to share her experiences as a domina, diva, and, yes, her one experience as a submissive with her readership. Varrin loves to experiment and to know what her submissives are feeling. To accomplish this, she will experiment on herself as much as possible. She finds self-bondage to be very interesting, and her wonderfully wild, creative, and erotic mind loves to invent new means of torture, humiliation, and edge play. Claudia is a major latex fetishist, loves any opportunity to show off her wardrobe and promote goodwill in the BDSM community. Her passion for shoes has been out-stripped by her passion for latex. Her favorite expression? "Kiss like you've never been kissed before; love like you've never been hurt before; sing as if no one is listening; dance as if no one is watching; and live life to the fullest, because you never know which moment will be your last."

PUBLISHED WORKS:

1997   *The Anne Rice Reader,* edited by Katherine Ramsland, Ph.D., fully accredited chapter entitled "How Do They Rate? Eliot Slater and Lasher as Love Slaves"

1998   *The Art of Sensual Female Dominance: A Guide for Women*, Kensington Books/Citadel Press, NYC, hardcover edition (out of print)

2000   *The Art of Sensual Female Dominance*, Kensington Books/ Citadel Press, NYC, in seventh paperback printing (also available in German and Spanish)

2001   *Erotic Surrender: The Sensual Joys of Female Submission*, Kensington Books/Citadel Press, NYC, hardcover edition

2002   *NYFU: New York Fetish Underground Guide*, Kensington Books/ Citadel Press, NYC, paperback edition

2003   *Erotic Surrender: The Sensual Joys of Female Submission*, Kensington Books/Citadel Press, NYC, paperback edition (also available in German)

2004   *Female Dominance: Rituals and Practices*, Kensington Books/ Citadel Press, NYC, hardcover edition (also available in German)

2005   *The Female Dominant: Games She Plays*, Kensington Books/ Citadel Press, NYC, trade paperback edition

2005   *Female Dominance: Rituals and Practices*, Kensington Books/ Citadel Press, NYC, trade paperback edition

2006   *Female Submission: The Journals of Madelaine,* Kensington Books/Citadel Press, NYC, hardcover edition

TELEVISION APPEARANCES AND MOVIE INTERVIEWS:

Maury 1994
Geraldo 1994
The Joan Rivers Show 1995
Real Personal with Bob Berkowitz 1994, 1994, 1995, 1996 (four-time guest panelist)
Playboy Channel's *Sextetera* 18 airings in January 2002
No Body Is Perfect, a movie by Raphael Sybilla, Paris, France, 2004

SPEAKING ENGAGEMENTS:

Aural Sex, Rubber Ball, London, England 1998
Dom/Sub Friends, NYC, 2001, 2002, 2005
Kink in the Carribean, Jamaica, West Indies, 2001
The Nutcracker Suite, NYC 2002

PUBLIC APPEARANCES AS A SPECIAL GUEST:

Rubber Ball, London, England, 1996, 1997, 1998, 1999, 2000, 2002, 2003, 2004, 2005
Euro-Perve, Amsterdam, Holland, 2000, 2001
Libertine Ball, Philadelphia, 1999
Alter Ego, Fort Lauderdale, Florida, 2001, 2002, 2003, 2004, 2005
Miss Fetish NYC Pageant, NYC, honored guest, 2000; contest judge, 2001
Kink in the Carribean, Jamaica West Indies, 2001
Black and Blue Ball, NYC, 1995, 1996, 2000, 2001, 2002, 2003, 2004, 2005
Leather Pride Night, NYC, 1996, 2000, 2001, 2002, 2003, 2005
Fetish in Paradise, Man-Ray Club, Boston 2002
Boston Fetish Flea Market, Boston, 2002
Nuit Demonia, Paris, France, 2002, 2003, 2004, 2005
The Playground, Fort Lauderdale, Florida, 2002, 2003
The Other World Kingdom, 2003, 2004, Awarded Sublime Lady Citizenship June 2004, 2006
The Houston Latex Party, 2004

Torture Garden's 13 Birthday Bash, London, England, 2004
Club Rub, London, England, 2004, 2005
Subversion, London, England 2005

MAGAZINE AND BOOK INTERVIEWS:

Playgirl Magazine, USA
Dresseuse Magazine, Paris, France
Mistresses of the Night, by Mistress Rene, Extreme Ink, Madison
  Wisconsin
Demonia Magazine, Paris, France
Desire Magazine, London, England
DDI, US

CONTRIBUTING AUTHOR:

American Dommes
Fetish Magazine
Mistress Mine

REVIEWS OF PUBLISHED WORKS (PARTIAL LISTING):

Publisher's Weekly, US
Skin Two Magazine, UK
Marquis, Germany
Desire Magazine, UK
Anima Publications, US
The Boston Globe, US
Toronto World and Globe, Canada
Prometheus Magazine (the official magazine of The TES Society), US
Kirkus Review, US
Dresseuse Magazine, France
Secret Magazine, Belguim
Dominatrix Directory International, US
Massad, Holland
Demonia Magazine, Paris, France